Canada by Bicycle

From Vancouver to St. John's

Published in Canada by

Dirty T-Shirt Productions

www.canadabybicycle.com

Written by Steve Langston

Edited by

Leah Dixon
Sheldon Birnie
Annik Adam

Cover design:
Jacob Quinlan

ISBN 978-0-9812428-1-1
Printed in Canada
November 2016

Fifth Printing

contents

The Country

Geographically, Canada occupies the majority of northern North America. Canada borders the United States of America to the south as well as to the northwest. To the east of the country is the Atlantic Ocean, to the west is the Pacific Ocean and to the north is the Arctic Ocean. With an area of 9 093 507 kilometres^2, Canada is the second largest country in the world, next to Russia. Canada's 243 000 kilometre coastline is the longest in the world.

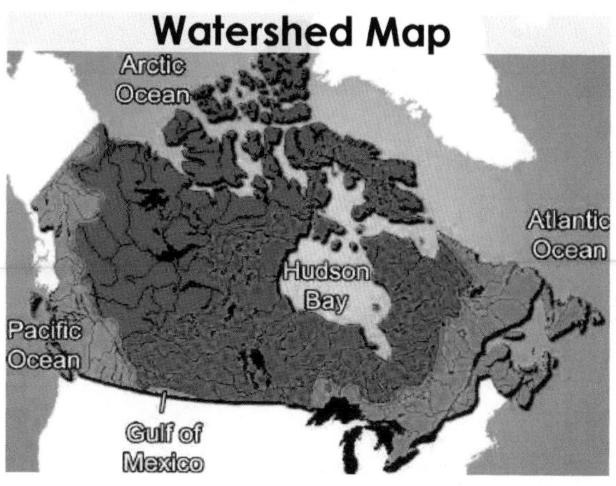

Canada is sparsely populated, with a population density of 3.5 inhabitants per square kilometre. Most of the country's inhabitants live along the southern border, near the United States.

Canada's major economies include mining, agriculture, forestry and tourism.

Canada is one of few developed nations that are net exporters of energy. This is largely contributed to by abundant hydroelectricity in the provinces of British Columbia, Québec, Ontario, Saskatchewan and Manitoba. Large oil and gas resources are located in Alberta, British Columbia, Saskatchewan, the northern territories and Newfoundland.

All population counts in this book are based on the 2006 Canadian Census. At the time of this census the population of Canada was 31 612 897.

The Tour

Because Canada is such a huge country with a relatively short summer season, it was necessary for me to schedule some long days of cycling. This ensures that cyclists can take days off to be tourists, and still finish before the snow falls.

As you pedal your bicycle across Canada from campsite to campsite, with all the equipment that you will need to live a happy, sustainable life, you will experience this vast country in a way impossible by plane, train or automobile.

Bike touring is the ultimate way to get to know an area. Expect to be approached by inquiring locals who want to know what you are up to. Through these encounters you will hear their stories and gain knowledge not possible while traveling by automobile. It will amaze you.

Each day is a unique adventure, where you will be challenged by weather, road and the physical demands of traveling without an automobile. Canada is a gigantic country. It will take endurance, patience and a positive attitude to bike from coast to coast.

In average weather conditions, a beginner cyclist can expect to ride around 20 kilometres per hour. This means that if you need to bike 100 kilometres, you will be on your bike and pedaling for around five hours. Breaks for lunch, rest and hydration will add another hour or two. If everything goes as planned, with no major mechanical failures, wrong turns or impromptu soccer games, you can expect to arrive at your destination eight or nine hours after you leave.

Upon arrival at your campsite, you set up your tent, unload your gear and have a shower. Afterwards you can relax, have a drink, prepare your meal and check out any local tourist attractions.

Canada is located far north of the equator meaning that summers bring long days, plenty of sun and sometimes-volatile weather. Summer solstice, on June 22nd, brings over 15 ½ hours of daylight to all locations on the *Canada by Bicycle* route.

Although people have biked across Canada year round, you will have the best results if you bike between May 1st and October 1st. It is likely that you will find campgrounds open and weather more agreeable during these times.

This tour is designed to start in Vancouver, British Columbia and end up in St. John's, Newfoundland. I have written this book that way because there is a prevailing west wind in Canada.

This means that it is more likely to have a wind out of the west, but it is possible to encounter many consecutive days with wind out of the east. I have met people biking both directions. Make the decision for yourself.

Please consult www.canadabybicycle.com regularly for updates to the tour, special offers and a chance to comment on the tour. If there is any information you feel would be helpful to others, you can let me know on this website.

Budget

Bike touring is an affordable way to see any area. A generous budget for this tour would be $60 CAD per day, per person. This budget will cover the essentials of groceries, camping, bike tubes and the occasional meal out. If you can travel with a friend the cost of camping will be much lower. Some private campgrounds in Canada can charge up to $30 CAD per night for camping. Splitting that cost with a friend will make your trip more affordable.

Blackhawk camping is the act of setting up your tent in an area that is not designated for camping. Most cycle tourists Blackhawk camp at least once in a while, while some bike tourists do it every night. Personally, I prefer to stay in a campground but have had some memorable evenings spent camped next to lakes and rivers. Also, sometimes you will want to go further or less than the scheduled campground making Blackhawk camping a good alternative. If you Blackhawk camp, bring lots of water to your campsite, clean up any mess that you make and be aware of your surroundings. An ideal Blackhawk site is close to a river or lake for swimming and washing dishes.

Before You Go

Before setting out on any bike tour it is necessary to be in reasonable physical condition. Don't be intimidated. This bicycle tour is achievable by any person that is fit and determined. Because bicycling is a non-impact activity, your body will recover from a hard day of exertion much quicker than from high-impact activities.

I recommend completing at least one short bike tour prior to leaving on your first long bicycle tour. Pick a campground approximately eighty kilometres from your home and load your bicycle with everything you will need for the evening including your tent, stove, cookware, clothing, sleeping bag, sleeping pad and groceries. Upon arrival, set your equipment up, cook dinner and do something fun like explore the area, have a bonfire or throw a Frisbee. In the morning, cook breakfast and cycle home.

On this trip you can test out your equipment and adequately assess your level of fitness.

The many kilometres between campgrounds can be intimidating for a first-time bike tourist. Keep in mind that you have an entire day to get to your destination. Get an early start and give yourself lots of time for breaks, rest and food. Many people break up their day into small, manageable increments, stopping approximately every ten kilometres.

The most common bicycle tour injury is a straining of the knees from cycling with a seat positioned too high or low. The repetitiveness of riding your bike all day can quickly turn a small ache into a serious injury.

Here is a quick way to determine if your seat is properly positioned: While riding your bike bring a pedal down to the very bottom of its cycle. At this point your knee should be bent slightly, but no more than 20°. If you are unsure, get fitted at a reputable bike shop.

Another strategy to ensure that you have a happy and healthy bike tour is to limit the amount of cargo that you are carrying on your bike. When packing you may deem an extra pair of shoes or hard cover book necessary, but when climbing a steep hill you will think otherwise! Pack only what is necessary and nothing else. If you find yourself lacking something while on the road, purchase it then.

Basic knowledge of bike mechanics is recommended before you head out on a bike tour. This includes being able to fine-tune your brakes, fix a flat tire or adjust your seat height. There are many bike shops on this route, but problems inevitably arise when you are far from one.

Take a bike repair course at a local college or read a book on the subject before you depart. If you are taking your bike in for a tune-up, ask if you can watch what is being done and don't be afraid to ask questions. Bike store employees are usually cyclists and will be interested in your trip.

Safety is always a concern when sharing the roads with trucks, cars and motorcycles. Whenever possible, the roads you'll ride will be both well constructed, yet lightly traveled. It is important to be aware of the traffic patterns in the area that you are cycling. Expect traffic to be brisk weekdays in the hours around 8 AM as people are heading to work and around 5 PM for those heading home.

When on the highway, cycle on the shoulder whenever possible. Where there is no shoulder, stay as close as possible to the right hand side of the road. If cycling with a partner or in a group, ride single file in a tight pack or else far enough apart that a motorist will pass you separately, as opposed to one prolonged, more dangerous pass.

Make sure you are familiar with how to signal your intentions of turning and stopping properly to motorists before starting your bike tour. A friendly wave to vehicles passing safely is always recommended! Most of Canada is sparsely populated; there is a good chance you will run into these motorists in the next town you visit.

The Bike

The ideal touring bike is one that is sturdy and light. Because almost all of your cycling will be on pavement, the ideal bike for highway riding has touring tires, which have little grip especially compared to a mountain bike tire. This allows for easier cycling due to less friction between the tire and the road.

Suspension is heavy and takes energy away from your task of traveling quickly and safely down the road, thus not recommended.

Traditional cantilever brakes are the best for bike touring. They are light, easy to fix and affordable. Parts are readily available at all bike shops. Disc brakes are very effective at stopping your bike, but hard to fix and heavy. Hydraulic brakes are nearly impossible to fix without heavy, complex tools.

Although there are touring-specific bicycles, many people tour on average-looking mountain bikes, without suspension. This style of bike can be purchased brand new for a few hundred dollars and is sturdy, reliable and readily available.

Race style bikes can also work well for bike touring. Make sure your bike is heavy-duty enough to withstand the stresses of bike touring.

In an ideal world you could walk into a bike store and buy a touring specific bike with no concern for price. Unfortunately, price is a concern and it is often necessary to tour on a bike that is not specifically designed for touring. I have seen people successfully tour on both mountain bikes and racing bikes. When purchasing a bike that is not intended for touring there are a few things you need to keep in mind.

Make sure that the rear wheel has sufficient clearance from the frame so that you can replace the rear-tire with a larger tire and still have clearance for the wheel to spin. Many race style bikes only leave enough room for race-style tires, which quickly deteriorate when hauling your heavy cargo. Also, if your wheel gets slightly bent you want the tire to remain clear of the frame.

If you are planning on using saddlebags, make sure that you can mount racks onto the bike. This requires threaded holes just above the rear axle.

Buy a touring specific seat specific to your gender. Your rear end will thank you.

Handlebars

The two types of handlebars most common on touring bikes are a flat handlebar or a drop handlebar, which curls down. Flat handlebars keep you in a more upright position and keep stress off of your arms but increases your wind resistance. Drop bars put more stress on your arms and hands but position you into a more aerodynamic position. Both types of bars are acceptable.

Wheels

In my experience, the most common bicycle problem that cyclists encounter while touring is chronic spoke breaking. Most wheels are not meant for the heavy load of a cycle tourist. Twisting and heaving on the wheel will snap an inferior spoke. As soon as one spoke is broken, it places more stress on the remaining spokes. If possible, have your rear-wheel's spokes replaced with the thickest gauge spokes that your bike shop has on hand before leaving on your trip. Make sure to acquire a few extras for when you are on the road.

Another way to ensure that you do not break too many spokes is to limit the amount of cargo that you are carrying. Bring only what is necessary.

Most mountain bikes have 26 inch or 650 millimetre rims while most race bikes have 28 inch or 700 millimetre tires. 28 inch tires allow the cyclist to ride faster than with 26 inch tires and are recommended for bike touring.

Older race bikes sometimes have 27 inch rims. I do not recommend traveling with this type of wheel as it is difficult to find replacement parts while on the road.

Tires

Spend as much money as you possibly can on tires. I got a good deal on an expensive set of tires and decided to splurge on them. I did not have a single flat from Vancouver all the way until Thunder Bay. I finally had to change them because they were seriously deteriorating. Make sure the tires that you buy are flat-resistant and high-quality. Feel the tires, if they feel thick and tough they are much better than tires that seem thin and easily ripped.

Visually inspect your tires on a regular basis for wear and tear. I generally don't carry a spare tire, only tubes, so it is important to replace your tire before it becomes too worn down.

One of the worst situations that you can encounter on the road is a ripped tire from hitting a sharp rock or other debris. When this happens your tire tube will be exposed and you will suffer from chronic flat-tires.

I noticed this problem on my bike as I got off of the ferry in Port-aux-Basques, Newfoundland. Knowing that the nearest bike store was around 250 kilometres away in Corner Brook, I had a lot of anxiety. In an attempt to fix the hole in my tire I trimmed a narrow strip off of the plastic cover of my journal and duct-taped it inside the tire, covering the hole. I made it to Corner Brook and bought a new tire but did not install it. The makeshift hillbilly patch lasted over 900 kilometres to St. John's. Don't forget this trick!

Make sure you know how to patch a punctured tube before you leave on your trip. Also, it is a good idea to bring along a tire pressure gauge. It is more likely that you will get a flat from your tire being under-filled than over-filled.

Pedals

You can tour with either traditional platform pedals or clip-in pedals. If using platform pedals, I recommend adding a basket (toe strap) to keep your foot aligned and in place.

Clip-in pedals are the norm for bicycle racing and it would be difficult to argue that they are not more efficient than platform pedals. However, clip-in pedals require a specific shoe that matches the pedals. Most people would then need to carry another pair of shoes to wear while exploring a city or going on a hike. This means you are carrying two pairs of shoes, which is a significant amount of cargo. There are now clip-in shoes available that are reasonable for strolling around a city. Make the decision with the help of a knowledgeable bike store employee.

I tour with platform pedals with a toe-strap and use running shoes that are appropriate for climbing a mountain or dining in a nice restaurant. I generally pair this with a light pair of sandals, which are good for airing out feet after a long day of pedaling. Some bike shop employees will tell you that you would be crazy to bike without clip-in shoes. I biked across the country with baskets and sneakers and had no problems. If you can, try both types and make your decision based on your financial situation and advice from your bike shop.

Carrying Your Gear

There are two ways to carry your gear. One is a trailer, and the other is the more traditional saddlebag system.

Trailers are effective. They allow you to haul large amounts of gear, without sacrificing maneuverability. They are expensive, however, and may be heavy for some people. Use a one-wheeled trailer as they perform much better than trailers with two wheels.

Saddlebags are small bags mounted to racks on the rear and sometimes front of your bike. They are easily removed, often waterproof and preferred by many cyclists. Saddlebags are usually more affordable and always lighter than a trailer.

If you choose to tour with saddlebags make sure that the rack(s) you mount your saddlebags to are high-quality. A rack designed to carry your homework or a few groceries will likely fail when you hit a bump at a high speed while supporting your worldly possessions.

Most people bungee cord their tent, mattress and sleeping bag to the top of the rear rack and fill the saddlebags with the rest of their gear. Consider purchasing a water-proof bag that you can fill with your sleeping bag and tent that will attach securely to your rack and keep your gear dry during precipitation.

Gear For Your Bike

Fenders for the front and rear tires of your bicycle are recommended. They will help keep you and your gear dry while biking through rain.

Most cycle tourists mount a small, detachable bag on their handlebars. This is a great spot for valuables, guidebooks, maps, cameras, music, food and other items that you want to keep closely available. The bag can be removed quickly when you want to leave your bike unattended for a few minutes. Known as handlebar bags, they are available at your local bike shop.

I recommend mounting an LED light to the front and rear of your bike. Nobody plans to ride after dark or in low-light situations but it will inevitably happen. A flashing light will make you visible to motorists.

Make sure your bike is equipped with a properly calibrated cycle computer. These affordable computers will help you interact with this guidebook more effectively, help you set an appropriate pace and break the monotony of a long day on the road.

Gear For You

Having proper clothing with you when you are bike touring will help to make your trip more enjoyable.

Make sure you have water-proof pants and jacket in case of rain. You'll also need a few pairs of cycling shorts as well as a casual pair for relaxing in after your day is over. Bring a few shirts to ride in that are made of a material that will wick away moisture and dry quickly. Cotton is not a good choice for bike touring. Pack one pair of pants that will be suitable for wearing around camp as well as for visiting museums or going out for dinner. Pack at least three pairs of socks. I generally pack one casual t-shirt and something with long sleeves appropriate for layering in cooler weather.

For cold weather, I recommend a fleece sweater as it will layer well, insulate you and pack easily.

Make sure you have a pair of gloves to protect your hands and bring you warmth both while cycling and while enjoying your evening. Bring a touque to help preserve body heat.

If you bike across the country you will undoubtedly experience both hot and cold weather. I recommend traveling with long underwear for the cold stretches.

Wear a helmet at all times while bicycle touring. Not only will it protect your brain in the event of a collision, but the helmet will help to protect your face from the elements while allowing heat to escape from your head.

Make sure to bring along a pair of sunglasses to block both the sun's rays as well as bugs and debris.

Make sure you don't hit the road without the following:

- A small hand operated tire pump for inflating bike tubes.
- Duct tape. DO NOT FORGET THE DUCT TAPE!
- Zip-ties. You can fix practically anything with zip-ties and duct tape.
- Tire irons used to get the tire on and off of the rim when changing a flat.
- A patch kit for fixing flat-tires.
- An extra tire tube or two. Make sure the valve type and size are appropriate for your bike rim.
- Chain breaker used to fix a broken chain.
- Extra link for your chain.
- Chain grease and an old toothbrush.
- A multi-tool with screwdriver bits and hex keys.
- A pair of pliers or an adjustable wrench.
- A spoke tool and extra spokes.

Camping Gear

A good tent is extremely important. It must be lightweight, waterproof and of the appropriate dimensions for your needs. Make sure your tent is large enough to shelter both yourself and your belongings in case of rain.

Make sure that you are familiar with your tent and how to set it up properly before you leave on your trip. Even the best tent, if set up improperly, will leak during rain.

A sleeping pad is important to keep you off of the ground and provide proper rest. Although inflatable mattresses are comfortable, in my bike tour experience they have proven to puncture easily and are difficult to patch. Thermarest makes a comfortable, uninflatable mattress that poses no risk of puncturing.

Make sure that your sleeping bag is appropriate for the temperatures that you will be experiencing. Remember that sleeping bag temperature ratings are only applicable if paired with an insulated pad.

Pillows are optional. Many bike tourists fill the compression bag from their sleeping bag with a sweater to make a pillow, but there are some inexpensive, compact travel pillows on the market.

Food

There are few idle moments when bike touring. You wake up in the morning looking to quell the hunger pangs in your stomach caused by your race car metabolism!

Breakfast is essential and is usually prepared at your campsite upon awakening. Next, you need to pack up your gear and load your bicycle. Once you are fed and your bicycle is packed, you are ready to hit the road.

Lunch is a great way to break up the monotony of cycling all day. Eating lunch in a restaurant can be a great way to meet people and enjoy a cooked meal but sandwiches prepared under a tree taste delicious as well!

Dinner, the highlight of your day, is a grand affair, as you are attempting to replace some of the 5000 or so calories that you have burned off while cycling! You can eat almost whatever you want while bike touring and not come home carrying the extra few pounds common with most traditional vacations.

Although cooking gear such as a stove, plate, and cookware add weight to your bike, I recommend traveling with them so you can prepare your own food. Restaurant portions are often insufficient to support the caloric requirements of bike touring and not always available close to camping spots.

Multi-fuel stoves are recommended for bike touring. They run on a variety of fuel from lighter fluid to gasoline. Gasoline is excellent because it is available globally so you will not be searching for a camping store to purchase a specific fuel. Multi-fuel stoves are very small. Including bottle, they fit into a nylon bag about the size of a shoe.

The type of cookware you carry will depend on how many people that you are traveling with. For one or two people I recommend using a small wok as you can use it to boil and fry. If there are more than two people on your tour I recommend a pot to accompany your wok. With a pot and a wok you can combine them to make a double boiler dutch oven allowing you to bake and cook many more types of food.

Bring along unbreakable cutlery and a plastic or metal plate (frisbees make great plates / bowls / frisbees). You should also bring a folding knife that you can use to cut vegetables and perform any tasks that should arise. Carry a small scrub pad and some biodegradable soap for cleanup.

Pack a few spices and a small, resalable bottle of oil to carry with you. Purchase the rest of your grocery products day-by-day. Make sure you have bottles with you to carry a minimum three liters of drinking water to keep you hydrated.

Packing Your Bike

Greyhound Bus and most airlines will not accept bikes that are not packed in a cardboard box or hard case. Most bike shops will pack your bike into a box for a fee, but they also will either give or sell to you at a low price a bike box so you can pack your bike yourself.

To pack a bike in a box, you need to take off the pedals, turn the handlebars sideways and remove the wheels from the frame and then release the air. Reference the internet for more information.

Don't forget that the threaded stud on the pedal on the chain side of the bike is threaded normally, but the other pedal is left-hand thread and must be turned clockwise to remove.

The maple leaf has symbolized Canada for hundreds of years. Aboriginals have annually held a spring harvest to collect the sap of maple trees.

This maple leaf is symbolized on the National Flag of Canada on a red flag that is twice as long as it is high. Centered on this red flag is a white square, which surrounds an 11-point maple leaf. The white square is exactly half as long as the entire flag.

This flag became Canada's official flag on February 15, 1965, which is now celebrated annually as National Flag of Canada Day.

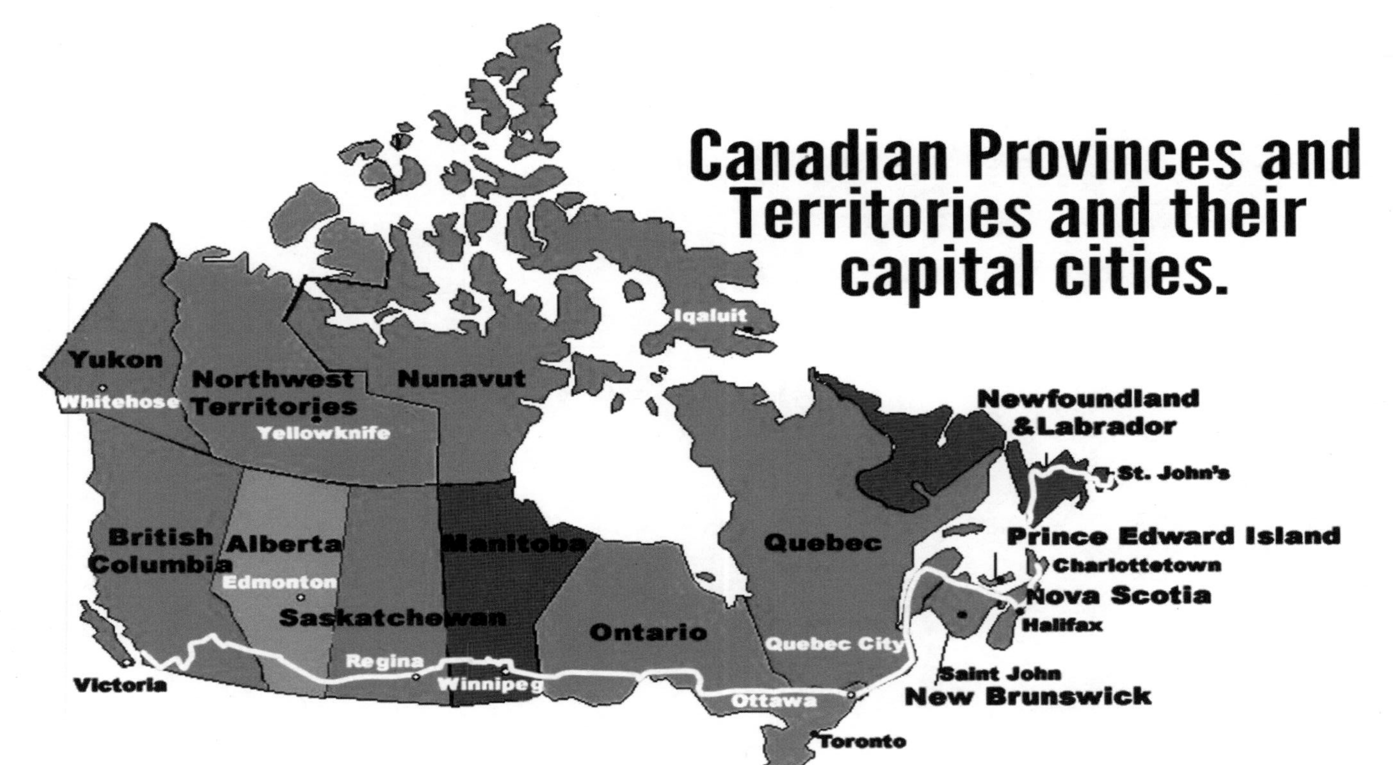
Canadian Provinces and
Territories and their
capital cities.
Yukon
Whitehose
Northwest
Territories
Yellowknife
Nunavut
Iqaluit
British
Columbia
Victoria
Alberta
Edmonton
Saskatchewan
Regina
Manitoba
Winnipeg
Ontario
Ottawa
Toronto
Quebec
Quebec City
Newfoundland
&Labrador
St. John's
Prince Edward Island
Charlottetown
Nova Scotia
Halifax
Saint John
New Brunswick

Province:	British Columbia
Population:	4 113 487
Area:	944 735 km^2
Industry:	Forestry, mining, tourism, arts, marijuana.
Highlights:	Vancouver and Stanley Park, Allison Pass, Okanagan Valley, Rogers Pass.

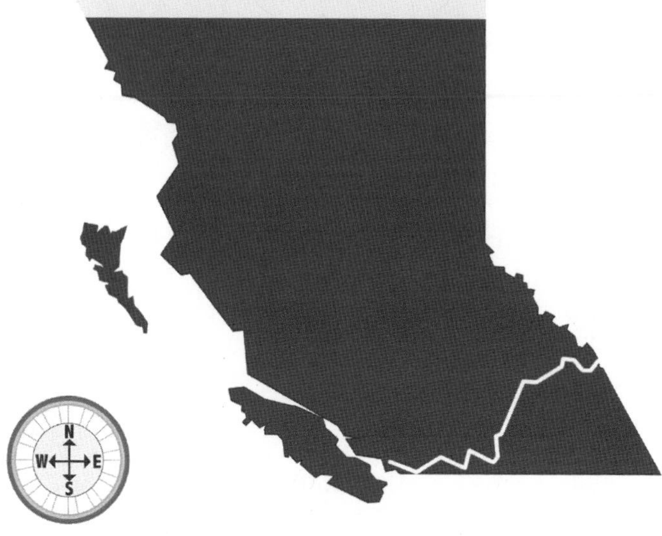

Vancouver to Mission's Rainbow Valley Trout Farm (66.2 K)

Home of the 2010 Winter Olympics, Vancouver is a densely populated metropolis where skyscrapers mingle with towering cedars, snow-capped mountains and the Pacific Ocean. The land is rich with First Nations history.

Vancouver is a cultural melting pot; only 48% of the city's inhabitants list English as their first language. Visitors to Vancouver have the opportunity to experience many authentic international cultures such as Chinese, Punjabi, Japanese and Filipino.

No visit to Vancouver would be complete without a stroll or bike through Stanley Park, where this trip begins. The natural beauty of this green space rivals any in the world. A nine-kilometre cycle path circles the park and will allow you to expediently visit trees that stretch up to eighty metres in the air while cycling amongst unique gardens and Totem poles.

Vancouver has many fine beaches within city limits, which are accessible by public transit. My favourite is Wreck Beach, next to the University of British Columbia (UBC). From the UBC main bus loop, walk west for five minutes down University Boulevard to UBC Gate 6. Turn right on Northwest Marine Drive and walk for 100 metres to a long set of stairs that leads you to the beach.

On a clear day you will be stunned by Vancouver's views. To the north is the Sunshine Coast, while to the south the snow capped volcano, Mount Baker, towers in the state of Washington. Vancouver Island appears to the west.

Vancouver is the most cycle-friendly city in Canada, boasting more than 300 kilometres of bike routes. Drivers expect to see cyclists and tend to give them ample room. Bikes are allowed on the Sky Train light rail system and there are mounts on the front of most buses. If mounting a bike onto the front of a bus, ensure it is securely fastened. Don't be afraid to ask the bus driver for assistance to ensure your bike does not bounce off and get run over.

There are no campgrounds in close proximity to downtown Vancouver, but there are many hostels that welcome bike tourists including the SameSun Hostel and Hostelling International's Vancouver Downtown, both conveniently located downtown.

Today you will bike out of busy Vancouver, into Port Moody, through Port Coquitlam and then Maple Ridge. Expect dense traffic on HWY 7 as it follows the Fraser River. Enjoy small climbs, fast cycling and the view of the mountains ahead of you. You will be climbing up them in the days to come.

Try to start cycling after 9:00 AM and focus on arriving at your campsite before 4:00 PM to avoid rush-hour traffic.

Your destination for the evening, Sun Valley Trout Park, is a former fish farm turned campground. Located 66 kilometres from Vancouver, the campground is an ideal first day ride; long enough to get in a good work out, but short enough that if you have kinks to work out in your body or bike, you can still arrive before dark. A few kilometres east of the campground, on the west side of Mission, you'll find a large grocery store where you can pick up supplies for the evening.

Kilometre Log

0.0 Cycle southeast out of Stanley Park on Causeway Road.

0.5 Causeway Road turns into West Georgia Street. Continue on West Georgia Street.

3.0 West Georgia Street turns into Georgia Viaduct.

3.7 Take exit ramp on your right towards Main Street.

4.0 Turn left onto Main Street.

4.5 Turn right onto East Hastings Street / HWY 7A.

9.4 East Hastings Street / HWY 7A intersects with Cassiar Street / HWY 1.

10.1 East Hastings Street / HWY 7A becomes Hastings Street / HWY 7A.

15.4 Road turns slightly to the right and becomes Burnaby Mountain Parkway.

17.3 With Simon Fraser University on your left bike through a lush park. Burnaby Mountain Parkway curves slightly right and becomes Gaglardi Way.

20.0 Take a left turn onto Broadway.

20.6 Broadway turns into Como Lake Avenue.

21.0 Take a 45° left turn onto Clarke Drive.

23.2 Follow Clarke Drive for 2.2 kilometres, you are now in Port Moody.

26.1 Turn right onto St. Johns Street / Barnet HWY / HWY 7A.

28.5 Road is now Barnet HWY / HWY 7A and no longer St. Johns Street. Pass through a major intersection.

31.2 Barnet HWY / HWY 7A turns into Lougheed HWY / HWY 7.

34.1 Continue on Lougheed HWY / HWY 7 through an industrial part of Maple Ridge. Cross the Pitt River.

44.1 Take a slight right onto the Haney Bypass which skirts the Fraser River.

46.7 Regain the Lougheed HWY / HWY 7 and stay on this highway for 18.9 kilometres.

46.9 Cross over Kanaka Creek.

65.6 Watch for signs for the Sun Valley Trout Park, which will be on your left side. Turn left onto Nelson Street.

65.9 Turn right onto Silverdale Avenue.

66.2 Enter Sun Valley Trout Park Campground.

Lessons learned from Brent Lane:

"To anyone who is thinking about bike touring, I suggest that you acquire a bike that is specifically made for touring and hauling gear. The money that you will save by using a bike that may be older or not made for touring will quickly be spent on repairs and delays. Having a reliable bike will allow you to enjoy a beautiful day of riding across the tremendous Canadian countryside."

West Vancouver
North Vancouver
Norgate
Lynn Creek
Dollarton
Burrard Inlet
Seymour Creek
West Point Grey
Kitsilano
Vancouver
W 16th Ave
University of British Columbia at Vancouver
University Endowment
Quilchena
Granville St
Main St
Knight Road
Knight St
Riley Park/ South Cambie
Grandview Woodlands
Willingdon Heights
Renfrew Heights
Cascade Heights
Kingsway
Victoria-Fraserview/ Killarney
Burnaby Lake Park
Westridge
99
99A
1
5 KM
Stanley Park 1
Wreck Beach 2
Vancouver SameSun Hostel 3
HI Vancouver Downtown 4
Vancouver International Airport 5

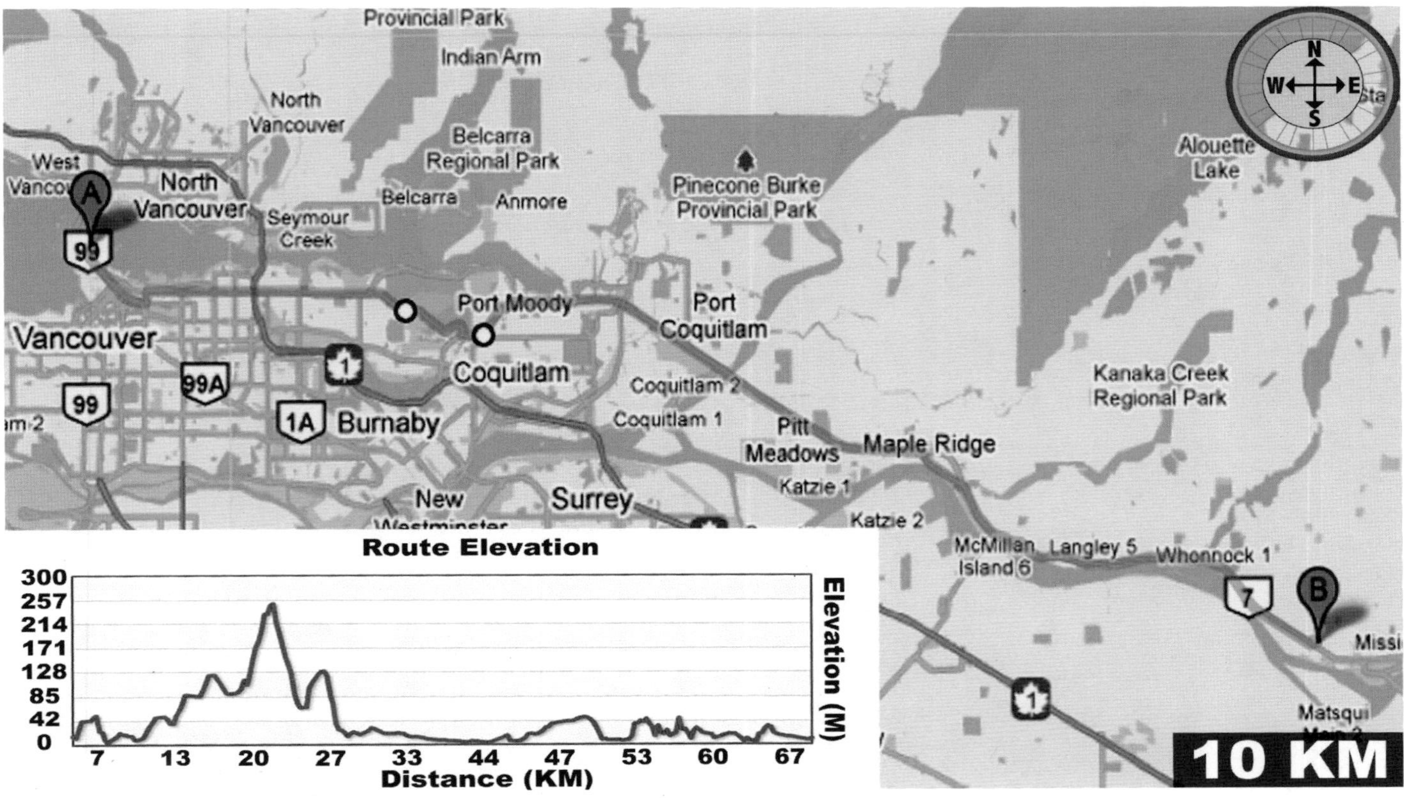

Provincial Park
Indian Arm
North Vancouver
Belcarra Regional Park
West
North Vancouver
Seymour Creek
Belcarra
Anmore
Pinecone Burke Provincial Park
Alouette Lake
A
99
Port Moody
Port Coquitlam
Vancouver
Coquitlam
99A
99
1
Coquitlam 2
Coquitlam 1
1A
Burnaby
Pitt Meadows
Maple Ridge
Kanaka Creek Regional Park
Katzie 1
New
Surrey
Katzie 2
McMillan Island 6
Langley 5
Whonnock 1
7
B
Matsqui
N
W
E
S
10 KM
Route Elevation
300
257
214
171
128
85
42
0
7
13
20
27
33
44
47
53
60
67
Distance (KM)
Elevation (M)

Rainbow Valley Trout Park to Hope's Coquihalla Campground (89.5 K)

The fertile Fraser River Valley will continue to guide you as you climb slowly towards Hope. HWY 7 runs parallel to HWY 1, which is preferred by big rigs (large, industrial trucks), so you can expect a pleasant ride on the Lougheed Highway / HWY 7. This area is mostly rural but you can expect to see regular commercial establishments where food and water are available.

Mission, population 34 505, is a quiet, friendly town along the shore of the Fraser River. People live in Mission because of its tranquil setting, small town feel and location just across the river from Abbotsford.

If you are having any problems with your bike or gear, stop at Wenting's Cycle on the east side of Mission. The staff offers expert advice and understands the unique needs of touring cyclists. They offer no-nonsense advice and will get you set up properly. Make sure not to leave Mission without spare tire-tubes, a patch kit and an extra link in case you break a chain on the coming climbs.

The highlight of your day will be Brio Springs, a natural spring on the left side of the highway that is hard to miss. Cool, clean water runs out of a pipe year-round making it a great place to fill your water bottle and take a break from riding.

The 6 185 people that call Hope home are proud of their locally produced chainsaw carvings and the area's natural beauty. Hope is located at the confluence of the Fraser and Coquihalla Rivers. Hope's bike store is called Cheyenne Sports.

Your destination for the evening is Hope's Coquihalla Campground. The campground is set in a forest and has campsites next to the Coquihalla River.

Kilometre Log

0.0 Leave Sun Valley Trout Park on Silverdale Avenue cycling west.

0.3 Take your first left turn onto Nelson Street.

0.5 Take your first left onto Lougheed HWY / HWY 7. Through Mission, HWY 7 is known as Railway

Avenue. Remain on this highway until you reach the west side of Hope.

13.7 Dewdney. Take a right turn here to remain on HWY 7.

13.9 Cross over a bridge over a tributary of the Fraser River.

24.2 Cross over the Fraser River.

28.0 Pass a campground called The Campground.

37.9 Cross over picturesque Harrison Lake.

41.7 Brio Springs.

51.8 Take a right turn to stay on HWY 7.

53.3 HWY 7 and HWY 9 merge in Agassiz.

84.4 Watch for signs indicating exits to HWY 1 and Hope. Exit right and circle counter-clockwise 180° before descending towards a bridge over the Fraser River on HWY 1.

85.0 In Hope, HWY 1 is known as Water Avenue. After crossing the Coquihalla River, follow HWY 1 / Water Avenue as it skirts the river.

86.6 Turn left onto Wallace Street.

87.1 Turn right onto 6th Avenue.

87.7 Take your third left onto Kawkawa Lake Road.

89.5 Enter Coquihalla Campground on your right hand side.

Coquihalla River

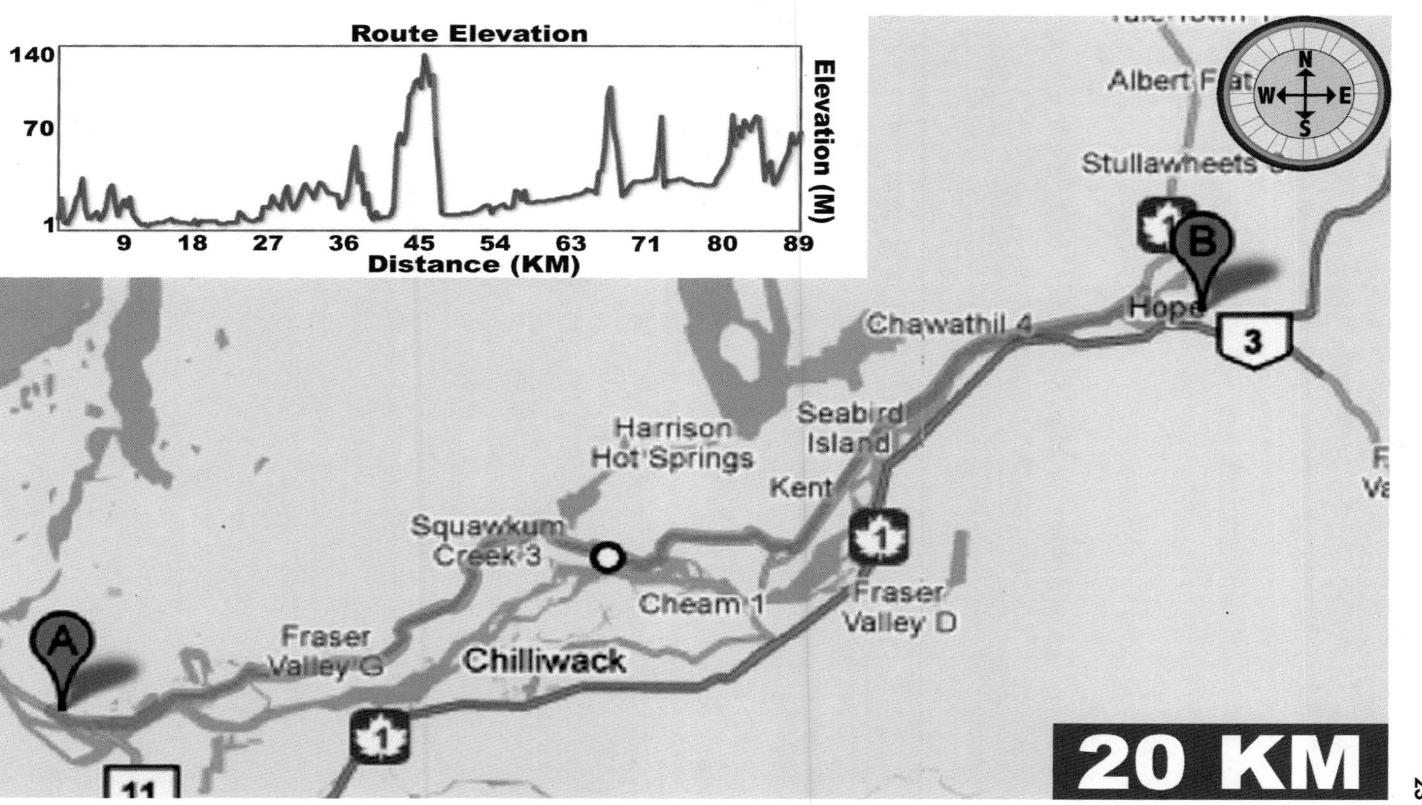
Route Elevation
140
70
1
9
18
27
36
45
54
63
71
80
89
Distance (KM)
Elevation (M)
Albert Flat
Stullawheets
N
W
E
S
B
Hope
3
Chawathil 4
Seabird Island
Harrison Hot Springs
Kent
1
Squawkum Creek 3
Cheam 1
Fraser Valley D
A
Fraser Valley G
Chilliwack
1
11
20 KM

Coquihalla Campground to E.C. Manning Provincial Park's Lightning Lake Campground. (71.0 K)

Today's ride is the most physically demanding of the entire trip. When you conquer Allison Pass, you will know you have the physical and mental strength to complete any day on this tour.

Your destination is Lightning Lake Campground in E.C. Manning Provincial Park.

Known to locals as Manning Park, this 708 kilometre^2 park is a legendary test to cyclists. Manning Park has diverse geography that includes wet coastal mountains, snow capped peaks, alpine meadows, chains of small lakes and flowing riverbeds. This protected area provides diverse habitat for the park's wildlife, which includes grizzly bear, wolverine, mountain beaver as well as 206 species of birds.

Stock up on groceries before you leave Hope as there are no grocery stores until you reach Princeton, 134 kilometres away. Leave Hope on HWY 3, the Crowsnest Highway. Expect temperatures to soar while climbing these unnerving, steep hills.

Climb for 18 kilometres out of Hope and be amazed at the devastation caused by the Hope Slide. During the morning hours of January 9, 1965, a small earthquake triggered the rock slide in which four people perished under an estimated 46 million cubic metres of debris.

After leaving Hope Slide you will cycle through the Sunshine Valley, a residential area with no stores. The residents are friendly and will fill your water bottles. Watch out for bears in this area!

Allison Pass is in the middle of Manning Park and separates the Skagit and Similkameen river drainages to the east and west respectively. The climb to the summit seems to go on forever. Don't rush up this beast. Take frequent short breaks to keep your morale high and legs fresh. Stop and take a picture at the summit and get ready for an exhilarating downhill towards Manning Lodge, which is next to the turnoff to Lightning Lake Campground.

Lightning Lake is 4 kilometres south of HWY 3 and is only open from early June until early October. It is the only campground in Manning Park with showers. Manning Lodge offers hostel type accommodations at a reasonable rate for the solo traveler, especially during spring and fall which is the off-peak season in this area. Use of the hot tub is included.

Contact Discover Camping to book campsites in any British Columbia Provincial Park especially on weekends during July and August.

Kilometre Log

0.0	Take a left turn out of the campground on Kawkawa Lake Road.
0.3	Take your first left turn onto 7th Avenue.
0.7	Take your first left turn onto Old Hope Princeton Way.
2.2	Turn left to merge onto HWY 3.
6.0	Intersection of HWY 5A / Coquihalla HWY. Stay right on HWY 3 / Crowsnest HWY.
17.2	Climb steadily to the site of Hope Slide.
20.4	Sunshine Valley.
42.2	West entrance of E.C. Manning Provincial Park.
59.4	Allison Pass Summit, elevation 1342 metres.
66.6	Manning Lodge.
65.8	Watch for signs and turn right towards Lightning Lake Campground on HWY 3B here.
70.8	Take a left turn.
71.0	Arrive at Lightning Lake Campground.

Lessons learned from Reghan Bieber:

I wish someone had told me that chafing was not just a "guy thing." Unfortunately, I had to learn the hard way. Who knew that the underwear you put on in the morning clearly defined your attitude for the day? My advice for the new female bike tourist is simple and straight forward. Put down the lace ladies, keep that cute thong at home, swallow your pride and wear comfortable underwear and those ugly things called bike shorts. Believe me, if you want to have a blissful relationship with your bike and body, choose your garments and textiles wisely. Remember, bike touring is not a fashion show!

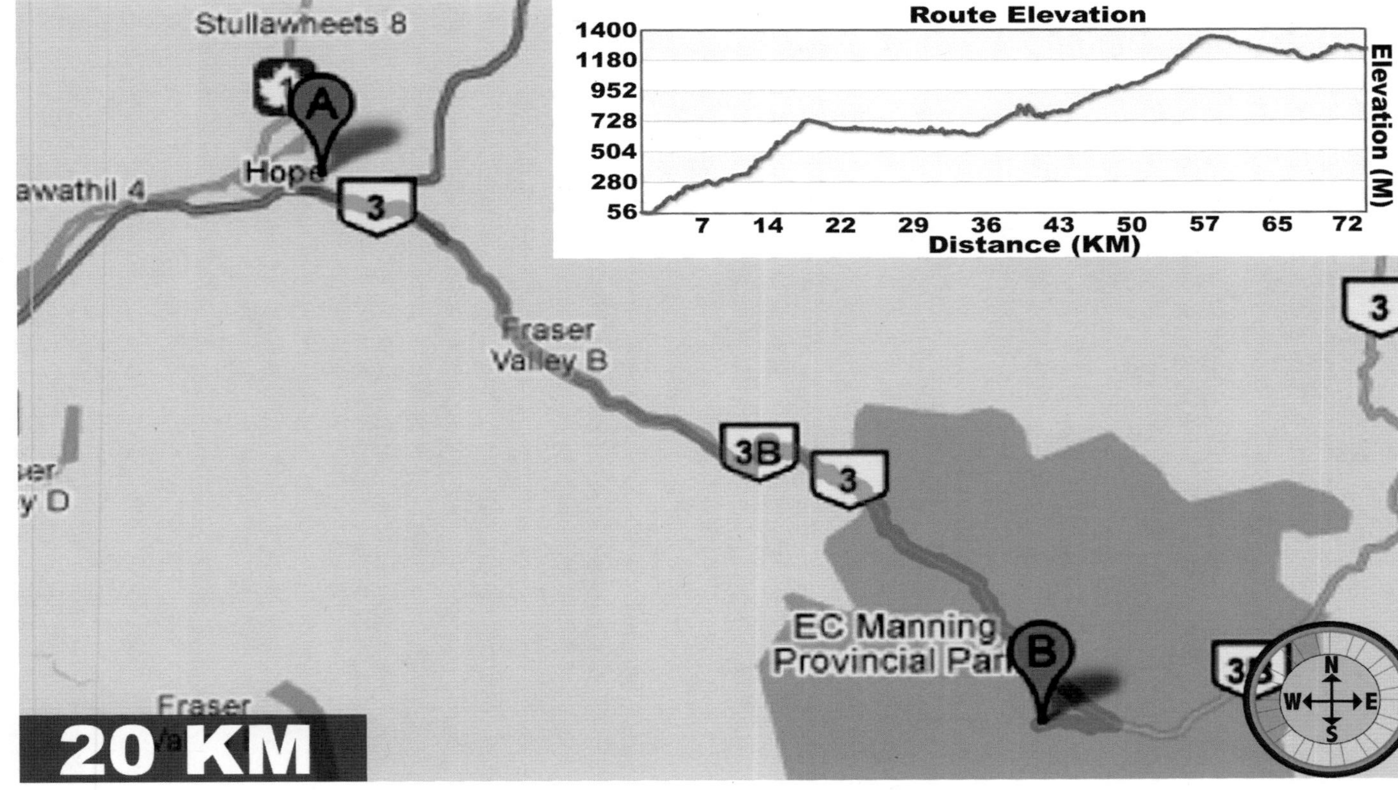

Stullawheets 8
A
Hope
awathil 4
3
Fraser Valley B
3B
3
EC Manning Provincial Par
B
Fraser
20 KM
N
W
E
S
Route Elevation
1400
1180
952
728
504
280
56
7
14
22
29
36
43
50
57
65
72
Distance (KM)
Elevation (M)

Bears

Bears are common in many parts of Canada. If you encounter one on the side of the road try to commandeer a car to drive between you and the animal, which will rarely initiate aggression. Prevention is your best defense against having a scary encounter with these giant mammals.

While camping, maintaining a clean campsite is of paramount importance. In bear country, locate your camp kitchen downwind of your tent by at least 50 metres.

Most campsites with bears in proximity will provide a secure locker to store your food. If this is not available, consider leaving your food bag in a washroom overnight. Do not under any circumstances store food in or near your tent. Also, remember that the clothes that you cooked your dinner in will smell like food so have a separate pair of garments to sleep in and store your cooking clothes away from the tent.

If there is nowhere appropriate to store your food, tie it to a rope and heave it over a tree limb out of the reach of bears.

I did not carry bear spray while I biked across Canada, but did meet one cyclist with a can of bear spray attached to his bike. At the time I thought it was unnecessary but when I woke up to a large animal sniffing my tent I wished I had a can of bear spray to protect myself!

Lightning Lake Campground to Bromley Rock Provincial Park: (92.9 K)

Congratulations on conquering Allison Pass. You will remember that climb for the rest of your life. However, you are not yet finished with extreme climbs. Although not as high, Sunday Summit, on the east boundary of Manning Park will challenge you comparably to Allison Pass. After climbing Sunday Summit, the ride to Princeton will be smooth and scenic.

Today you will start cycling along the stunning Similkameen River, which appears shortly after Manning Lodge. This waterway is one of the most beautiful and untouched rivers in Canada's south. Every year anglers from all over the world flock to the area to fish for Cutthroat and Rainbow Trout.

Pack plenty of water; the only place to fill your bottles is at a small gas station and restaurant at the eastern boundary of Manning Park.

The landscape and climate will change dramatically today as you approach Princeton. Trees will be larger, plants lusher and the weather milder.

Enjoy the dramatic descent into Princeton, population 2 610. Grocery stores will be visible from the highway as you enter. If your bike needs some love, head to Backroads Bike Shop. Princeton is the place to acquire supplies before continuing down the road to Bromley Rock Provincial Park.

Your destination for the evening, Bromley Rock Provincial Park, is located at a traditional First Nations fishing site and is a great place for a swim. Visitors flock to the area to relax on the sandy beach or to start a tubing adventure down the river to Stemwinder Provincial Park. There are showers on site, but bring drinking water with you as there is often a boil-water advisory in the park. The campsites are picturesque, placed on the banks of the Similkameen. Camping is permitted all year long although services are only guaranteed from late April until late September.

Kilometre Log

0.0	Leave Lightning Lake Campground heading north.
0.2	Take a right turn onto HWY 3B.
5.2	Turn right onto HWY 3. Remain on this highway all day.
21.2	East boundary of Manning Park.
21.3	Small gas station and restaurant.
39.3	Sunday Summit, elevation 1 284 metres.
70.0	Enter Princeton.
72.1	Cross over the Similkameen River.
73.3	River's Edge Campground is on the left side of the highway.
74.8	Princeton Municipal Campground.
92.9	Bromley Rock Provincial Park.

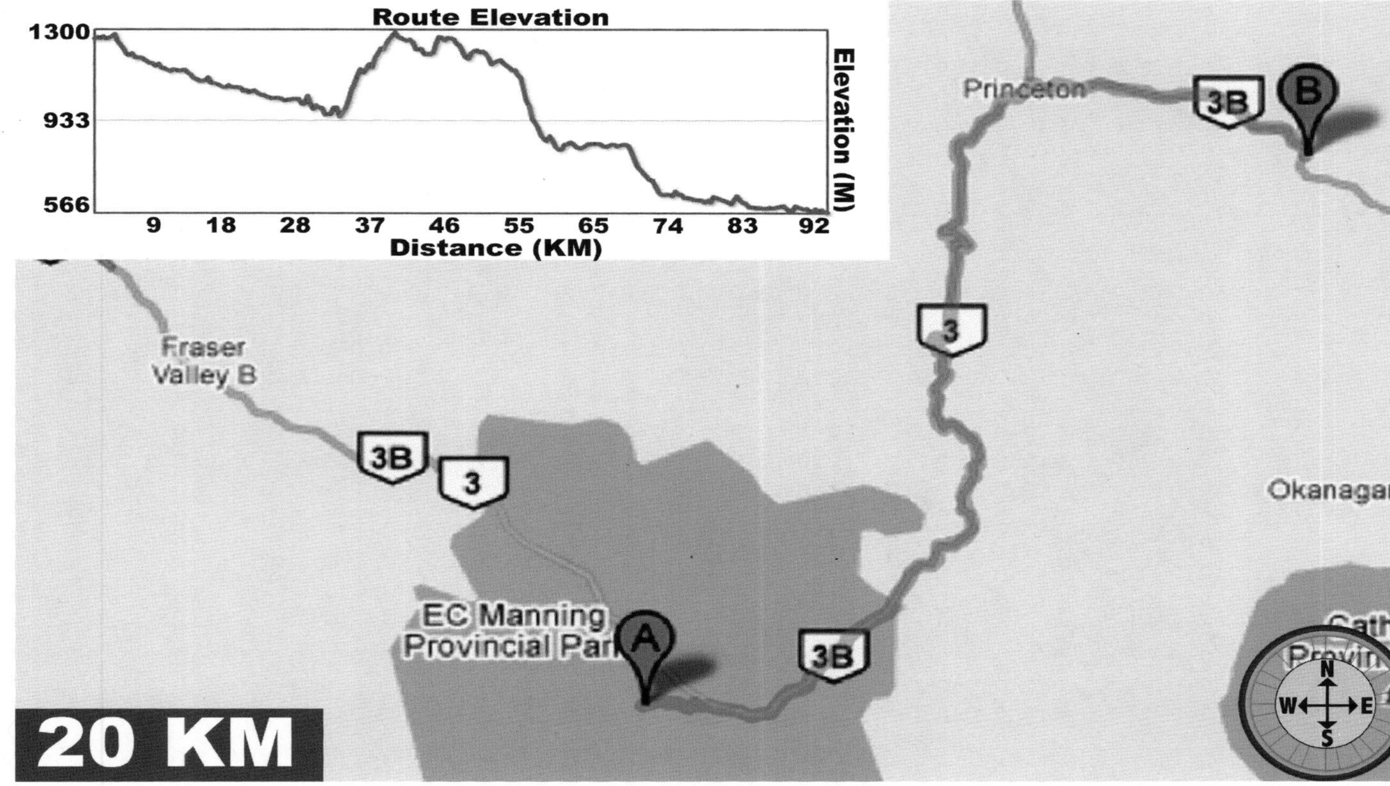
Route Elevation
1300
933
566
9
18
28
37
46
55
65
74
83
92
Distance (KM)
Elevation (M)
Fraser
Valley B
3B
3
EC Manning
Provincial Par
A
3B
3
Princeton
3B
B
Okanagan-
N
W
E
S
20 KM

Bromley Rock Provincial Park to Okanagan Provincial Park: (115.3 K)

Enjoy easy pedaling all day on the mostly downhill ride to Penticton. You will feel like an all-star cyclist gliding effortlessly along the banks of the Similkameen in this warm, temperate part of Canada.

Just before the town of Hedley is Stemwinder Provincial Park, a small pine-dotted picnic and camping area on the Similkameen River. If swimming, use caution as the river is cold and the current strong. Watch for poison ivy along the banks.

Poison Ivy is a small green deciduous plant characterized by three leafs and a lack of thorns. It produces an itchy rash when it contacts the skin of most people.

At the turn of the 20th century, Hedley was a thriving gold mining town. A large mill processed gold from the neighbouring Nickel Plate Mountain. Declining resources and fires in the community led to Hedley's economic decline. Presently, Hedley is a small village catering to tourists. Check out the Hedley Mining Museum and meet some of the locals that often sell textiles out of their front yards.

The area between Hedley and Keremeos is densely populated with large, white antelope.

Although you can bypass Keremeos, population 1 289, consider checking out the charming town. Its name is derived from the Similkameen dialect of the native Okanagan word keremeyeus, meaning "creek which cuts its way through the flats." Keremeos is famous for bountiful harvests of fruits and vegetables. It is also renowned for its superior wine growing potential. Keremeos has a campground called Eagle Campground & RV Park.

Leave Keremeos and continue cycling towards Penticton through orchards and verdant agriculture land. Watch for wind gusts on some of the long downhill sections.

At Keremeos, HWY 3 splits and HWY 3 goes south before heading east towards Alberta along B.C.'s southern border. HWY 3A and HWY 3B head north where they merge with HWY 97 near Skaha Lake. HWY 97 is a busy double-lane. It will be your trail until intersecting with HWY 1 at Sicamous.

Skaha Lake forms the southern border of Penticton, which is bordered on the north by Okanagan Lake. Penticton, population 31 909, is a popular tourist and retirement destination. It is famous for peaches, beaches, golf and especially wine. Penticton was known by the Salish First Nation as Pen-Tak-Ton, meaning "a place to live forever."

Penticton's British Columbia Wine Information Centre is a good place to learn about wine and wine tourism in the Valley. Residents of the Okanagan Valley take great pride in area vineyards and the quality of wine they produce. Many wineries operate throughout the Okanagan valley and offer tourists a unique chance to taste wines and tour vineyards.

If you do not have time restrictions, consider staying the night in Penticton and going wine touring at Naramata Bench.

Camping is available at the south end of town at Wright's Beach RV Park & Campground. Freedom Bike Shop is available for any repairs or supplies you may need. The Okanagan is a beautiful, but expensive place to visit. Real estate prices are sky high, and this is reflected in campground prices.

After leaving Penticton, expect HWY 97 to be busy, especially during July and August. Wear bright coloured clothing and cycle with confidence. Other than the dense traffic, the ride to Kelowna is enjoyable with Lake Okanagan on your right and rugged, rocky cliffs on your left.

Summerland, population 10 828, is aptly named as it has some of the warmest temperatures in Canada, with a mean summer temperature of 21° C. The town is situated on a long hill. One exit to the city is at the bottom of the hill and the other is at the top. Summerland is a good place to acquire supplies to prepare for your evening in Okanagan Lake Provincial Park.

Stay at either the South or North Campground in Okanagan Provincial Park. The South Campground opens first, generally around April 1st, and closes at the beginning of October. Located on the shores of Lake Okanagan, this campground offers sandy beaches and is surrounded by Ponderosa Pine and sagebrush.

Kilometre Log

0.0 Leave Bromley Rock Provincial Park on HWY 3 heading south.
11.9 Stemwinder Provincial Park.
16.9 Exit to Hedley.
44.4 Keremeos, population 1 289. Turn left onto Keremeos Bypass Road.
45.0 Take a left turn to stay on Keremeos Bypass Road / HWY 3A.
46.8 Take a left turn to return to HWY 3.
61.9 Climb steadily to the south end of Yellow Lake where there are washrooms and a rest area.
76.1 HWY 3 dead-ends into HWY 97. Turn left heading north on HWY 97.
84.1 Wright's Beach Campground on the shore of Skaha Lake.
84.5 Penticton Regional Airport.
84.9 Cross a bridge over the canal and turn left onto Channel Parkway / HWY 97.
89.0 Road veers to the right and becomes Railway Street / HWY 97.
89.7 Take a left turn onto Eckhardt Avenue W / HWY 97.
90.5 Eckhardt Avenue W / HWY 97 turns right and becomes only HWY 97.
96.0 Kickininee Provincial Park with camping and showers.
96.8 Soorimpt Provincial Park.
97.8 Pyramid Provincial Park picnic grounds.
101.1 Summerland.
115.0 Turn right into Okanagan Provincial Park.
115.3 Okanagan Provincial Park South Campground.

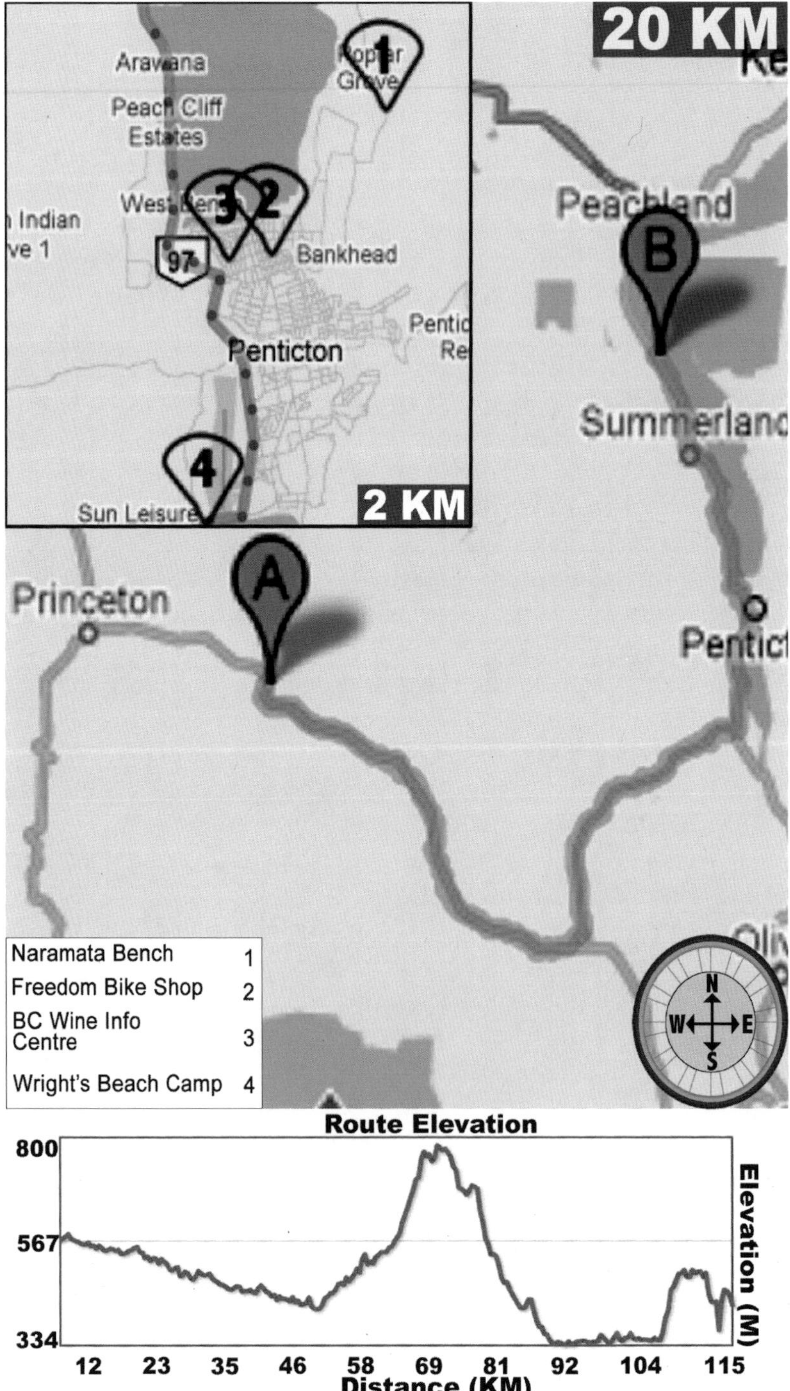

20 KM
2 KM
Aravaana
Poplar Grove
Peach Cliff Estates
West Bench
Indian
ve 1
97
Bankhead
Penticton
Pentic
Re
Sun Leisure
Peachland
Summerland
Princeton
Pentict
Oliv
N
W
E
S
Naramata Bench 1
Freedom Bike Shop 2
BC Wine Info Centre 3
Wright's Beach Camp 4
Route Elevation
800
567
334
12
23
35
46
58
69
81
92
104
115
Distance (KM)
Elevation (M)

Wine tasting near Penticton

The Okanagan Valley was formed glacially during the Tertiary and Quaternary periods around 10 000 years ago. Ice as thick as two kilometres scraped the surface and left behind sedimentary deposits along its borders.

The system of long, narrow lakes in the Okanagan Valley are a result of this glacial activity.

Okanagan Valley

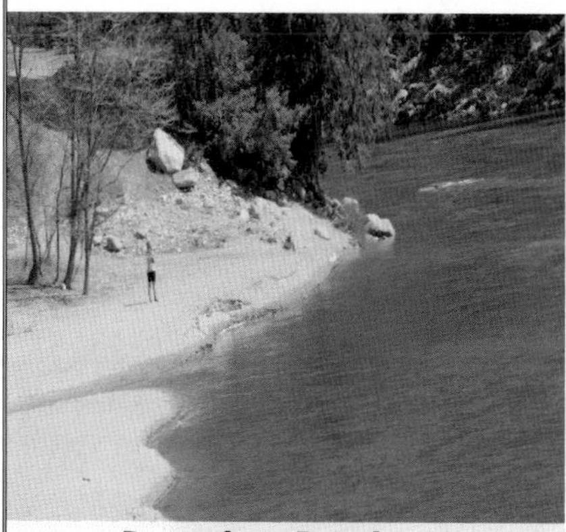

Bromley Rock

This system of lakes drains towards the south into the Okanagan River, which meets up with the Columbia River in Washington and heads west towards the Pacific Ocean.

Okanagan Provincial Park to Vernon's Swan Lake RV Park: (95.7 K)

The congested, noisy HWY 97 continues to hug Lake Okanagan as you cycle north towards Vernon.

If you are traveling through this area in the summer, expect the trees to be covered in flowers or fruit. July and August brings a festival-like atmosphere to the Valley as gleeful residents celebrate the quality grapes grown in the area.

The first town you will cycle through today is Peachland, population 4 883, where Hainle Vineyards became the first ice wine maker in North America.

Enter Kelowna by crossing the William R. Bennett Bridge, which spans Lake Okanagan. Named after former B.C. Premier William R. Bennett, nine floats keep the bridge poised stoically on Lake Okanagan.

In the summer, tourists flock to Kelowna for golf, the wine industry and other outdoor pursuits. In the winter, the city boasts world-class skiing and snowboarding at four area resorts. The area also has many trails for snowshoeing and cross-country skiing.

If you want to spend a night in Kelowna, check out Willow Creek Campground. Also, if you need a bike shop, talk to the staff at Cyclepath. If you are pining for a roof over your head, SameSun Hostel is a happening, friendly hostel.

Leave the city of Kelowna heading north. First pass Kelowna International Airport and cycle towards Oyama, a small clean town nestled between Wood Lake to the south and Kalamalka Lake to the north.

As you near Vernon, population 35 944, you will cycle along the shore of Kalamalka Lake and then up a large hill that separates you from Vernon. Descend rapidly into the city where you can purchase supplies for the evening.

The Okanagan Valley was occupied exclusively by the Interior Salish First Nations people until fur traders arrived in 1811. In the 1850s, gold was discovered and mining joined cattle ranching as the area's major economic industries. The town was known as Priest's Valley until 1887, when the town changed its name to Vernon.

If you need work done on your bike head to Olympia Cycle & Ski.

Swan Lake RV Park and Campground is located just north of Vernon and off of HWY 97. In my opinion, the small detour taken up old Kamloops Road is compensated for by the idyllic setting of this campground along the shore of Swan Lake.

Kilometre Log

0.0	Leave Okanagan Lake Provincial Park South Campground heading towards HWY 97.
0.3	Turn right onto HWY 97.
9.4	Peachland.
17.9	Intersection of HWY 97 and 97C.
34.2	William R. Bennett Bridge.
35.5	Enter Kelowna on HWY 97 / Harvey Avenue.
40.2	Harvey Avenue / HWY 97 becomes Okanagan HWY / HWY 97.
50.4	Kelowna International Airport.
52.8	Ellison Lake.
58.9	Winfield.
61.7	Wood Lake.
68.4	Oyama.
78.5	Kekuli Bay Provincial Park.
69.2	Kalamalka Lake.
72.5	Road narrows to one lane.
85.3	Enter Vernon on HWY 97 / 32nd Street.
90.0	Turn left on 43rd Avenue.
90.5	Turn right onto Old Kamloops Road.
95.7	Swan Lake RV Park and Campground.

Lessons learned from Stacie Bourgeois:
Pack clothing that can be worn both on and off your bike. Bring items that are versatile enough to help you cope with the ever-changing weather. The ideal type of clothing will dry quickly and be water resistant. Minimizing your cargo to the bare essentials is hard, but doing so will make life easier. Less to pack up, less to carry, less to wash...less is better!

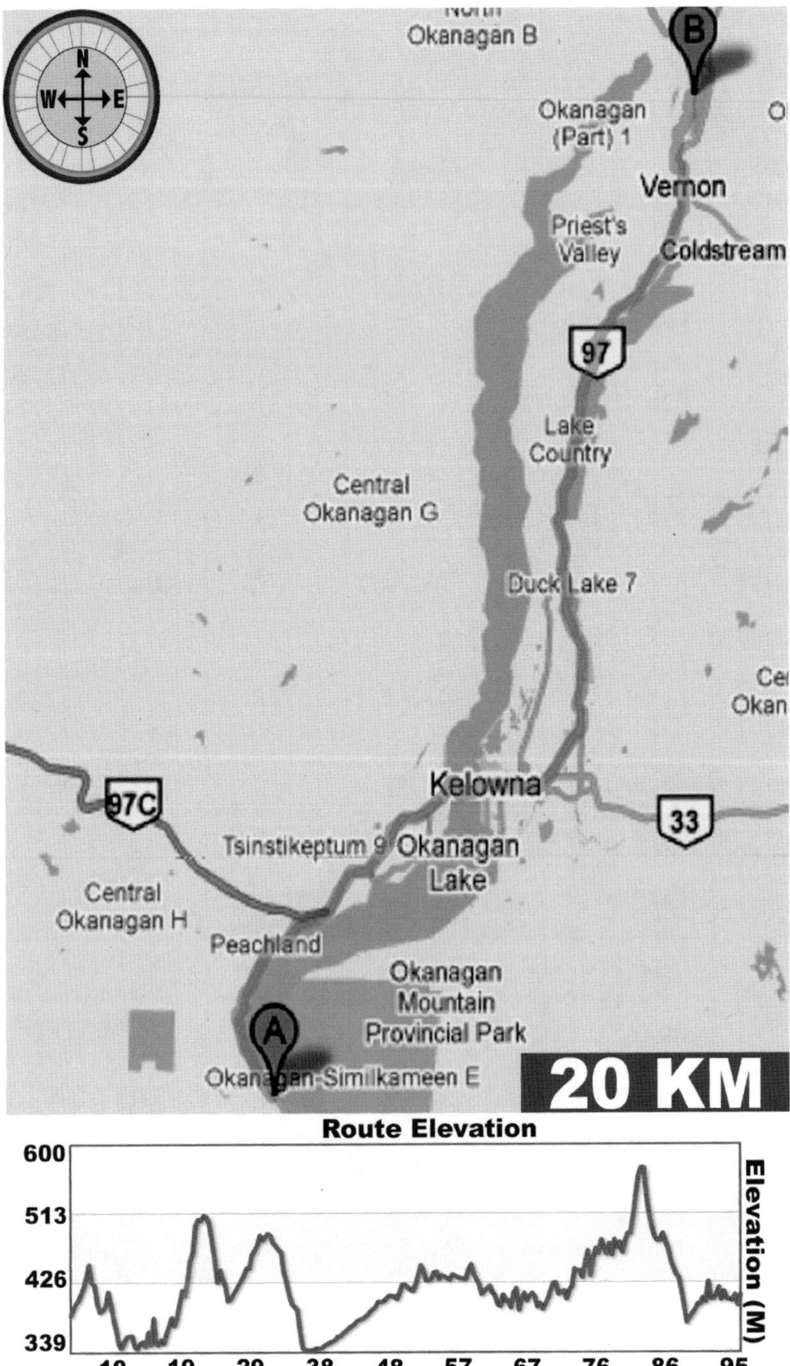

North
Okanagan B
Okanagan
(Part) 1
Vernon
Priest's
Valley
Coldstream
97
Lake
Country
Central
Okanagan G
Duck Lake 7
Kelowna
97C
33
Tsinstikeptum 9
Okanagan
Lake
Central
Okanagan H
Peachland
Okanagan
Mountain
Provincial Park
Okanagan-Similkameen E
20 KM
Route Elevation
600
513
426
339
Elevation (M)
10
19
29
38
48
57
67
76
86
95
Distance (KM)

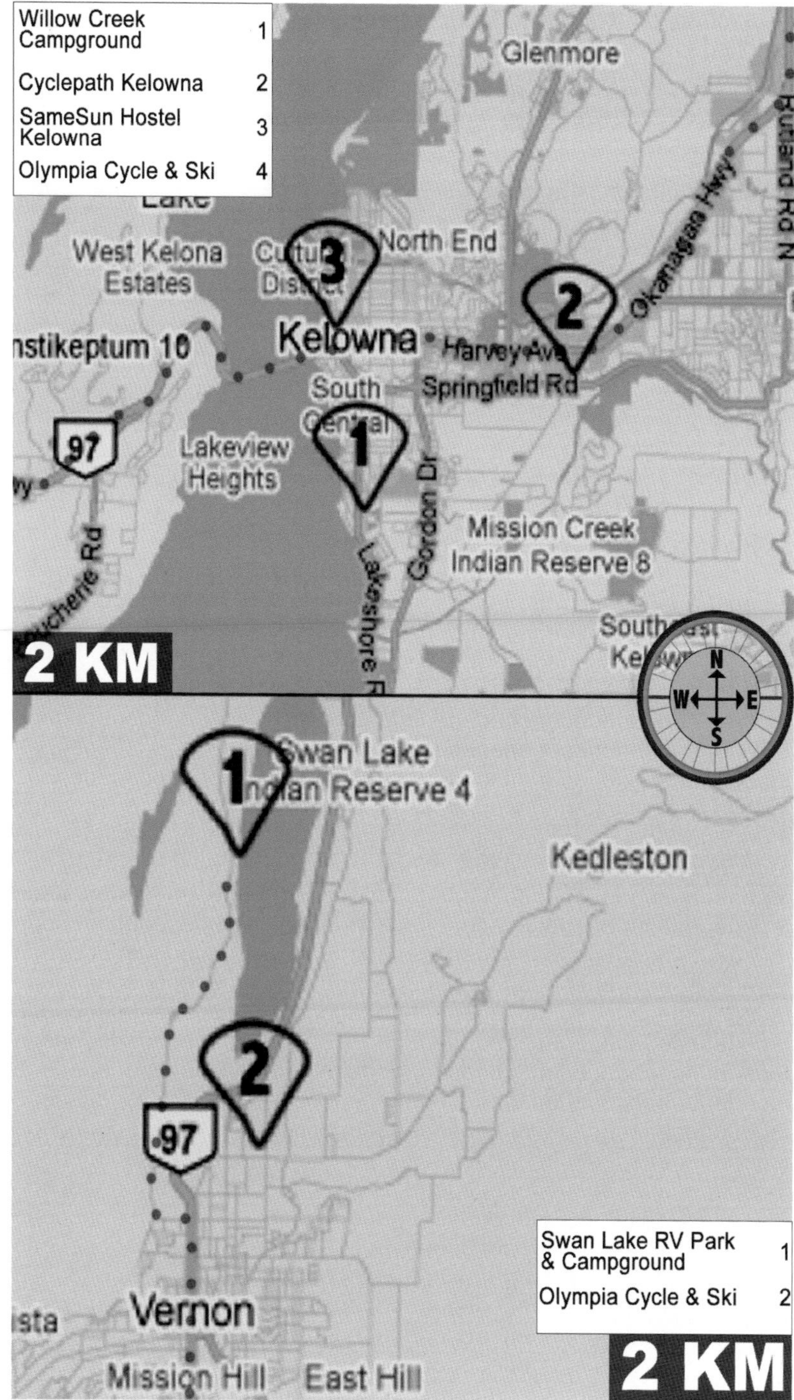
Willow Creek Campground 1
Cyclepath Kelowna 2
SameSun Hostel Kelowna 3
Olympia Cycle & Ski 4
Glenmore
Rutland Rd N
Okanagan Hwy
West Kelona Estates
North End
Kelowna
Harvey Ave
Springfield Rd
South Central
97
Lakeview Heights
Gordon Dr
Lakeshore Rd
Mission Creek Indian Reserve 8
2 KM
N
W
E
S
Swan Lake Indian Reserve 4
Kedleston
97
Vernon
Mission Hill
East Hill
Swan Lake RV Park & Campground 1
Olympia Cycle & Ski 2
2 KM

Swan Lake RV Park & Campground to Revelstoke's Lamplighter Campground: (140.1 K)

Today you will leave behind the sunny confines of the Okanagan Valley, biking first through the Shushwap Valley along the shores of Mara Lake towards Sicamous. Here you will turn right to head east towards Alberta. Expect a cooler climate from Sicamous to Calgary.

The next two days of cycling to Golden are lengthy. I have scheduled these long days with overnight stops in towns offering grocery stores and supplies. Expect to be on your bike for up to eight hours a day. Start your day early and take short breaks at regular intervals.

The first town you will visit after leaving your campsite is Armstrong. If you are hungry and have some spare time, consider touring the Village Cheese Company, a cheese factory based on the estate winery concept.

Continue through Enderby, a small town on the banks of the Shushwap River, with the Enderby cliffs towering overhead. Check out the tidy downtown with many shops and services reminiscent of earlier days.

Rugged, rocky shorelines with sandy beaches starkly contrast the dark blue water of Shushwap Lake. The lake consists of four arms that form a shape similar to the letter H. Salmon Arm is to the southwest, Anstey Arm to the northeast, Seymour Arm to the north and the main lake is to the west. Throngs of tourists flock to this area in the summertime to cruise the lake in giant houseboats.

Sicamous, population 3 192, is known as the Houseboat Capital of Canada. Stock up on supplies here before leaving as there are scant services between Sicamous and Revelstoke. Camping and groceries are available in Sicamous.

Expect to notice a distinct change in both landscape and temperature after leaving Sicamous. HWY 1 cuts through the sweeping views of large mountains covered in coniferous trees and often snow. Listen for waterfalls in this area; you will often hear them prior to seeing them.

HWY 1 will be your trail from here until Regina. Generally, traffic flows briskly down a double-lane highway next to large paved shoulders, which are ideal for bike tourists. With a few exceptions, you will not suffer through many long climbs.

Engineers have designed the highway with large freight-hauling trucks in mind, thus grades are usually mellow.

Take a break at the Last Spike. Soak up the park surrounding the spot where the last spike was driven into the ground to signal the completion of the cross-continental Canadian Pacific Railway on November 7th, 1885. The completion of this railroad linked the east and west coast and was a major factor in British Columbia's decision to join the Canadian Confederation. There is a small gift shop with washrooms here.

Kay Falls is one of the more stunning waterfalls on the entire route across the continent. Stop and enjoy its splendor for a moment before pushing onto Revelstoke.

Revelstoke is a small mountain town on the shores of the Columbia River. The town site is located just north of where the Illecillewaet empties into the Columbia and a short distance to nearby Mt. Revelstoke National Park. Locals appreciate the area for its natural beauty and opportunity for an array of outdoor pursuits including hiking, cycling and rafting in the summer. In the winter, locals head to Revelstoke Mountain Resort, famous for the mass amount of powder snow that accumulates in this area. If you want to sound like a local, refer to the town as Revy.

The 2 000 kilometre Columbia River originates around Columbia Lake and the adjoining Columbia Wetlands just south of Invermere. It flows north through Golden before taking a hard left turn to begin heading south around the Selkirk Mountains. The river flows through Revelstoke, then into Washington where it heads towards the Pacific Ocean to form the border between Washington and Oregon. The Columbia River descends an average 40.9 centimetres per kilometre, which is why the river has been so thoroughly exploited for hydro-electricity production.

Lamplighter Campground is a quiet campground located near both HWY 1 and historic downtown Revelstoke. Flat grassy lots as well as laundry and free wireless internet make the Lamplighter a sound choice. Cross the Columbia River into downtown to purchase supplies for the evening. Revelstoke's bike shop, Flowt Bikes and Skis is located downtown. If you need a roof over your head check out Revelstoke's SameSun Hostel.

Kilometre Log

0.0 Leave Swan Lake Campground on Old Kamloops Road heading north.
2.8 Old Kamloops Road runs into HWY 97. Turn right onto HWY 97.
4.3 Turn left onto HWY 97A and head north.
17.1 Exit to Armstrong.
30.7 Enderby.
37.0 Exit to HWY 97B. Continue heading north on HWY 97A.
41.6 Grindrod.
50.3 Whispering Pines Campground.
53.3 Mara Lake Provincial Park. No camping available.
66.2 Sicamous.
68.5 HWY 97 dead-ends into HWY 1. Turn right on HWY 1.
80.6 Road splits to double lane with large shoulder.
81.6 Sicamous KOA Campground.
82.8 Cedars Campground.
83.4 Cross over Eagle River.
87.3 Malakwa. Small gas station on highway.
90.3 Craigellachie & The Last Spike.
91.2 Eagle River Campground.
92.2 Small gas station.
111.2 Crazy Creek Resort.
111.9 Kay Falls.
122.1 Three Valley Gap Hotel on Three Valley Lake.
135.8 Smokey Bear Campground.
139.5 Descend towards Revelstoke and the Columbia River Valley. Turn right onto HWY 23.
139.8 Turn left onto Nixon Road.
140.1 Lamplighter Campground.

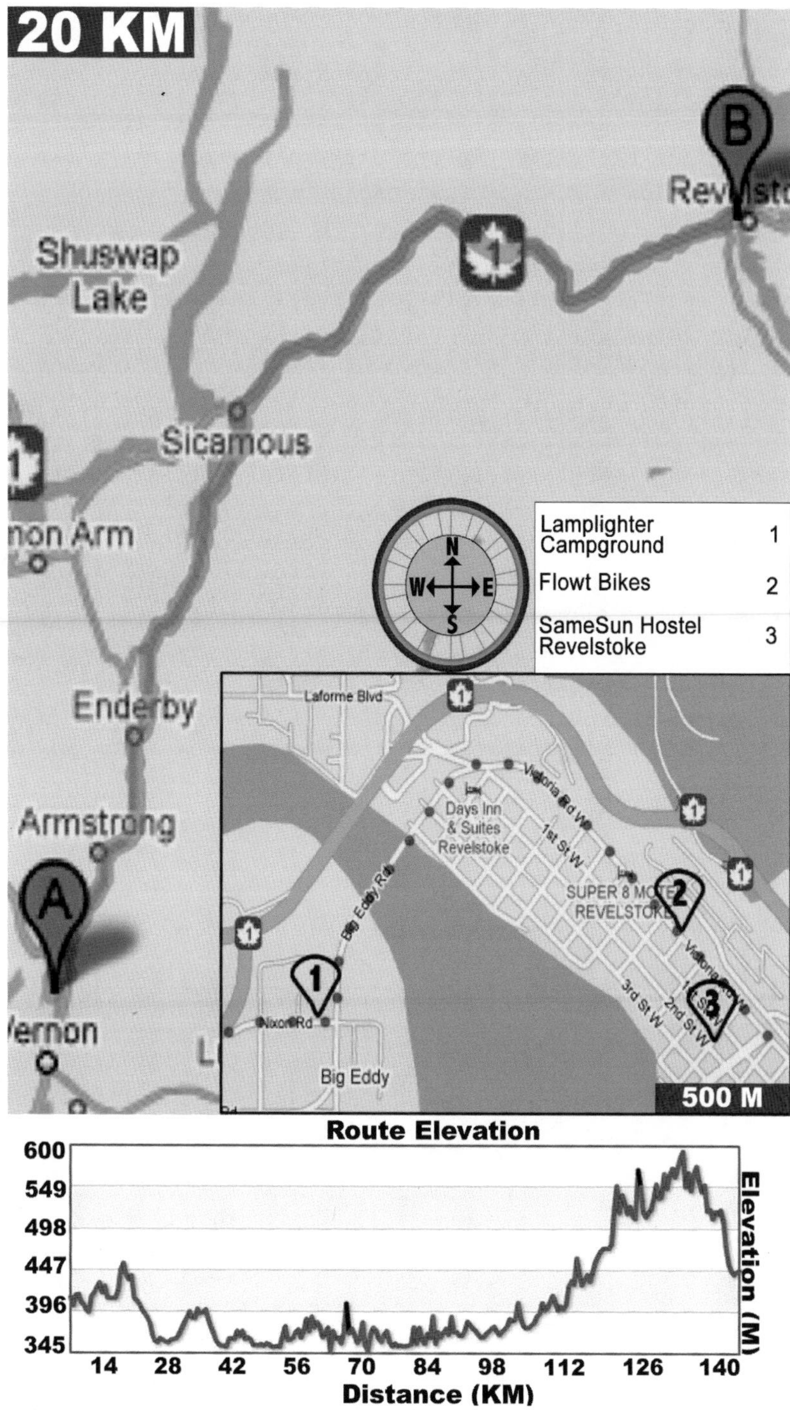
20 KM
Shuswap Lake
Sicamous
Enderby
Armstrong
Lamplighter Campground 1
Flowt Bikes 2
SameSun Hostel Revelstoke 3
Laforme Blvd
Days Inn & Suites Revelstoke
Victoria Rd W
1st St W
SUPER 8 MOTEL REVELSTOKE
3rd St W
2nd St W
Nixon Rd
Big Eddy Rd
Big Eddy
500 M
Route Elevation
600
549
498
447
396
345
14
28
42
56
70
84
98
112
126
140
Distance (KM)
Elevation (M)

Lamplighter Campground to Golden Municipal Campground: (152.3 K)

Today's ride will take you through both Mount Revelstoke and Glacier National Parks.

Mount Revelstoke National Park, founded in 1914, is small compared to most national parks, with an area of only 260 kilometres^2. The park preserves many epic attractions such as the world's only inland rainforest and ancient stands of old growth western red cedar. Don't miss the Giant Cedars hiking trail to view some of these monster trees.

Extensive clear-cut logging in the area surrounding the park combined with the park's small size has caused stress on the park's ecosystems. Its ecological integrity is being threatened by local development and ecological isolation.

Glacier National Park was established in 1886. It covers 1 349 kilometres^2 of mostly glaciated area. The Columbia Mountain range dominates the park, which is known for steep rugged slopes, a warm, moist climate and old growth cedar. Wildlife such as mountain caribou, mountain goat, black and grizzly bear call this area home. More information is available at the Parks Canada Rogers Pass Discovery Centre located near the summit of Rogers Pass.

Each August, wildflowers burst dramatically into bloom in the alpine meadows of both Mount Revelstoke and Glacier National Park.

Rogers Pass, elevation 1 330 metres, in the Selkirk Mountains, is the highest point on the impressive highway route between Golden and Revelstoke.

American Major A.B. Rogers discovered Rogers Pass in 1881. Construction of the railroad in this area was complete by 1885.

To me, Rogers Pass was not as fierce as I had imagined. When we reached the sign indicating we were there, my group and I were surprised. We had expected a long hard climb rather than what proved to be a gentle ascent.

The Rogers Pass area is home to the first and only tunnels on the *Canada by Bicycle* route. Some of these tunnels are short and safe, others are long and scary. Before entering a tunnel, make sure there is no traffic approaching from behind and then pedal hard! Ensure that you have a flashing light on your bike to alert motorists of your presence.

Make sure to remove your sunglasses before entering, as some of the tunnels are very dark. Do not panic because of the lack of light, your eyes will quickly adjust and your surroundings will become visible. Look down for painted lines on the road to orient you. The noise of passing traffic can be very loud and unnerving, so be ready for it. As scary as the tunnels are, it beats being swept off of your bike by an avalanche!

Weather in this area can be very volatile. Don't rule out snow at any time of the year. The small gas station at Rogers Pass is your last chance for food or beverage before Golden.

The towering Selkirk Mountains catch warm, moist Pacific air from the coast and send it up from the earth causing it to cool and fall as precipitation. The massive amount of snow that falls in this area means that avalanches are a constant concern.

East of Rogers Pass the highway drops into the Rocky Mountain Trench, which separates the Selkirk and Rocky Mountain ranges.

Golden, population 4 373, is situated at the junction of the Columbia and Kicking Horse Rivers in the Columbia River Valley. The economy of this bustling mountain town is dominated by logging, tourism and the Canadian Pacific Railway. Check out the covered Kicking Horse Pedestrian Bridge at 8th Avenue North, spanning 46 metres across the river of the same name. This bridge is the longest free-standing timber frame bridge in Canada.

Kicking Horse River and Valley get their name from Dr. James Hector. In 1858, he was part of the Palliser expedition exploring Canada's west for both agricultural potential and a route for the Canadian Pacific Railway. Near Golden one of the packhorses fell into the river. While trying to pull the horse from the river it kicked Hector in the chest, causing him to lose consciousness. Mistaken for dead, Hector's crew began to dig his grave and stopped only after he regained consciousness a few hours later.

Your destination for the evening is the Golden Municipal Campground, set tranquilly beneath the bows of towering trees but only seconds from downtown. This campground is as nice as any you will find on your travels in Canada. If you want a roof over your head try the popular Kicking Horse Hostel. Check out Summit Cycle for any bicycle needs that you may have.

Kilometre Log

0.0	Leave Lamplighter Campground heading east on Nixon Road.
0.1	Turn left on Big Eddy Road.
0.7	Cross over the Columbia River.
0.8	After crossing the bridge Big Eddy Road becomes Wilson Street.
1.3	Wilson Street becomes Victoria Road West. Stay right.
2.8	Turn left onto MacKenzie Avenue.
2.9	Turn right onto Track Street East.
4.3	Track Street East dead-ends into Townley Street. Turn left.
5.2	Intersection of Townley Street and HWY 1. Turn right and head west on HWY 1.
8.5	Mt. Revelstoke National Park is on your left.
27.3	Skunk Cabbage Boardwalk. Washrooms available.
29.9	Giant Cedars Boardwalk.
31.5	Exit Mt. Revelstoke National Park.
35.4	Cross over Illicillaweet River.
48.7	MacDonald Shed avalanche tunnel.
48.6	Twin Shed avalanche tunnel.
49.1	Enter Glacier National Park.
49.3	Lanark Shed avalanche tunnel.
70.7	Rogers Pass and Rogers Pass Visitors Centre. Small service station.
74.8	Tupper Tunnel 1. This is a scary tunnel!
75.8	Tupper Tunnel 2. A much more enjoyable tunnel.
78.9	Mt. Shaugnessy Tunnel.
93.7	East boundary of Glacier National Park.
122.1	Descend rapidly into the Kicking Horse River Valley.
132.7	Blaeberry.
148.8	Exit right into Golden on HWY 95.
149.1	Road circles 270° clockwise where it merges with 10th Avenue North.

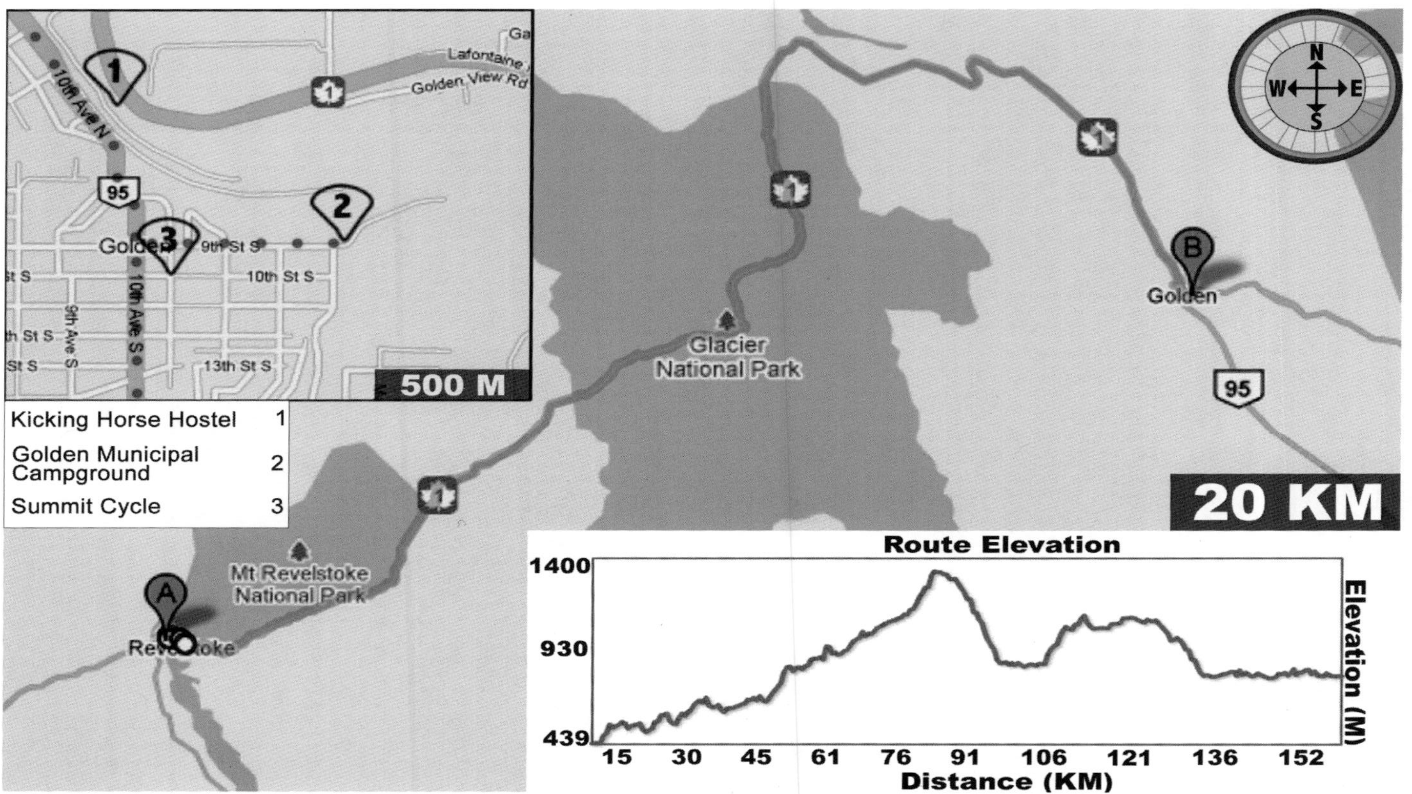
Golden View Rd
Lafontaine
10th Ave N
95
Golden
9th St S
10th St S
10th Ave S
9th Ave S
13th St S
500 M
Kicking Horse Hostel 1
Golden Municipal Campground 2
Summit Cycle 3
Glacier National Park
Mt Revelstoke National Park
Revelstoke
Golden
95
20 KM
W
E
N
S
Route Elevation
1400
930
439
15 30 45 61 76 91 106 121 136 152
Distance (KM)
Elevation (M)

150.8 Cross over Kicking Horse River.

151.2 At intersection of 10th Avenue South & 9th Street South turn left.

152.3 Bike for five blocks to Golden Municipal Campground at the intersection of 14th Avenue South and 9th Street South.

Golden Municipal Campground to Lake Louise Campground: (85.0 K)

There is a small store in Field, but I recommend you purchase supplies in Golden for the ride to Lake Louise as you will not find any large grocery stores until Banff.

Yoho National Park was established in 1886 to represent the western slopes of the Rocky Mountain region. Yoho is an expression for awe and wonder in the Cree language. This 1 313 kilometre^2 National Park is famous for its waterfalls, namely Takakkaw Falls and Wapta Falls, which are most robust during the summer months.

Positioned at the foot of Mount Stephen, Field is the administrative centre for Yoho National Park and home to the Park's Visitor Centre. I encourage you to cross over the Kicking Horse River into this quiet mountain town. It has a few small shops and restaurants that give off good vibes. Make sure to stop and speak with one of the knowledgeable staff at the Parks Canada Visitor Centre. If you are feeling energetic they will direct you to nearby trails that allow you to scramble to the top of some monster peaks.

Leave Yoho National Park and cross the Alberta border into Banff National Park. Prime Minister John A. Macdonald created this park in 1885, to quiet claims from over who was permitted to commercially develop the area. Macdonald originally set aside 26 kilometres^2 around the hot springs and named it Banff Hot Springs Reserve. From this small park, Banff National Park was born. Move your watches an hour ahead when you enter into Alberta.

Annual tourist visits to Banff National Park number over 5 million which does not include the millions more that pass through the area on HWY 1. Keep your eyes peeled for grizzly and black bear as well as cougar, lynx, wolverine, mountain goats and bighorn sheep.

The town-site of Lake Louise, including campgrounds and a small mall, are all in close proximity to both the Trans-Canada Highway and its name-sake, Lake Louise. Many hiking trails are located close by.

Emerald green Lake Louise drains into the Bow River via Louise Creek and is named after Princess Louise Caroline Alberta, the fourth daughter of Queen Victoria.

If you are in the mood for a pampering, whip out your credit card and pull into one of Canada's most famous hotels, Chateau Lake Louise on the east shore of it's namesake. Even if you don't want to drop the big bucks on this hotel, it is worth having a look around the hotel grounds and stunning Lake Louise.

Places of interest to bike tourists in Lake Louise Village include an awesome bakery, Wilson Mountain Sports for bike-parts and a Parks Canada Visitor Centre.

Northeast of HWY 1 is Lake Louise Ski Area, one of Canada's premiere ski hills, with 139 marked runs.

If five-star accommodation isn't your thing, wheel into the Lake Louise Tent Campground. Parks Canada has a separate campground for tents and soft-trailers because of the high density of bears in the area. Even though the campground is encircled with an electric fence, make sure your campsite is clean and food is stored responsibly.

Unfortunately, Lake Louise Tent Campground is open only from mid May to late September. If the campground is closed, check out Hostelling International Lake Louise.

Kilometre Log

0.0 Leave Golden Municipal Campground heading east on 9th Street South.

0.7 Turn right onto HWY 95 / 10th Avenue South.

1.2 HWY 95 / 10th Avenue South turns into HWY 95 / 10th Avenue North.

1.8 Take exit to HWY 1, circling 270° counter-clockwise.

2.7 Turn right onto HWY 1 and climb steadily out of Golden.

31.5 Enter Yoho National Park.

35.9 Wapta Falls.

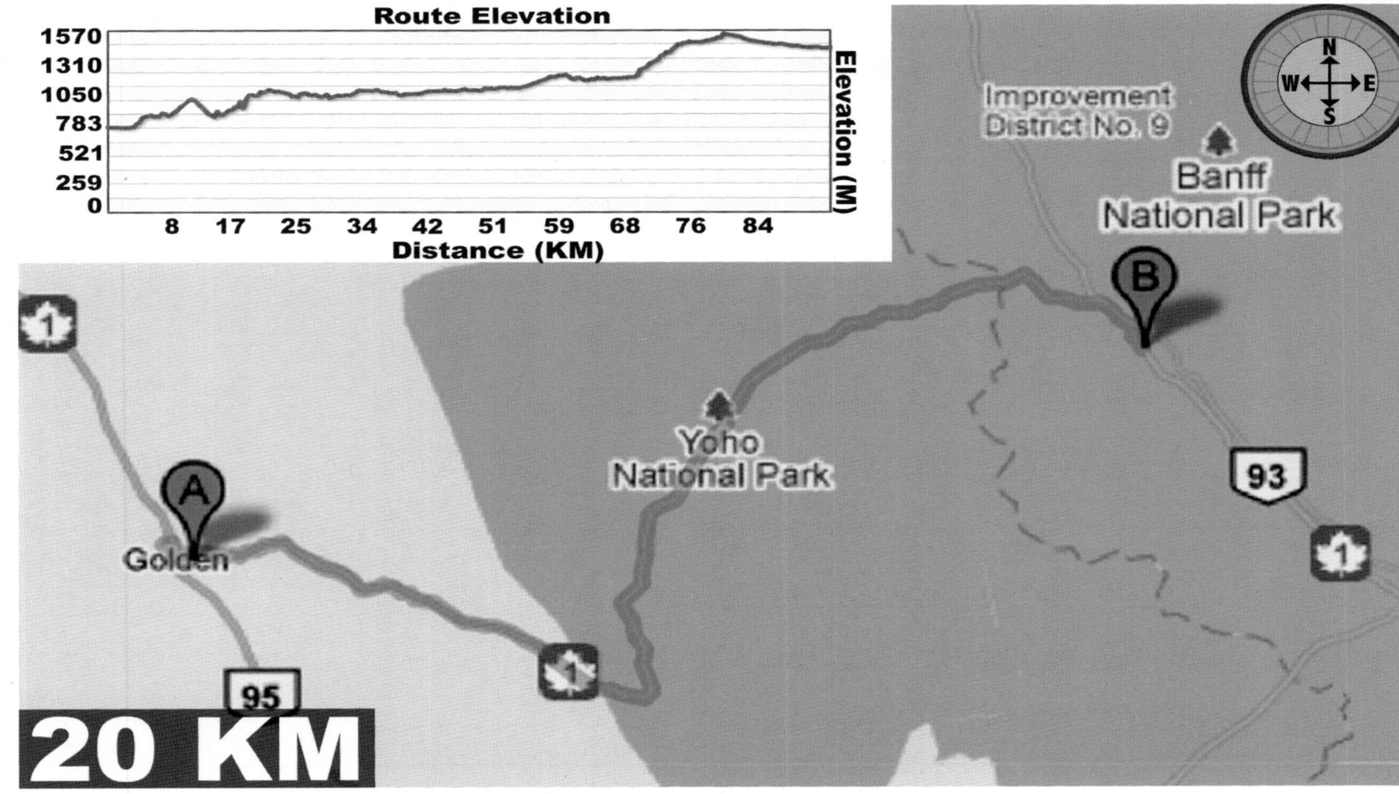

Route Elevation
1570
1310
1050
783
521
259
0
8
17
25
34
42
51
59
68
76
84
Distance (KM)
Elevation (M)
Improvement
District No. 9
Banff
National Park
N
W
E
S
B
1
Yoho
National Park
A
Golden
93
95
20 KM

37.2 Exit to Chancellor Peak Campground.
38.3 Exit to Hoodoo Creek Campground. Both of these campgrounds are open from early June to early September.
48.8 Pass over Ottertail River.
57.6 Exit to Field.
57.8 Parks Canada Visitor Centre.
65.0 Pass Spiral Tunnels on your left. These tunnels spiral to help trains easily gain elevation.
73.9 Cross the border of Yoho National Park and British Columbia and enter into Banff National Park and Alberta.
80.4 HWY 93 merges with HWY 1.
82.9 Turn right to exit into Lake Louise.
83.2 Turn right onto HWY 1A.
83.6 Turn left on Fairview Road.
84.8 Turn right into Lake Louise Tent Campground.
85.0 Lake Louise Tent Campground.

Lessons learned from Johanna Willows:
When bike touring, it's important to be honest with yourself when assessing your fitness levels. Take breaks when your body needs them and you will have a more enjoyable time.

Province:	Alberta
Population:	3 632 483
Area:	661 482 km^2
Industries:	Oil & gas, agriculture.
Highlights:	Banff National Park, Banff, Lake Louise, Calgary.

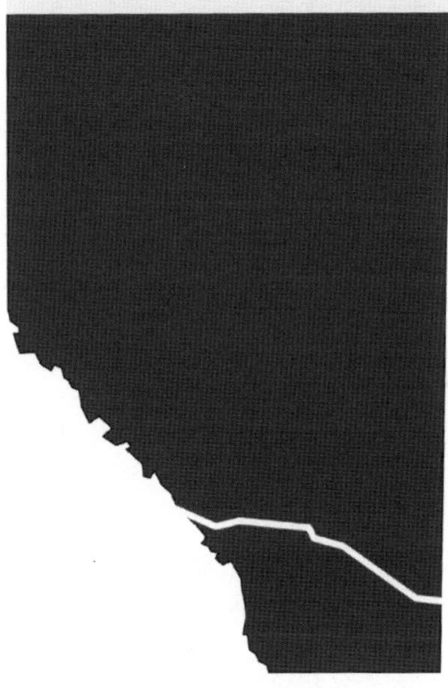

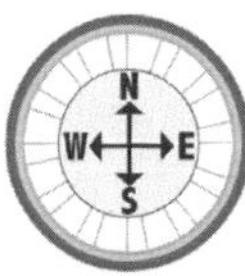

Lake Louise Campground to Canmore's Wapiti Campground: (76.3 K)

Enjoy an easy ride today along the Bow River through the Bow Valley. This river originates in the Wapta Icefield, which lays on the border of Banff and Yoho National Parks. The name Bow refers to the reeds that grow along its banks and were used by First Nations people to make bows for hunting. The Bow River is cold and clear, warming as it flows through Calgary before continuing southeast to join with the Oldman River in southern Alberta.

Before your arrival in Banff, you will bike past the exit to Sunshine Village ski hill, which is typically open until Victoria Day Long Weekend.

Parks Canada and Banff National Park have built wildlife corridors along this stretch of highway allowing wildlife to move safely between areas of habitat. Some corridors go under the highway while others allow animals to cross over top. The corridors over the highway look like a walking bridge, but provide safe passage for wildlife.

Situated at an elevation of 1 463 metres, Banff is Canada's highest elevated town. It is also known as the only ski town in the world that is busier during summer months than in the winter. Banff and its surrounding National Park got its name in 1884, from Lord Steven, a director of the CPR recalling his hometown of Banffshire, Scotland.

There are three exits into Banff and the town is a must see. It is surrounded by Mount Rundle, Sulphur Mountain, Mount Norquay and Cascade Mountain. Besides the ample shopping opportunities, Banff's downtown does have points of interest to a bike tourist. Mountain Magic Equipment is one of a handful of bike stores located downtown. SameSun Hostel will provide you with an affordable place to stay if you want to spend the evening enjoying Banff's legendary nightlife. Banff Park Museum National Historic Site is Canada's oldest natural history museum. It will take you back to 1903, when the museum was founded. Banff Springs Hotel, sister hotel to Chateau Lake Louise, is located on the south edge of town.

Banff's explosive growth from a small service centre in the late 1800s, to its present size of 6 700 permanent residents, plus tourists, has led to concerns from environmentalists about harm to the area's ecosystems.

While biking east towards Canmore, look to your right to catch views of Three Sisters Peaks. From left to right, they are known as Big Sister, Middle Sister and Little Sister. Big Sister has an elevation of 2 936 metres.

Your destination for the evening is Canmore's Wapiti Campground. HWY 1 bisects Canmore. This quiet campground with panoramic views is on the south (right) side of the highway as you approach Canmore from Banff.

For almost a century, the town of Canmore was an important coal-mining town. In 1979, the last coal mine ceased operation. This economic blow to the town of Canmore painted a bleak picture for its continued existence. However, shortly after the mines closed it was announced that Canmore would be the site of Nordic events for the 1988 Calgary Winter Olympics. This breathed new life into the small mountain town and was instrumental in helping Canmore transition from a small industrial town to its present state as a world-class tourism destination.

Grocery stores are available in Canmore. If you are looking to experience Canmore as it was over a hundred years ago, check out the Canmore Hotel, which has changed very little since the late 1800s.

Don't be surprised to see large group of cyclists whiz by you. Canmore is a training centre for skiing and its residents are notoriously active bike enthusiasts. Check out Rebound Cycle, located downtown, for any bike needs you may have.

If you are looking for a fun, challenging trail in the area, consider hiking to the abandoned teahouse up Mount Lady Macdonald. Ask a local for more information.

Wapiti Campground, elevation 1 309 metres, offers stunning views of the area.

Kilometre Log

0.0	Leave Lake Louise Tent Campground heading towards Fairview Road.
0.2	Turn right on Fairview Road.
1.2	Turn left remaining on Fairview Road as it angles towards HWY 1.
1.5	Fairview Road intersects with HWY 1.
24.9	Intersection of HWY 1 & HWY 93.
46.2	Exit to Sunshine Village.
48.8	Intersection of HWY 1 & HWY 1A.
54.5	Exit to Banff on Mt. Norquay Road.
56.6	Exit to Banff on Compound Road.
58.7	Exit to Banff on Banff Avenue.
71.6	East boundary of Banff National Park.
73.5	Harvie Heights.
75.3	Take your first exit right to Canmore.
75.5	Turn right onto HWY 1A.
76.2	Turn left off of HWY 1A onto Ray McBride Street.
76.3	Turn left into Wapiti Campground.

Lessons learned from Ben McManes:
Reliability, versatility and packability are the three keys to a successful pack. Load your bike with all your gear at least once before leaving on your trip. This will give you a chance to make sure everything fits and gives you a chance to identify and discard unnecessary items. Test your gear before you leave. You don't want to be on the road when you find out your rain jacket absorbs water instead of repelling it.

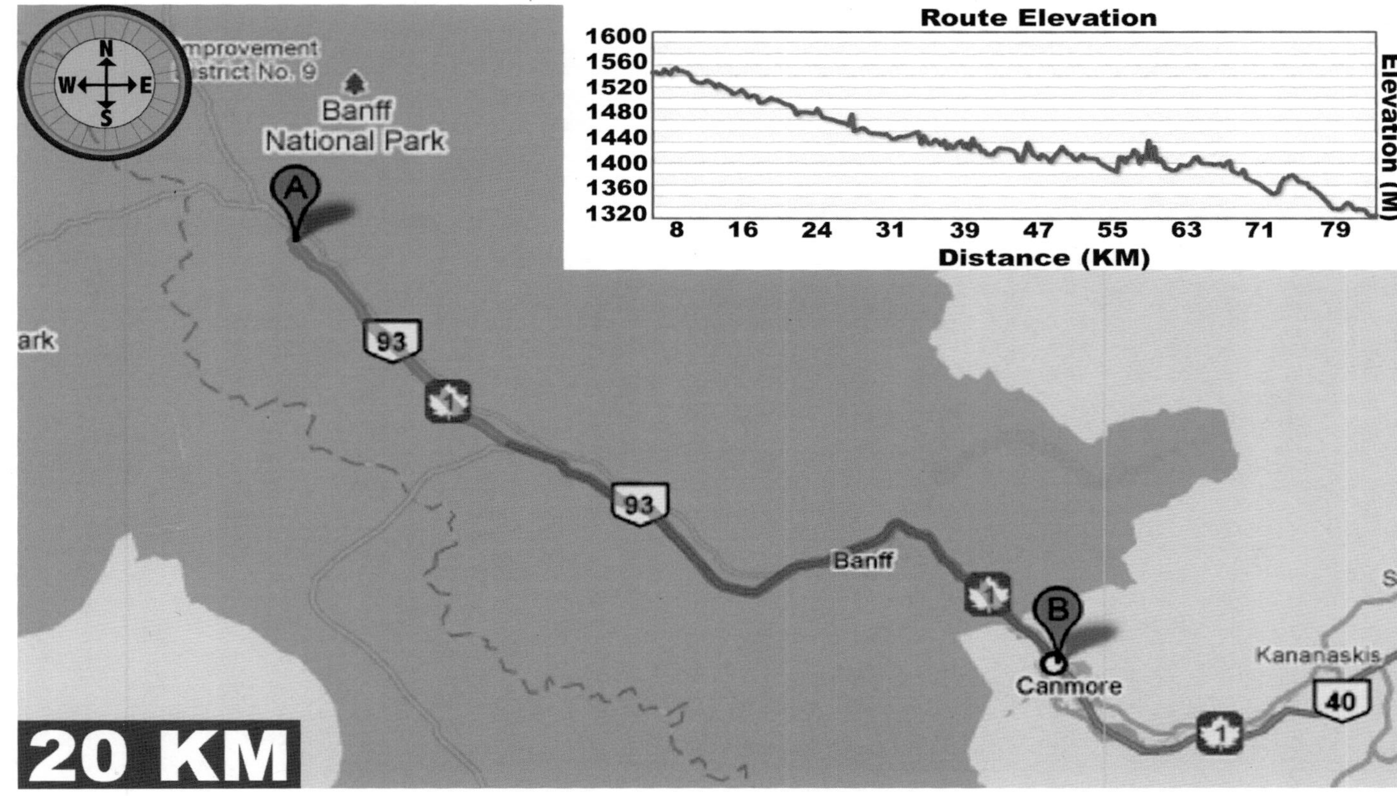
Route Elevation
1600
1560
1520
1480
1440
1400
1360
1320
Elevation (M)
8
16
24
31
39
47
55
63
71
79
Distance (KM)
N
W
E
S
Banff
National Park
A
93
1
93
Banff
1
B
Canmore
Kananaskis
40
1
20 KM

Wapiti Campground to Calgary West Campground: (90.5 K)

Watch the horizon open up as you leave the mountains behind you. The road to Calgary has two and sometimes three lanes, always with a massive shoulder. I have directed you to the highway immediately after leaving Wapiti Campground. If you need to visit Canmore, there are many opportunities to regain the highway from the east side of town.

The first settlement that you will ride through is Deadman's Flats, a small village just east of Canmore, with a restaurant on the highway at a large truck stop. The origin of the name Deadman's Flats is not definitive. One legend is that two Aboriginal people were hunting in the area that was at the time a national park, when they saw Park Wardens approaching. Knowing that hunting in the area was illegal, they smeared themselves with the blood of the dead beavers that they had hunted and played dead. When the startled wardens found them they left to get help to deal with the situation. When the warden was out of sight, the men "rose from the dead," and returned to camp with their beavers.

Climb up Scott Lake Hill to an elevation of 1 410 metres and then race down the other side of it and enter the prairies! This area is known for gusting winds and lack of precipitation.

On a clear day you will be able to see Calgary long before you cycle into it. Calgary's distinctive skyline is surrounded by kilometres of urban sprawl. Calgary Tower is the most notable point on the Calgary skyline. It was briefly Canada's tallest building when it was constructed in 1968.

Calgary, with a population of 988 193, sits at the convergence of the Bow and Elbow Rivers. It was at this merging of waterways that the North West Mounted Police built a fort to protect the area's fur trade and to stop U.S. whiskey traders from entering the western plains of Canada in the 1870s.

Calgary has always been a boomtown that swells with population and prosperity when the price of oil and gas is high and busts when it is not. In 1947, the population of the city was about 100 000. By 1955 it had doubled.

HWY 1 intersects the city of Calgary and is known as 16th Avenue North through the city. Calgary streets are set up in a grid formation where avenues run from west to east and streets run from north to south.

Cyclists should avoid roads that end with Trail, as these are major freeways that are not friendly to cyclists. All streets and avenues end with a combination of two cardinal directions (NW, NE, SE, SW), which indicate the quadrant of the city that the street or avenue is located in.

On the west side of Calgary is Canada Olympic Park, which was built for the Winter Olympics that Calgary hosted in 1988. Just looking at the towering ski jump will send shivers up your spine. Canada Olympic Park is used for skiing, snowboarding, ski jumping, luge, skeleton and bobsled both recreationaly and competitively.

Another famous building in Calgary is the Saddledome. Built in 1983, the inverted hyperbolic paraboloid's unique design creates pillar-free view from all seats and also reduces interior volume. The design was strictly functional with no thought that it resembled a saddle and would become a symbol for Calgary's cowboy heritage.

People from all over the world move to Calgary for its clean air, many parks, employment opportunities and proximity to the Rocky Mountains. Calgarians have risen to affluence largely on the back of the oil and gas industry. This burgeoning middle class has fueled a demand for single-family dwellings. Combine that with few geographical barriers to growth and a perceived endless supply of gas and oil and you end up with a sparsely populated city that is connected to the core area with massive highway-style arteries.

If you are passing through Calgary in early July, treat yourself to a day off and take in the Calgary Stampede. Calgarians favourite festival is the world's largest outdoor rodeo and a Calgary tradition since 1912. During Stampede, residents and tourists get into the spirit by dressing in traditional western attire and decorating their homes and businesses.

If you are limping into Calgary with bike problems, hit Bow Cycle & Sport on the west side of the city.

There is a campground on both the east and west side of the city, both located near HWY 1. Calgary West Campground is on the west side of town and Mountain View Camping is on the east. Both cater to motor homes but permit tents. Calgary is spread over a massive area, meaning that both of these campgrounds are far away from the centre of the city. I am going to give directions to Calgary West Campground, but don't be afraid to hit a hostel in the centre of town, as it will give you an opportunity to see Calgary up close.

If staying at Calgary West Campground you will have to cycle into Calgary to acquire groceries for the evening.

Hostelling International's Calgary City Centre is located downtown; it comes highly recommended.

Kilometre Log

0.0 Turn left out of Wapiti Campground and head north on Ray McBride Road.
0.1 Turn right on Mountain Avenue.
0.7 Turn left to merge onto HWY 1. Remain on this road until you can see Calgary.
1.5 Exit to Canmore.
2.2 Exit to Canmore.
3.5 Cross Cougar Creek.
4.1 Exit to Canmore.
5.5 Cross over the Bow River.
6.6 Last exit to Canmore.
10.7 Deadman's Flats.
16.0 Lac des Arcs.
27.1 Intersection of HWY 1 & HWY 1X.
31.3 Intersection of HWY 1 & HWY 40 & Stoney Nakoda Resort.
53.6 Scott Lake Hill.
56.7 Intersection of HWY 1 & HWY 68.
69.7 Cross Jumping Pound Creek Road.
73.8 Intersection of HWY 1 & HWY 22. Large truck stop and restaurant here.
85.2 Cloverleaf to exit the highway. Keep heading east.
88.9 Exit right off of HWY 1 .
89.1 Continue heading west on this road as it parallels HWY 1 as West Valley Road SW.
90.2 West Valley Road SW curves right to become 101 Street SW.
90.5 Turn right off 101 Street SW into Calgary West Campground.

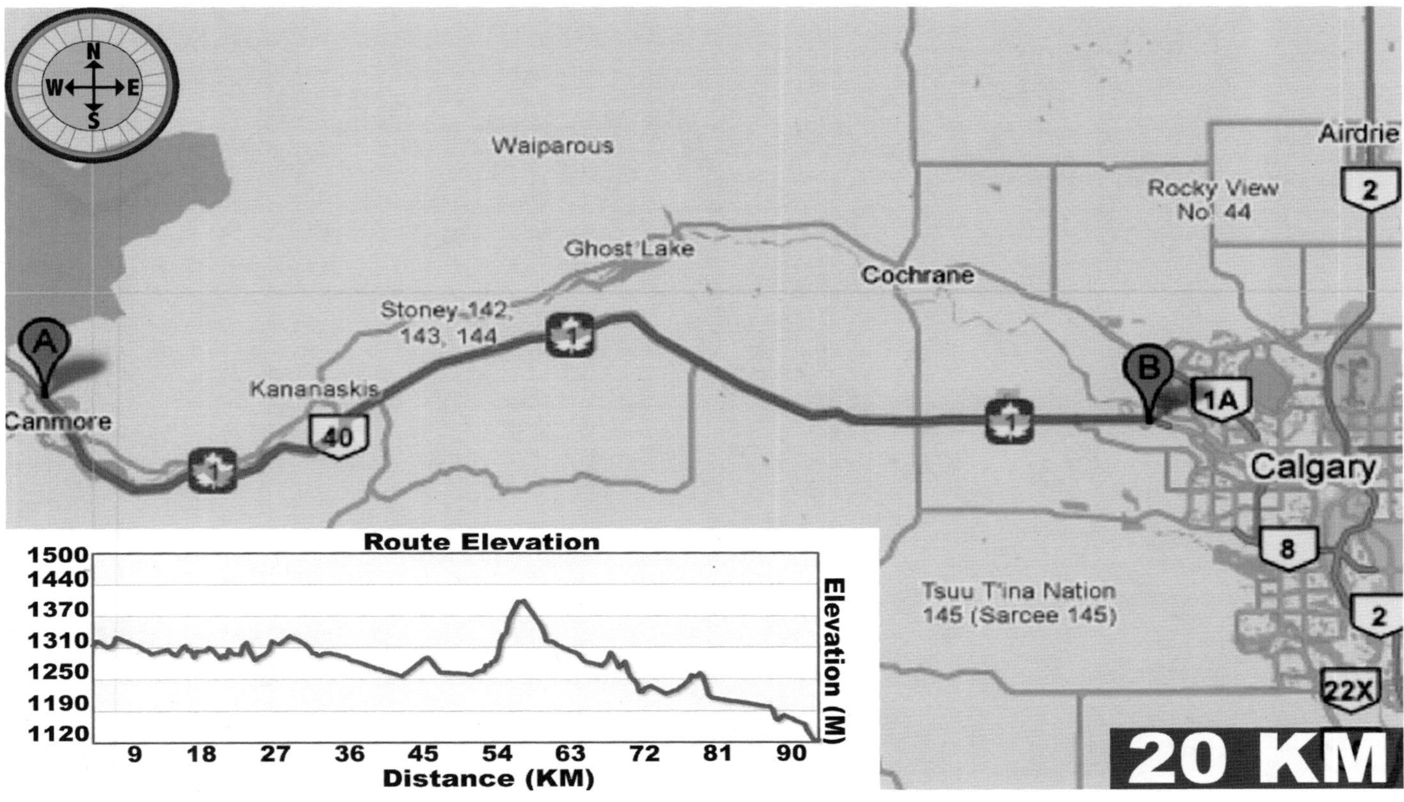

N
W
E
S
Waiparous
Airdrie
Rocky View No! 44
2
Ghost Lake
Cochrane
Stoney 142, 143, 144
1
A
Kananaskis
B
1A
Canmore
40
Calgary
8
Tsuu T'ina Nation 145 (Sarcee 145)
22X
Route Elevation
1500
1440
1370
1310
1250
1190
1120
Elevation (M)
9
18
27
36
45
54
63
72
81
90
Distance (KM)
20 KM

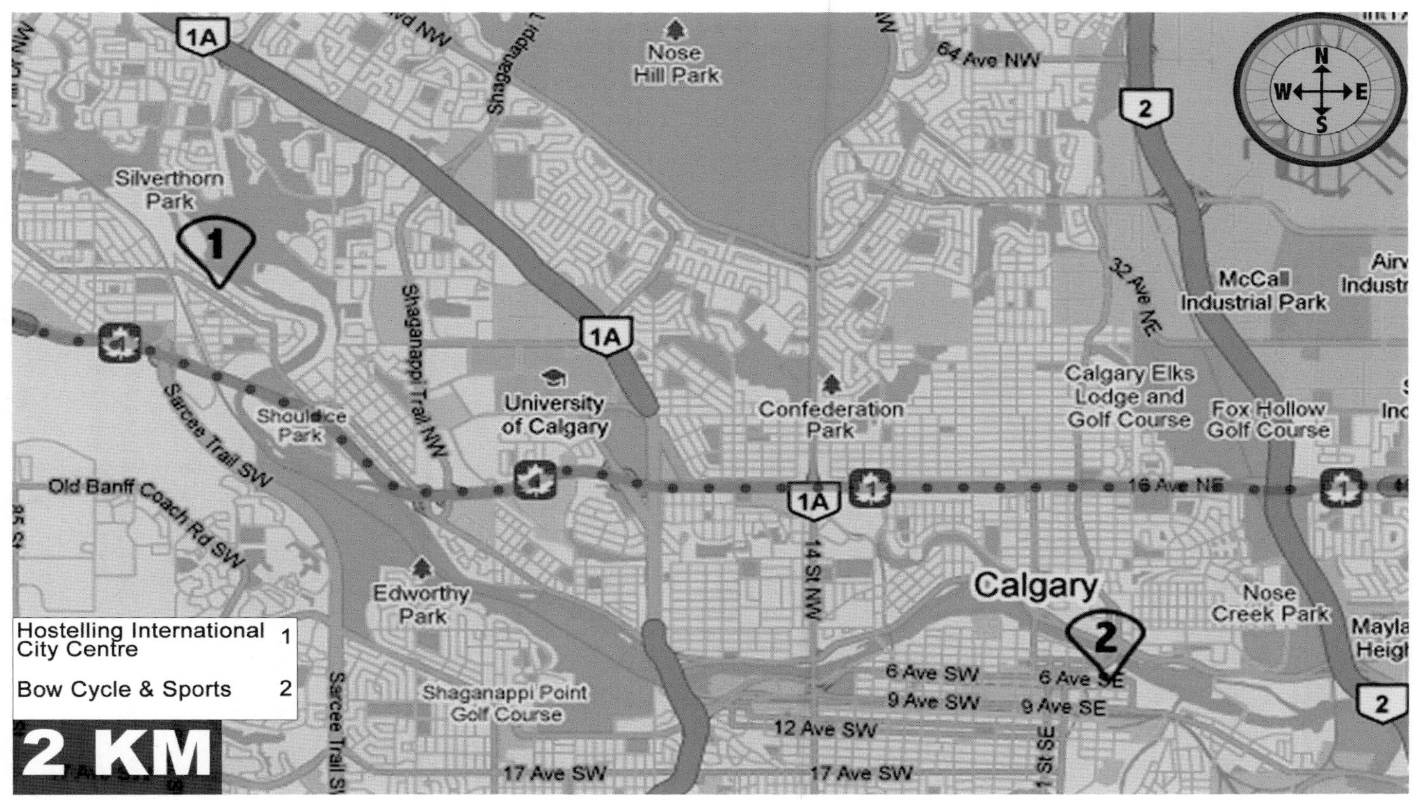
Nose
Hill Park
64 Ave NW
Silverthorn
Park
1
1A
2
McCall
Industrial Park
32 Ave NE
Shaganappi Trail NW
University
of Calgary
Confederation
Park
Calgary Elks
Lodge and
Golf Course
Fox Hollow
Golf Course
Shouldice
Park
Sarcee Trail SW
Old Banff Coach Rd SW
16 Ave NE
14 St NW
Edworthy
Park
Calgary
Nose
Creek Park
2
Hostelling International City Centre 1
Bow Cycle & Sports 2
Shaganappi Point
Golf Course
6 Ave SW
6 Ave SE
9 Ave SW
9 Ave SE
12 Ave SW
17 Ave SW
17 Ave SW
1 St SE
2 KM
N
W
E
S

Calgary West Campground to Bassano Campground: (154.2 K)

Weather will play an important role in how you remember the prairie section from Calgary to Regina. With a west-wind, you will cycle effortlessly, watching serene farmland blur by.

If the wind is in your face, this stretch will be truly challenging.

After cycling over the mountains you will undoubtedly be in good physical condition. The battle with wind is not so much physical as mental.

Whatever happens, you cannot let yourself become dejected. Think of the many worse things that you could be doing with your life at that point and push on. If you are in a group, cycle in a tight pod, with the leader breaking wind for the rest of the group. Alternate who rides out front so everyone can rest his or her legs.

Don't expect to make fabulous time when facing high wind. You can cycle easily at 15 km/h into a headwind, but it will take a Herculean effort to increase your speed to 20 km/h. Lower your expectations and don't kill yourself. Start your day early, and take short breaks every ten or fifteen kilometres, giving yourself manageable goals to focus on.

Leave the hustle and bustle of Calgary behind as you head east on HWY 1. Expect an adequate shoulder next to double lane highway all the way to Regina.

The first town to pop up out of the prairie is Chestermere, population 11 262. Chestermere is centered on Chestermere Lake, which was created in 1906, by damming the Kinniburgh Slough and diverting water from the nearby Bow River. People enjoy living in Chestermere for its lake, small town feel and proximity to Calgary.

Next cycle through Strathmore, population 11 335. Strathmore sprung up as a stop for the CPR trains heading west to the mountains. It now serves as an agricultural hub for the nearby farmlands.

The road jogs south after Strathmore. Where the road turns left to return heading east is the exit for Gleichen and the nearby Sik Sika First Nation. Gleichen has a few small stores and 2 exits allowing you to visit the town and return to the highway with little backtracking.

After the exits to Gleichen, expect to see wetlands along the sides of the highway. Wetlands are an important part of the ecosystem as they nurture waterfowl, prevent floods and naturally purify water. Because of their lack of direct economic benefit, wetlands have traditionally been modified from their natural state and drained for irrigation or flooded for use as lakes. Society is beginning to understand the significant role that wetlands play in ecosystem sustainability and efforts are being made to preserve what many experts consider to be the most biologically diverse of all ecosystems. Wetlands act as a buffer against floods and promote sustainable watersheds. When biking by a wetland you can often feel the air become notably cooler and hear the chirping of crickets and birds.

Your destination for the evening is the Bassano Campground, located centrally in Bassano and run by the town. Groceries are available in this small prairie town.

Kilometre Log

0.0	Leave Calgary West Campground, heading north on 101st Street SW.
0.3	101st Street SW curves left and turns into West Valley Road SW.
1.4	Turn right and curve 180° to gain HWY 1 E.
1.6	Head east on HWY 1 E.
4.0	Canada Olympic Park.
5.9	Intersection of 16th Avenue NW & Sarcee Trail.
6.8	Cross over the Bow River and cycle through Shouldice Park.
9.3	Intersection of 16th Avenue NW & Shaganappi Trail NW.
11.5	Intersection of 16th Avenue NW & Crowchild Trail NW.
17.7	Intersection of 16th Avenue NW and Deerfoot Trail / HWY 2.
25.9	Exit Calgary.
31.6	First exit to Chestermere.
34.0	Second exit to Chestermere.

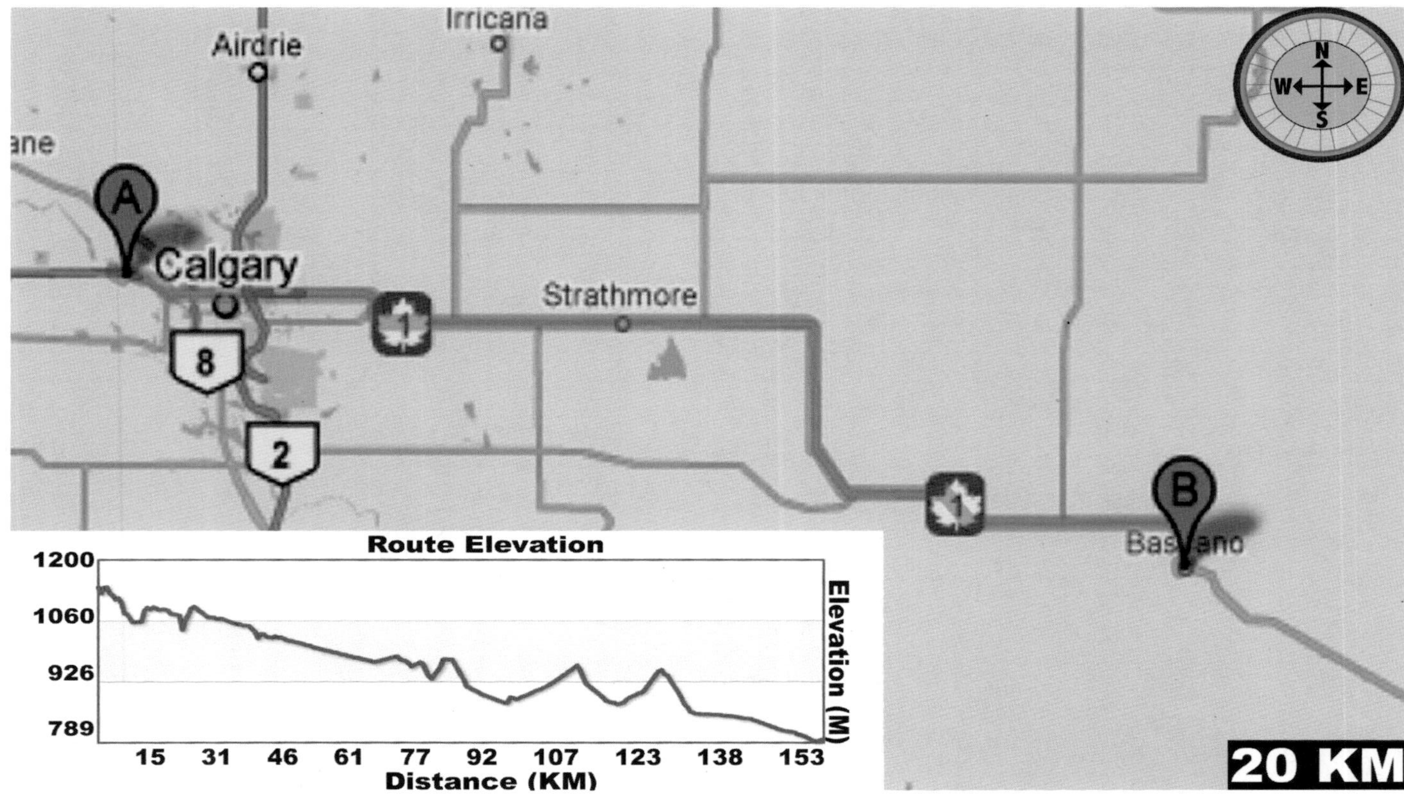
Irricana
Airdrie
A
Calgary
1
8
2
Strathmore
1
B
N
W
E
S
Route Elevation
1200
1060
926
789
15
31
46
61
77
92
107
123
138
153
Distance (KM)
Elevation (M)
20 KM

44.4 Intersection of HWY 9 & HWY 1.
63.8 Strathmore.
68.8 Strathmore Highway Camping.
73.6 Intersection of HWY 1 & HWY 21.
86.3 HWY 1 turns 90° to the right.
103.3 Exit to Gleichen on HWY 547.
107.3 Intersection of HWY 1 & HWY 901.
117.8 Intersection of HWY 1 & HWY 842.
133.4 Intersection of HWY 1 & HWY 56.
152.8 Turn right into Bassano on 6th Avenue.
153.7 Turn left at 6th Street.
154.2 Head four blocks to the intersection of 6th Street and 2nd Avenue to Bassano Campground.

Bassano Campground to Medicine Hat's Gas City Campground: (155.4 K)

Today is another long day of cycling across flat prairie. Make sure that you have plenty of liquid as there are long distances between towns. There are virtually no trees in the area to block the sun and wind. You can quickly become dehydrated.

Pedal first into Brooks, population 12 498, which is known as "The City of 100 Hellos," due to the diverse global population that comes to work in the local agriculture industry. Brooks has a small Kiwanis Campground.

South of Brooks is the Brooks Aqueduct, which was built by the Canadian Pacific Railway Company (CPR) during the 1910s. An aqueduct is a channel used to transport water. This massive elevated canal helped move water from the Bow River to the dry land near Brooks and serves as testament to the hardworking and enterprising pioneers that developed this region. The Brooks Aqueduct is now defunct and is a National and Provincial Historic Site. Tours are available in the summer for a small fee.

Past Brooks is Tillebrook Provincial Park. Although a nice campground in proximity to the highway, it offers the visitor little more than a pleasant place to camp for the evening.

Stop at the side of the road today and read about the first natural gas discovery that took place very close to the highway in 1883 while CPR employees were looking for water to service their train line.

If you see brigades of army vehicles in the area, don't be surprised. It will most likely just be the soldiers from nearby CFB Suffield training.

Before entering Medicine Hat, cycle through Redcliff, the greenhouse capital of the prairies. Commercial greenhouse farming became successful here because of abundant sunlight, inexpensive natural gas and proximity to HWY 1.

Medicine Hat lies at the intersection of HWY 3 and HWY 1 on the banks of the South Saskatchewan River. The name Medicine Hat comes from the Blackfoot word for the eagle tail feather headdress worn by Medicine Men. The city is known for its vast energy resources, especially natural gas. If you need a bike shop, head to Cycle Path.

From HWY 1 you can't miss the giant tee-pee originally designed for the city of Calgary during the 1988 Olympics and moved to its present site in 1991.

The giant teepee overlooks the Blackfoot Buffalo Jump. A buffalo jump was traditionally used by aboriginal people to kill buffalo. They herded the giant animals towards the steep drop at high speeds so they could not stop before they went over the cliff's edge.

The Medicine Hat Gas City Campground is a city run campsite on the west outskirts of the city. This campground is a popular place during summer months. Laundry facilities and a small convenience store are available on-site.

Kilometre Log

0.0 Cycle away from Bassano Campground heading north on 6th Street.
0.6 Turn right on 6th Avenue.
1.4 Turn right onto HWY 1.
5.1 Intersection of HWY 1 & HWY 550.
38.4 Intersection of HWY 1 & HWY 36.
46.8 Brooks.
56.3 Tillebrook Provincial Park.
59.0 Intersection of HWY 1 & HWY 875.
67.5 Intersection of HWY 1 & HWY 876.
113.6 Intersection of HWY 1 & HWY 884.

Near Field, British Columbia

Chinook Winds

Chinook winds provide respite to the cold winters that are common in the plains area east of the Rocky Mountains. Chinook winds are caused by moist air from the Pacific Ocean traveling east that is forced to rise over the mountains. As the air mass gains elevation, it cools, condensing the moisture inside, causing it to fall as precipitation. The now dry air descends towards land as it enters the plains on the east side of the mountains and warms rapidly. This result is a warm, turbulent wind that raises the ambient temperature rapidly.

Swift Current, Saskatchewan

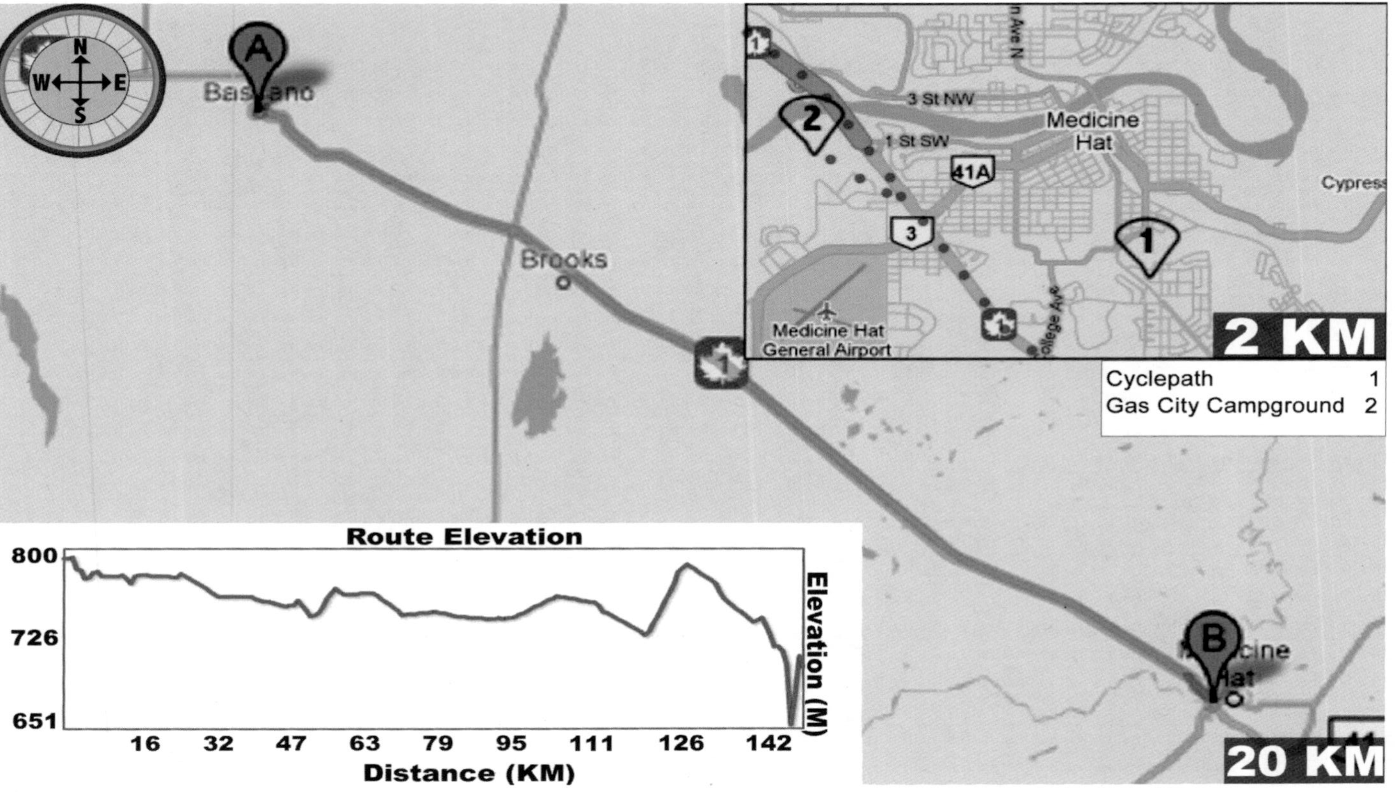
N
W
E
S
A
Bassano
Brooks
1
B
Medicine Hat
20 KM
1
3 St NW
Medicine Hat
2
1 St SW
41A
3
1
Cypress
Medicine Hat General Airport
College Ave
1
2 KM
Cyclepath 1
Gas City Campground 2
Route Elevation
800
726
651
16 32 47 63 79 95 111 126 142
Distance (KM)
Elevation (M)

140.4 Intersection of HWY 1 & HWY 524.
145.3 Redcliff.
152.4 Cross over South Saskatchewan River.
154.0 Turn right at 7th Street SW.
154.3 Turn right onto 11th Avenue SW.
155.4 Remain on 11th Avenue SW until you reach the campground gate.

Gas City Campground to Eagle Valley Campground: (91.6 K)

Purchase supplies before leaving Medicine Hat. The road to Eagle Valley Campground is desolate and lonely. Midway through your day you will cross the border of Alberta and Saskatchewan.

Pack sufficient water as the only place to fill your bottles is at the gas station and restaurant just past the halfway point in Walsh and at the rest area at the provincial border.

Your destination for the evening is Eagle Valley Campground, an oasis located just off of the highway. The campground is Caribbean themed and the owners are friendly. The entire campground is serviced with free wireless internet and laundry facilities are on site.

Saskatchewan is the only province in Canada that does not practice daylight savings time. Between March and November clocks in the province of Saskatchewan will be the same as the province of Alberta. From November to March Saskatchewan clocks will be the same as Manitoba. If you are traveling through after November but before March, adjust your clocks accordingly.

Kilometre Log

0.0 Leave Gas City Campground on 11th Avenue SW.
1.1 Turn left at 7th Street SW.
1.4 Turn right onto HWY 1.
1.9 HWY 3 intersects HWY 1 here. Remain on HWY 1.
8.7 Exit Medicine Hat.
14.3 Dunmore.
15.7 Intersection of HWY 1 & HWY 41. HWY 1 & HWY 41 are the same highway here.
31.7 HWY 1 / HWY 41 becomes HWY 1 here.

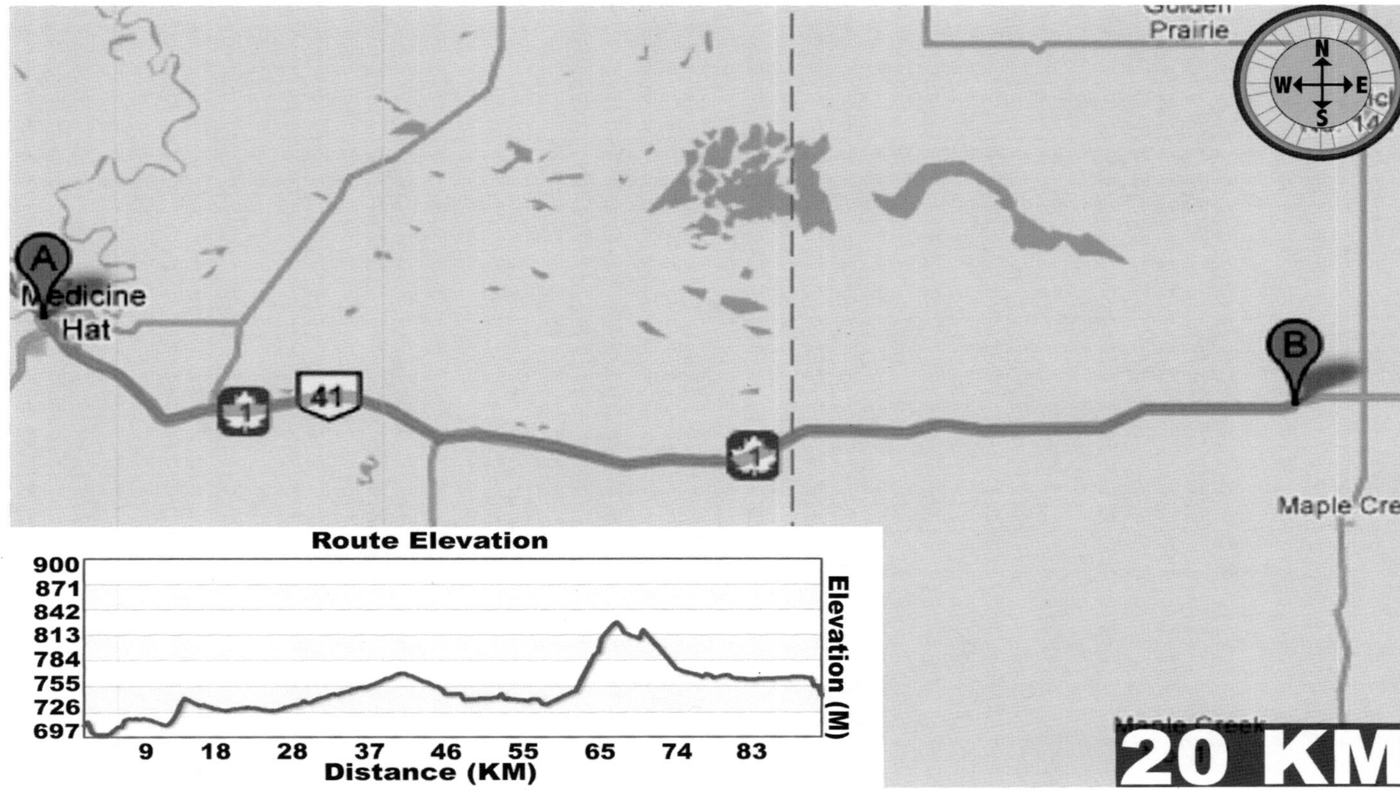
Prairie
N
W
E
S
A
Medicine Hat
1
41
1
B
Route Elevation
900
871
842
813
784
755
726
697
Elevation (M)
9
18
28
37
46
55
65
74
83
Distance (KM)
20 KM

36.2 Irvine. No services.
52.9 Walsh. Gas station, campground and restaurant.
56.4 Alberta & Saskatchewan border.
90.9 Turn right to Eagle Valley Campground.
91.1 Turn left to enter Eagle Valley Campground.
91.6 Eagle Valley Campground.

bald prairie

Province: Saskatchewan
Population: 1 034 974
Area: 651 900 km^2
Industries: Oil & gas, agriculture, potash, uranium.
Highlights: Regina, the Qu'Appelle Valley, Moose Jaw Tunnels, strong prairie tail-winds.

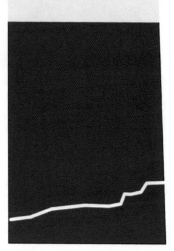

Eagle Valley Campground to Swift Current's Kinetic Park Campground: (135.6 K)

Early in the day look south into the distance to see the Cypress Hills which rise to an elevation of 1 468 metres. The hills form a drainage divide separating the rivers that drain to the Gulf of Mexico and those that drain to Hudson Bay.

The highway shoulder deteriorates before Tompkins but improves afterwards. Services are available on the highway. Watch the barbed wire fences that run parallel to the highway for birds.

Gull Lake, a small agricultural town at the intersection of HWY 1 and HWY 37, is home to giant wind-turbines that can be seen from a distance. Stiff prairie winds turn the 23 metre blades, generating power for Saskatchewan's electrical consumption. There is a gas station on the highway here.

Your destination for the evening is Swift Current. Swift Current Creek, the city's namesake, runs north to south through the east side of town.

There are private campgrounds at each end of the city on HWY 1, but I recommend camping at the city run Kinetic Exhibition Park. If you have some spare time, visit the Mennonite Heritage Village next to Kinetic Park or browse the Museum & Interpretive Centre adjacent to HWY 1.

Kilometre Log

0.0	Leave Eagle Valley Campground heading west.
0.4	Turn right towards HWY 1.
0.5	Turn right onto HWY 1.
1.2	Cycle over Maple Creek.
5.4	Intersection of HWY 1 & HWY 21. Service station and tourist information is available here.
29.8	Intersection of HWY 1 & HWY 614.
54.7	Tompkins and Shady Place Campground.
78.2	Intersection of HWY 1 & HWY 37 and Gull Lake.
100.6	Exit to Webb. No services on highway.
123.7	HWY 32 merges with HWY 1.
130.2	Enter Swift Current on HWY 1.
131.1	Intersection of HWY 1 & 11th Avenue NW. Turn right here.

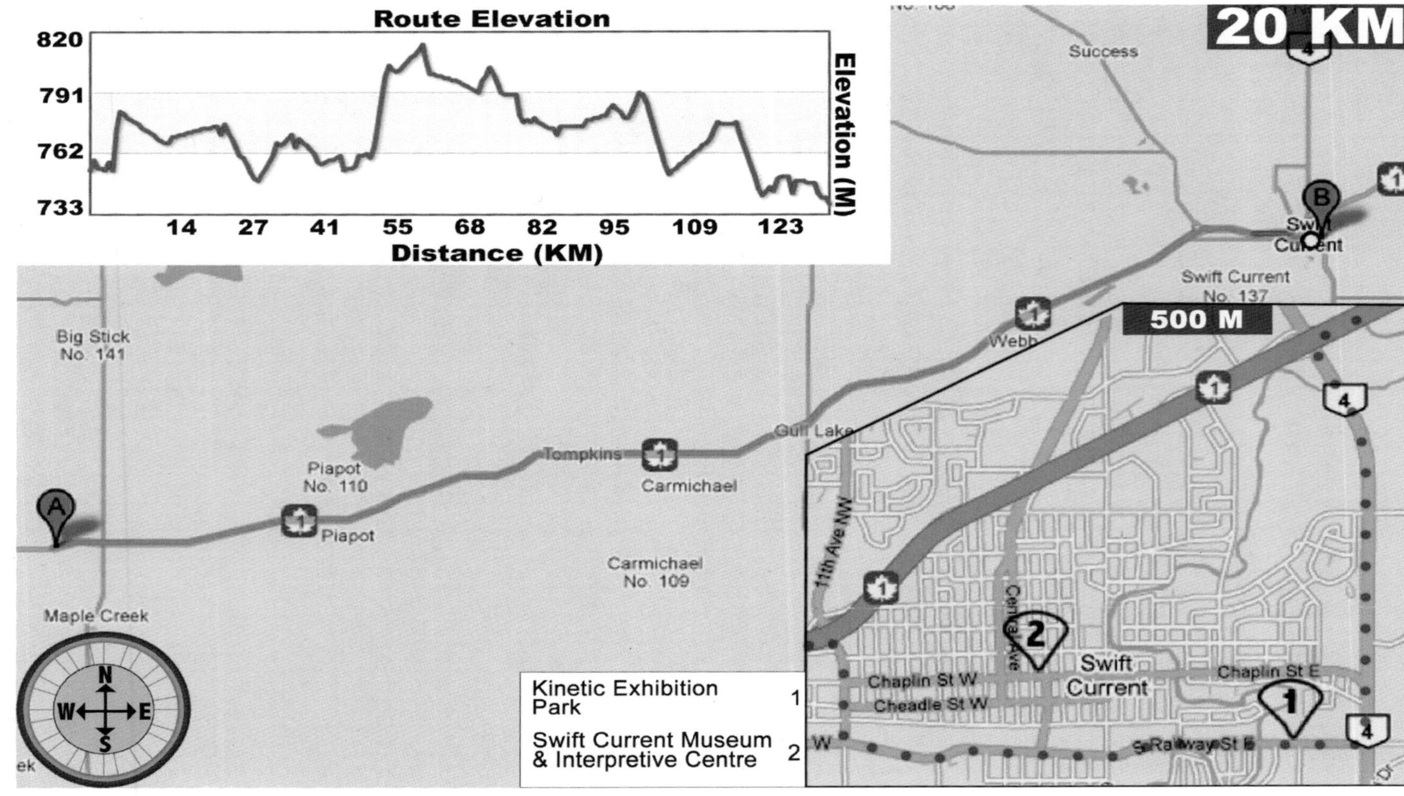

Route Elevation
820
791
762
733
14
27
41
55
68
82
95
109
123
Distance (KM)
Elevation (M)
20 KM
Success
Swift Current
Swift Current No. 137
500 M
Webb
Big Stick No. 141
Gull Lake
Tompkins
Carmichael
Piapot No. 110
Piapot
Carmichael No. 109
Maple Creek
11th Ave NW
Central Ave
Swift Current
Chaplin St W
Cheadle St W
Chaplin St E
S Railway St E
Kinetic Exhibition Park 1
Swift Current Museum & Interpretive Centre 2
N
W
E
S

131.6 After crossing the railway tracks, turn left on South Railway Street West.
135.2 Cross over Swift Current Creek.
135.6 Welcome to Swift Current Kinetic Park Campground.

Kinetic Park Campground to Besant Campground: (138.5 K)

The prairies have a beauty that I cannot adequately convey through words or pictures. One has to pass through the rolling fields of wheat, enjoying panoramic views and miles of emptiness, to gain an appreciation of it all.

The ground in this area is rich with deposits of Sodium Sulfate. Don't be surprised if you see a white film in the ditches or on the horizon. Sodium Sulfate is harvested using an evaporation process that separates the Sodium Sulfate from water. The result of this process is a product used in industrial applications like the manufacturing of detergents. Sodium sulfate has been mined in this area since 1947.

Chaplin Lake is designated by the Western Hemispheric Shorebird Reserve Network because it is vital bird habitat. Chaplin Lake is Canada's second largest saltwater lake. 67 000 birds have been counted in this area in one day. Birds flock to this area to feast on shore flies, brine shrimp and seeds from the shallow, salty water. Many birds use this area as a link between their winter home in South America and their nesting grounds in Canada's north. Some birds fly for over 70 hours without a break, making this stop a much-needed rest area. Stop at Chaplin's Interpretive Centre to learn more.

Climb the lookout tower in Chaplin Lake to view nearby Chaplin Lake and salt flats. Your destination for the evening is Besant Campground, just east of Mortlach. Mortlach, population 254, is famous for its Saskatoon berry Festival held annually on the first Saturday of July. There is a small grocery store here that is closed on Sundays. Check out Mortlach Museum where you can have your picture taken in their authentic jail cell.

The Besant Campground is located next to a small pond. There is a small store on-site and laundry facilities available. Debit and credit cards are not accepted. Watch the ground for cacti.

Kilometre Log

0.0 Leave Kinetic Park Campground heading east on South Railway Street East.

0.3 Turn left onto HWY 4.

2.8 Cross over Swift Current Creek.

3.2 Turn right off of HWY 4 onto HWY 1.

3.6 Cross over Swift Current Creek.

17.8 Waldeck. No services.

45.7 Exit to Herbert and Lone Eagle Campground.

50.0 Reed Lake.

59.3 Exit to Morse.

64.1 Intersection of HWY 1 & HWY 19. HWY 1 & 19 are the same here until Chaplin.

69.5 Highway splits around the town of Ernfold.

80.1 Cross over Chaplin Lake.

88.6 Chaplin.

101.8 Secretan.

116.1 Parkbeg.

130.1 Exit to Mortlach at intersection of HWY 626 & HWY 1.

136.6 Turn right off of HWY 1 towards Besant Campground.

138.5 Bike down a long tree-lined road until you see the campground office.

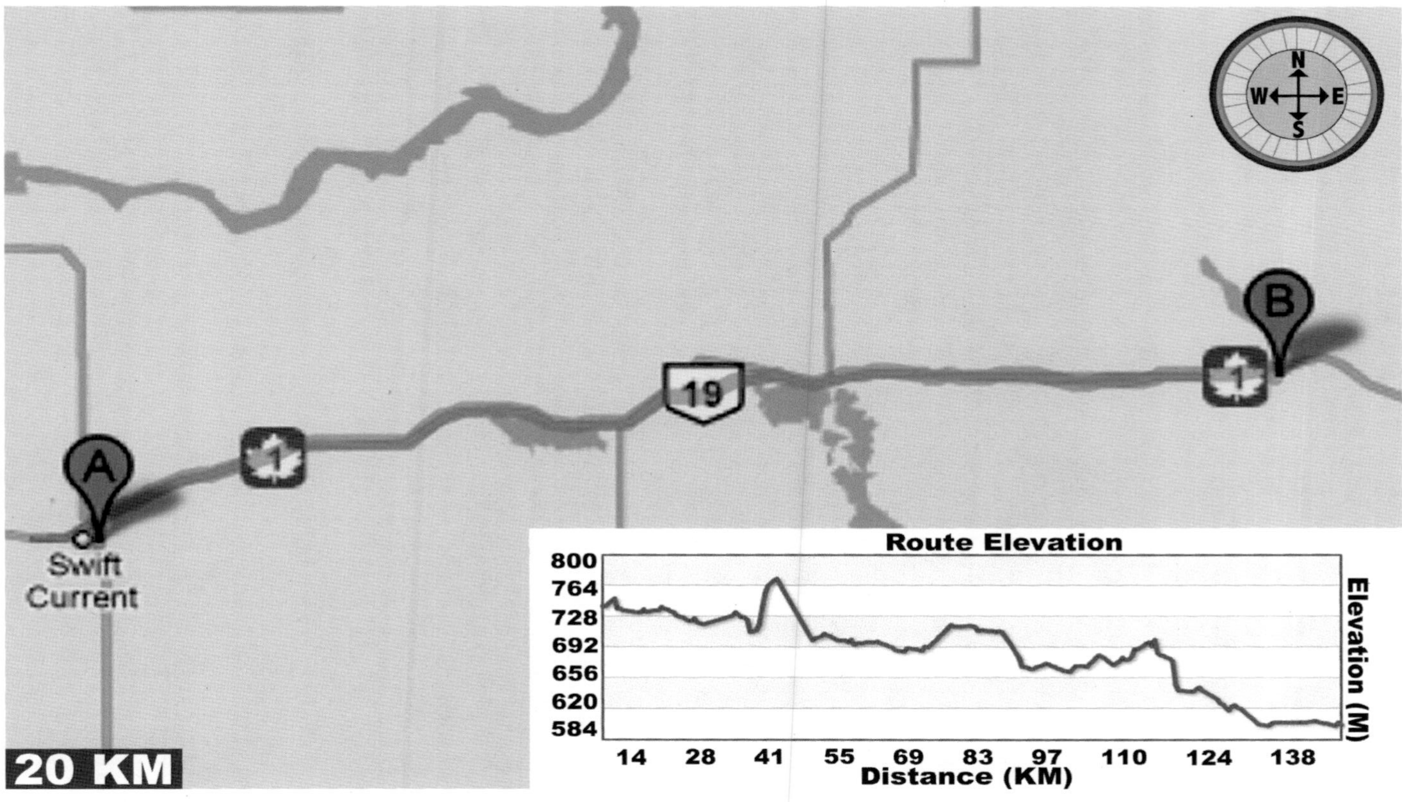

N
W
E
S
B
1
19
A
1
Swift Current
Route Elevation
800
764
728
692
656
620
584
Elevation (M)
14
28
41
55
69
83
97
110
124
138
Distance (KM)
20 KM

Besant Campground to Regina's Kings Acres Campground: (114.8 K)

Moose Jaw, population 32 132, sits on the banks of the Moose Jaw River. The city serves as a hub to the many small farming communities in the area, but also as a popular destination for tourists. If you want to spend the evening in Moose Jaw, check out River Park Campground.

In the early 1900s, most of Moose Jaw's buildings were heated with steam produced in coal boilers beneath the ground. A series of tunnels was developed to allow workers to service the equipment. During the Prohibition era in the early 1900s, these tunnels were used to produce liquor for both domestic use and export to the United States. Local legend is that Al Capone once lived in these tunnels to oversee their operation. Presently, over 100 000 people annually take the Tunnels of Moose Jaw tour that starts next to the train station in the city's downtown.

Regina, population 179 246, is Saskatchewan's capital city and home to the largest legislative building in Canada. Regina, meaning "Queen" in Latin, is also home to the world famous Royal Canadian Mounted Police Training Academy and the RCMP Heritage Museum.

Watch for green flags displaying the citizens of Regina's enthusiasm for their Canadian Football League (CFL) team, the Saskatchewan Roughriders. The team's fans are the most raucous in the country.

City planners can take credit for much of Regina's beauty. The city is focused around man-made Wascana Lake and over 300 000 trees in the city's parks were hand planted.

If you need work done on your bike head downtown to Western Cycle.

Your destination for the evening is Kings Acres Campground on the east side of the city, next to the Tourism Regina office. The campground offers free wireless internet, laundry and a small store.

Kilometre Log

0.0 Leave the campground heading north down the tree lined road.
1.1 Turn right onto HWY 1.
7.9 Intersection of HWY 1 & HWY 643.
12.8 Caronport. Services available on the highway.
32.4 Enter Moose Jaw on HWY 1.
33.9 Intersection of HWY 1 & Main Street N.
36.5 Mac the Moose.
39.6 Cross over Moose Jaw River.
44.4 Intersection of HWY 1 & HWY 301 (N) / HWY 39 (S).
98.9 Enter Regina on the southeast side of the city.
100.8 Exit right and circle 270° clockwise to gain HWY 6 / Albert Street.
106.7 Turn right off of Albert Street / HWY 6 onto Victoria Avenue.
110.5 Victoria Avenue becomes E Victoria Avenue / HWY 1.
112.9 Turn left onto Prince of Wales Drive.
113.4 Turn right and remain on Eastgate Drive.
114.8 Turn left into Kings Acres Campground.

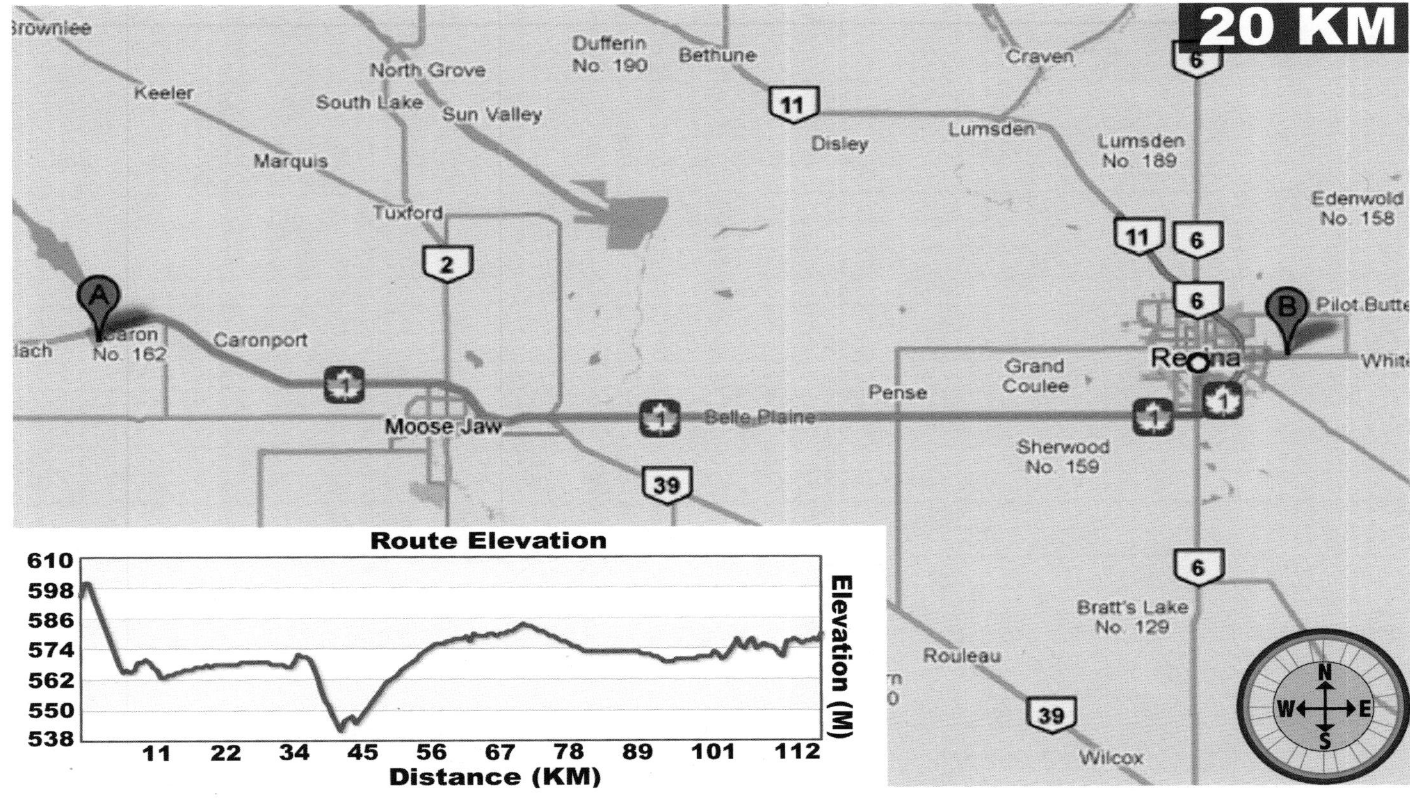

20 KM
Keeler
North Grove
South Lake
Sun Valley
Dufferin
No. 190
Bethune
Craven
Marquis
Tuxford
Disley
Lumsden
Lumsden
No. 189
Edenwold
No. 158
A
No. 162
Caronport
Moose Jaw
Belle Plaine
Pense
Grand
Coulee
Sherwood
No. 159
B
Bratt's Lake
No. 129
Rouleau
Wilcox
2
11
6
1
39
N
S
E
W
Route Elevation
610
598
586
574
562
550
538
11
22
34
45
56
67
78
89
101
112
Distance (KM)
Elevation (M)

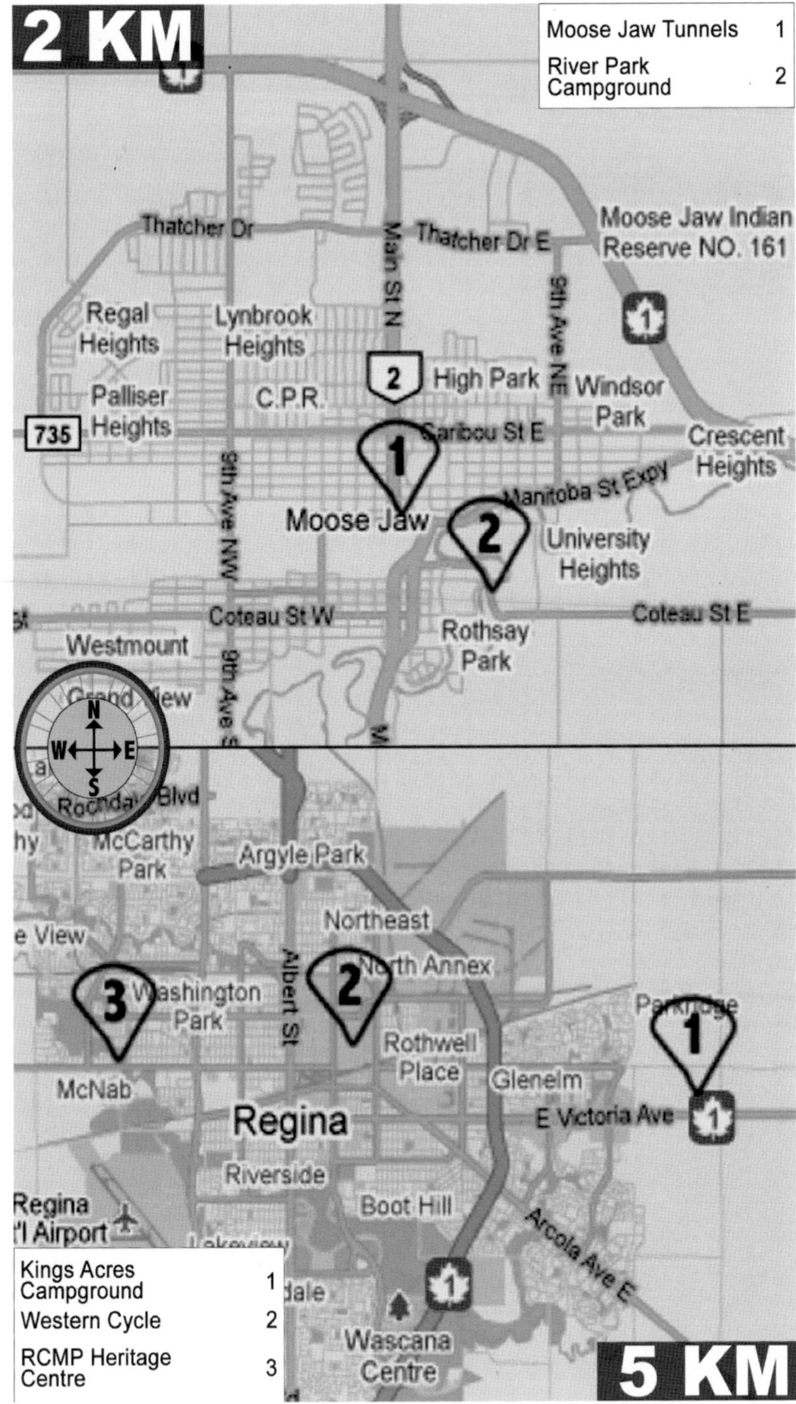
2 KM
Moose Jaw Tunnels 1
River Park Campground 2
Thatcher Dr
Thatcher Dr E
Main St N
9th Ave NE
Moose Jaw Indian Reserve NO. 161
Regal Heights
Lynbrook Heights
High Park
Windsor Park
Palliser Heights
C.P.R.
735
Caribou St E
Crescent Heights
9th Ave NW
Manitoba St Expy
Moose Jaw
University Heights
Coteau St W
Coteau St E
Westmount
Rothsay Park
N
W
E
S
McCarthy Park
Argyle Park
Northeast
Albert St
Washington Park
Rothwell Place
Glenelm
McNab
Regina
E Victoria Ave
Riverside
Boot Hill
Arcola Ave E
Wascana Centre
Kings Acres Campground 1
Western Cycle 2
RCMP Heritage Centre 3
5 KM

I have opted to veer off of HWY 1 from Regina and take a more northern route. The reason for this detour is that HWY 1 is notoriously dangerous in many parts of southern Manitoba with little or no shoulder. The northern route offers safer cycling, more services and better scenery.

By heading north you will explore the parkland area of Manitoba, becoming acquainted first with Lake Dauphin, then Lake Manitoba and further on Lake Winnipeg as well as the small Icelandic fishing village on its shores. Cycle through Whiteshell Provincial Park and check out an array of lakes and rivers that blend handsomely with boreal forest and granite ridges.

Manitoba's provincial parks are bargain priced and small bike stores are available in Melville, Yorkton, Dauphin, Selkirk and Kenora.

By taking this route you will miss Manitoba's capital city, Winnipeg.

Boreal forest

The setting sun silouetting boreal forest is an image that will be burned into your memory after this trip.

Characterized by a predominance of coniferous trees, boreal forest covers 35% of Canada, playing an important role in the country's economy as well as supporting diverse ecosystems. Boreal forest helps combat climate change as it produces oxygen and absorbs and stores carbon dioxide.

Boreal forest is present in a northern circumpolar band in Scandinavia, Russia and North America, occurring in areas with cold winters and short, cool, moist summers.

Kings Acres Campground to Melville Regional Park: (155.4 K)

Leave Kings Acres Campground on HWY 1 heading west. At Qu'Appelle head north towards Fort Qu'Appelle and the Qu'Appelle Valley. Qu'Appelle was once a bustling, significant town. It was expected to be the capital city of the Northwest Territories, which included this area in the 1880s, until Lieutenant Governor Edgar Dewdney made present-day Regina the capital. Qu'appelle is now a quiet prairie town.

You can shave 12 kilometres off of your total distance for the day by heading northwest on HWY 10 at Balgonie, but this is a notoriously rough highway. Make the decision based on your tolerance for bumps, long distance riding and type of bike that you are riding.

Zoom down the south side of the stunning Qu'Appelle Valley into the town of Fort Qu'Appelle, which sits nestled between Echo and Mission Lake. The Qu'Appelle Valley runs from west to east, starting at Diefenbaker Lake in Saskatchewan and ending where it meets the Assiniboine River Valley in Manitoba.

Legend states that the Qu'Appelle River and Valley got its name from a young Cree warrior named Three Eagles. Three Eagles was paddling up the river, having left his girlfriend behind at his camp. From his canoe he heard his name called. "Kâ-têpwêt??" Kâ-têpwê is the Cree word for "who calls" in English and translates to "qu'appelle" in French. The next day, Three Eagles returned to camp to find that his girlfriend had passed away in the evening, but not before calling his name into the night.

Fort Qu'Appelle is a friendly town tucked in a valley that overflows with tourists during summer months. There is a good grocery store and many restaurants available here, as well as the Fort Qu'Appelle Campground.

Highway conditions transition from good to marginal in this area. When roads are rough, take your time and make sure you don't hurt your wrists.

Climb out of the valley and head towards Melville. Melville is a quiet town that is growing rapidly due to the commodities boom currently happening in Saskatchewan.

If you need bike repairs check out Melville's Hometown Cycle & Sports. Your destination for the evening is Melville Regional Park, located on the northwest side of town set next to the baseball diamonds. Showers are available through a separate entrance to the small house at the entrance of the park.

Kilometre Log

0.0 Leave Kings Acres Campground heading west on Eastgate Drive.
1.9 Turn left onto Prince of Wales Drive.
2.2 Turn left onto East Victoria Avenue / HWY 1.
14.8 Intersection of HWY 48 / HWY 1. Exit to White City.
21.2 Intersection of HWY 1 & HWY 46.
22.0 Intersection of HWY 1 & HWY 364.
37.1 McLean.
50.7 Intersection of HWY 1 & HWY 35. Turn left here.
52.7 Enter Qu'Appelle on HWY 35.
70.6 HWY 35 & HWY 10 merge to become HWY 10 / HWY 35.
80.2 Enter Fort Qu'Appelle on HWY 10 / HWY 35.
81.0 HWY 10 / HWY 35 becomes HWY 10 as HWY 35 heads north. Remain on HWY 10.
81.6 Pass over the Qu'Appelle River.
82.6 Intersection of HWY 10 and HWY 56 E / HWY 22 W.
98.8 Intersection of HWY 10 & HWY 310. Exit to Balcarres.
151.9 Enter Melville on HWY 10.
154.8 Intersection of HWY 10 & HWY 47.
155.2 Turn right off of HWY 10 onto Prince Edward Street at the baseball diamond.
155.4 Welcome to Melville Regional Park & Campground.

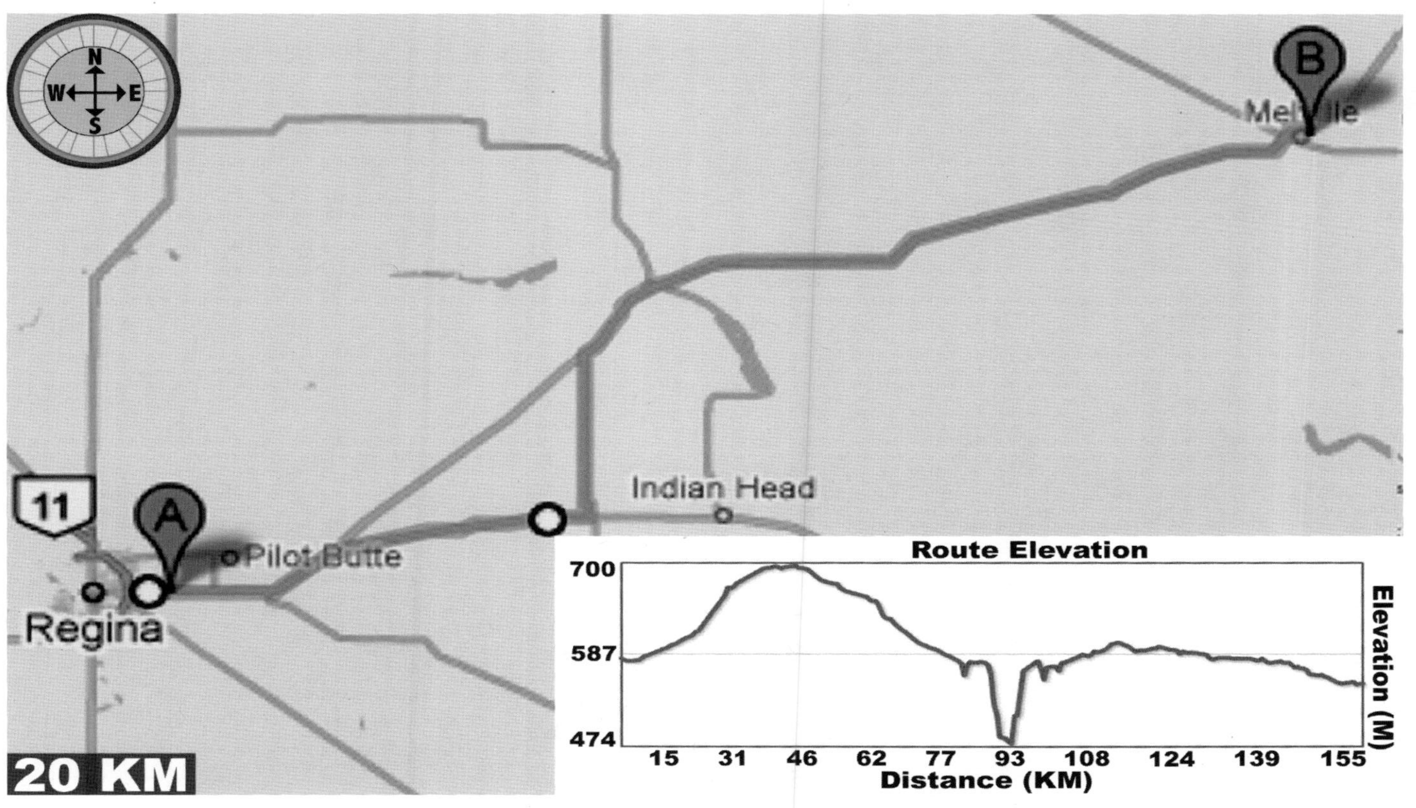

N
W
E
S
11
A
Pilot Butte
Regina
Indian Head
B
20 KM
Route Elevation
700
587
474
15
31
46
62
77
93
108
124
139
155
Distance (KM)
Elevation (M)

Melville Regional Park to Roblin Kin Park & Campground: (119.7)

Today you will make the transition from prairie to parkland as you cross from Saskatchewan into Manitoba. Parkland is generally covered with boreal forest and dotted with lakes, ponds and rivers.

Yorkton, population 15 038, gets its name from the group of settlers from York County, Ontario, that settled in this area in 1882. They came with hopes of farming the area's fertile ground. If you need a bike store, check out Hometown Cycle & Sports. If you would like to spend the evening here, check out the city-run campground on the west end of the city on HWY 16. The Yorkton Library offers free internet to guests and is conveniently located on Broadway Street West / HWY 16.

Leave Yorkton and head east towards Manitoba. Soon after arriving in Manitoba, you will plunge dramatically into the Shell Valley, home to Lake of the Prairies, which is not a lake but the dammed Shellmouth River. This man-made reservoir was completed in 1972, as part of a strategy to reduce the risk of flooding on the Assiniboine River in the south of Manitoba. The Shellmouth Dam is located at the south end of Lake of the Prairies. It controls the quantity of water flowing south. Ricker's Campground is located in the valley.

Climb out of the valley and cycle towards Roblin, population 964, which is also the Fly Fishing Capital of Manitoba. If you get into town early, check out the Roblin Leisure Aquatic Centre and enjoy the 112-foot water slide. Groceries are available in town.

Spend the night on the shore of Goose Lake at Roblin Kin Park and Campground. At $10.00 a night, the campground gets the nod as the most affordable on the trip.

Turn your clocks an hour forward when crossing the Manitoba border, unless you are crazy enough to be biking through this area between November and March!

Kilometre Log

0.0	Leave Melville Regional Park heading north on Prince Edward Street.
0.6	At the baseball diamond turn right on HWY 10.
36.1	Enter Yorkton on HWY 10.
38.0	Turn right on HWY 10 / Broadway Street West.
39.7	Yorkton Public Library in between Haultain Avenue and Laurier Avenue.
40.1	Broadway Street West turns into Broadway Street East.
40.4	Hometown Cycle off of 3rd Avenue North.
42.4	Exit Yorkton on HWY 10 / Broadway Street East.
80.1	Intersection of HWY 10 & HWY 8 (N) / HWY 80 (S). Exit to Wroxton.
101.9	Intersection of HWY 10 & HWY 369.
105.1	Border of Manitoba and Saskatchewan. Enter Manitoba on HWY 5.
106.3	Cross over Lake of the Prairies.
117.7	Enter Roblin.
118.6	Turn right at the intersection of HWY 5 & HWY 83.
118.9	Turn right onto Queen Street.
119.6	Turn right onto Goose Lake Drive.
119.7	Roblin Kin Park and Campground.

The Qu'Appelle Valley

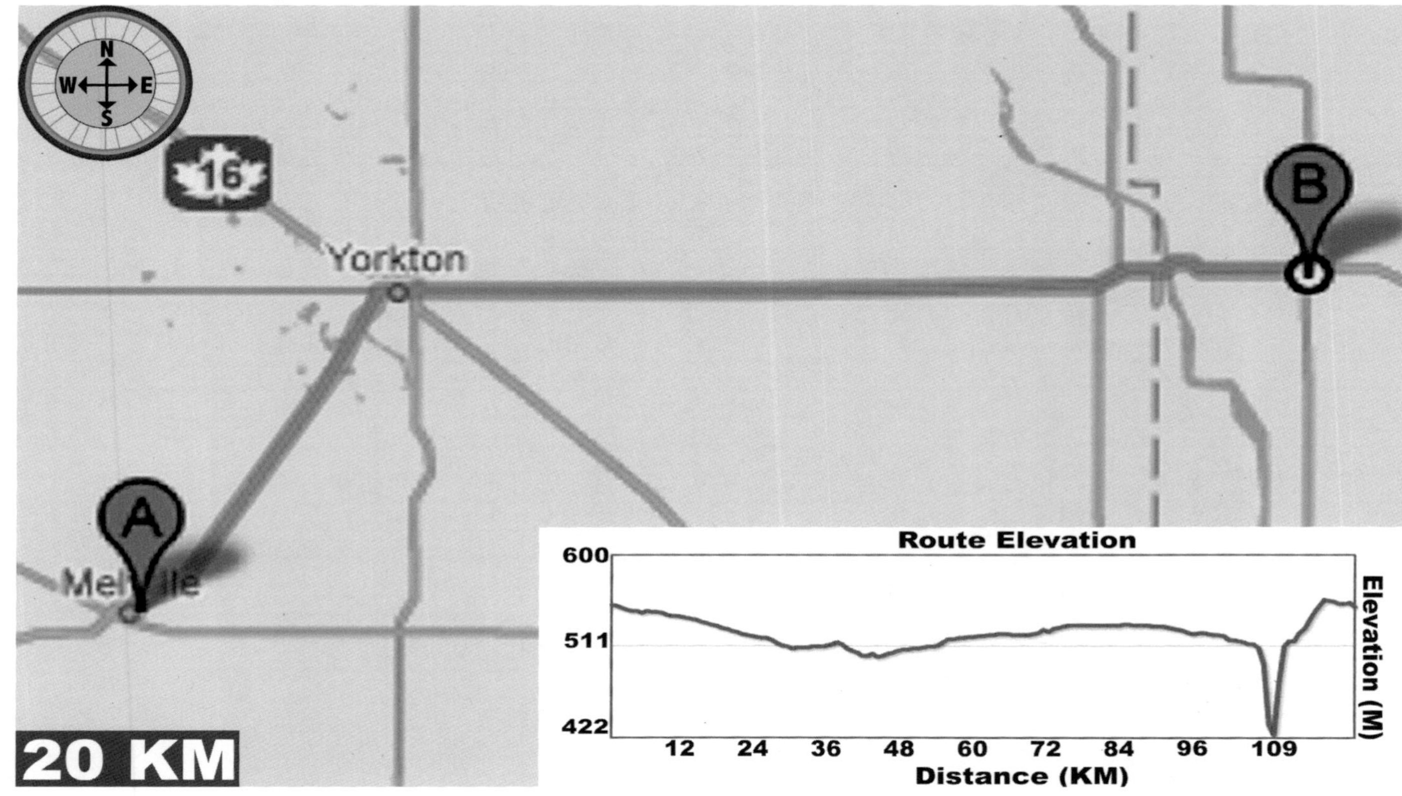
N
W
E
S
16
Yorkton
B
A
20 KM
Route Elevation
600
511
422
12
24
36
48
60
72
84
96
109
Distance (KM)
Elevation (M)

Province:	Manitoba
Population:	1 213 815
Area:	649 950 km^2
Industries:	Agriculture, forestry, mining, transportation, hydro electricity.
Highlights:	Lake Manitoba, Lake Winnipeg, Gimli, Whiteshell Provincial Park.

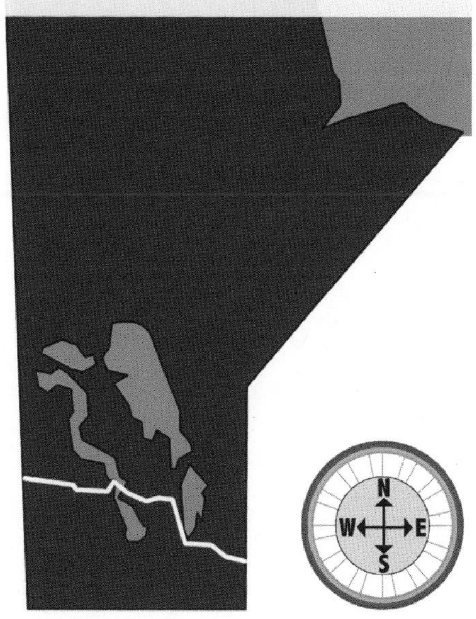

Roblin Kin Park to Rainbow Beach Provincial Park: (114.1 K)

Leave Roblin and head east towards Dauphin through sparsely populated parkland.

The first town that you will enter is Grandview. The town's website claims that in 1901, someone stood looking at the nearby Duck Mountains and made the statement, "What a grand view." Over a hundred years later the town still exists and has a campground in Wilson Park as well as a museum and many recreation facilities.

From Grandview head towards Gilbert Plains. If you have time, check out the Negrych Pioneer Homestead, a federally designated Heritage Site which is believed to be the most complete and best preserved Ukrainian farmstead in Canada. It includes a fully preserved working peech which is a massive log and clay cook stove that was once the heart of every Ukrainian home. Camping is available at Centennial Park next to the popular Gilbert Plains Golf Course.

The next town you will reach is Dauphin, population 7 906. Dauphin has everything that a bike tourist might need, including a bike store, hospital, grocery store, mall and many restaurants. Dauphin is famous for the country music festival that it hosts in the beginning of July each year just south of town. Dauphin is a Ukrainian town and many of the residents can still speak the language and observe traits from the old country. The north gate of Riding Mountain National Park is just south of town.

The bike east to Rainbow Beach Provincial Park is flat and easy. Expect light traffic except on weekends. Rainbow Beach presently has a small canteen for food and drinks. Full shower facilities are available and the view over Dauphin Lake is stunning. To reserve a site at any Manitoba Provincial Park call or visit their website.

Kilometre Log

0.0	Leave Roblin Kin Park and Campground heading east on Goose Lake Drive.
0.1	Turn left onto Queen Street.
0.8	Turn left onto HWY 83.
1.2	Turn right onto HWY 5.
48.2	Grandview.

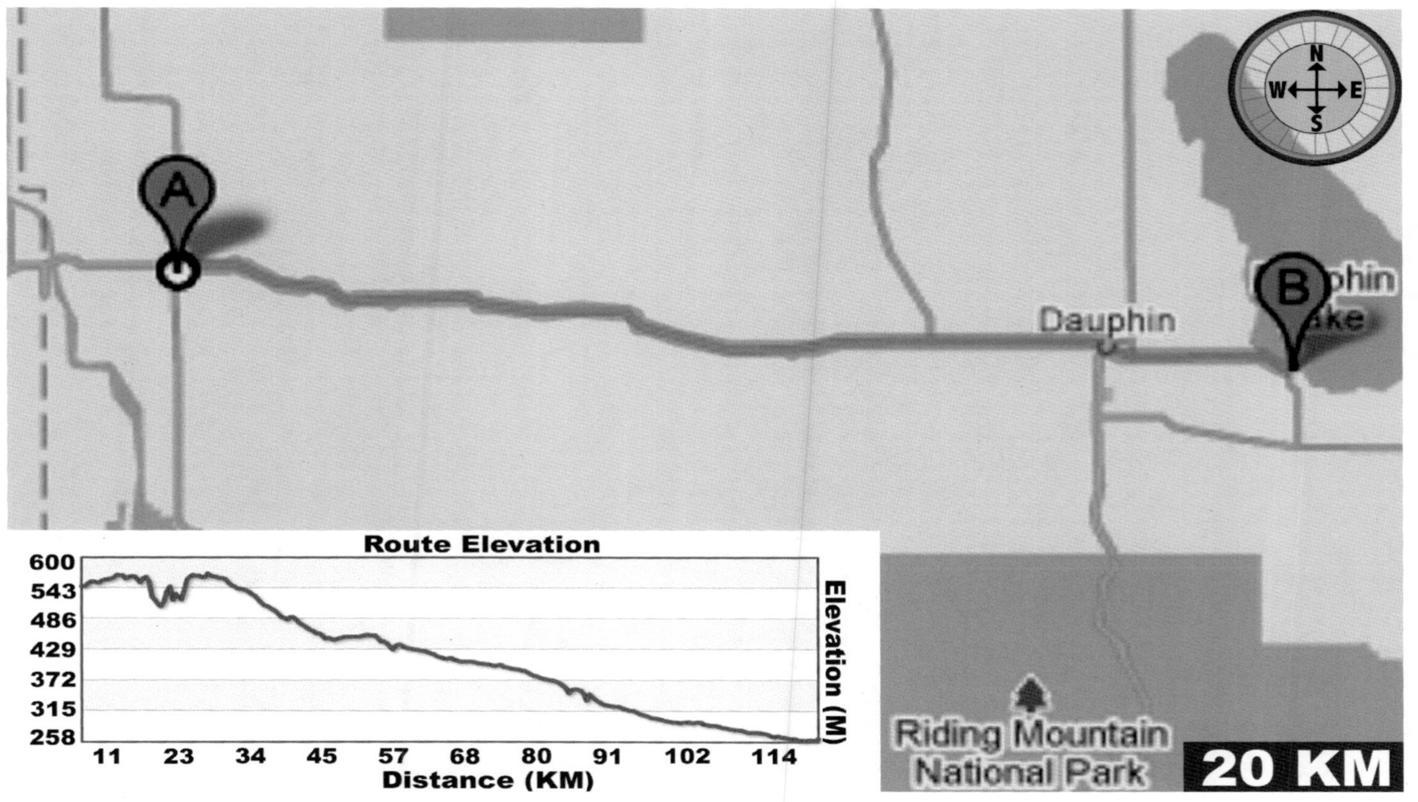
A
B
Dauphin
N
W
E
S
Riding Mountain
National Park
20 KM
Route Elevation
Elevation (M)
600
543
486
429
372
315
258
11
23
34
45
57
68
80
91
102
114
Distance (KM)

64.4 Intersection of HWY 5 & HWY 274 at Gilbert Plains.
78.1 Intersection of HWY 5 & HWY 10. The two roads merge here.
94.0 Intersection of HWY 5 / HWY 10 & HWY 362. Enter Dauphin on Second Avenue NW.
95.3 Turn right onto Main Street N / HWY 20A.
95.4 Turn left onto 1st Avenue Northeast / HWY 20A.
96.3 Exit Dauphin on HWY 20A.
98.2 HWY 20A becomes HWY 20.
114.1 Turn left to enter Rainbow Beach Provincial Park.

Rainbow Beach Provincial Park to Narrows West Resort: (97.8 K)

Today you will cycle through vibrant wetlands on a highway that is quiet and freshly paved with a small consistent shoulder

For the first part of your day you will have the northern slopes of Riding Mountain National Park to your right. Keep a keen eye on the skyline for bald eagles, which are common in this area. Riding Mountain National Park is located on the highest part of the Manitoba Escarpment, which stands in stark contrast to the surrounding prairie. The park is home to wolves, moose, elk, black bear, cougar and lynx.

Today you will get a glimpse of Lake Manitoba, Manitoba's second largest fresh water lake. Steady climbing for the first fifteen kilometres of the ride will get you warmed up for an enjoyable day. Ochre River, population 929, is the first town that you will cycle through after leaving Rainbow Beach Provincial Park. A small church converted to a coffee shop near the highway is a good place for a break.

As you approach Ste. Rose du Lac, the signage will be in both French and English. This bilingual town has a bank, pharmacy, campground and most services to please a cyclist. If you choose to enter Ste. Rose, make sure to check out the Grotto, an artificial cave handsomely decorated and used as a place of worship. The Grotto is located next to the campground, on your left hand side as you turn off the highway to enter town. Although your destination campground has a small store, consider purchasing your supplies here.

After Ste. Rose, Eddystone will be the only town to acquire food or water, so make sure you have adequate provisions.

Cross the bridge that spans over Lake Manitoba and you are at your destination, Narrows West Resort. The resort has a full restaurant, bar, hotel, campground, small grocery store as well as a liquor and beer vendor.

The province of Manitoba is named after this area. Manitou Wapow means "strait of the Manitou," in Cree. Manitou was later changed to Manitoba and adopted as the name of this province.

Keep an eye out for Lake Manitoba's legendary giant serpent Manipogo while exploring the area.

Kilometre Log

0.0 Leave Rainbow Beach Provincial Park biking southeast on HWY 20.
7.8 Ochre River.
9.0 Junction of HWY 5 & HWY 20. Turn left onto HWY 5.
27.1 Exit to Ste. Rose du Lac.
28.5 HWY 5 turns to the right. Continue straight on HWY 68.
57.3 Eddystone.
97.8 Narrows West Resort & Campground.

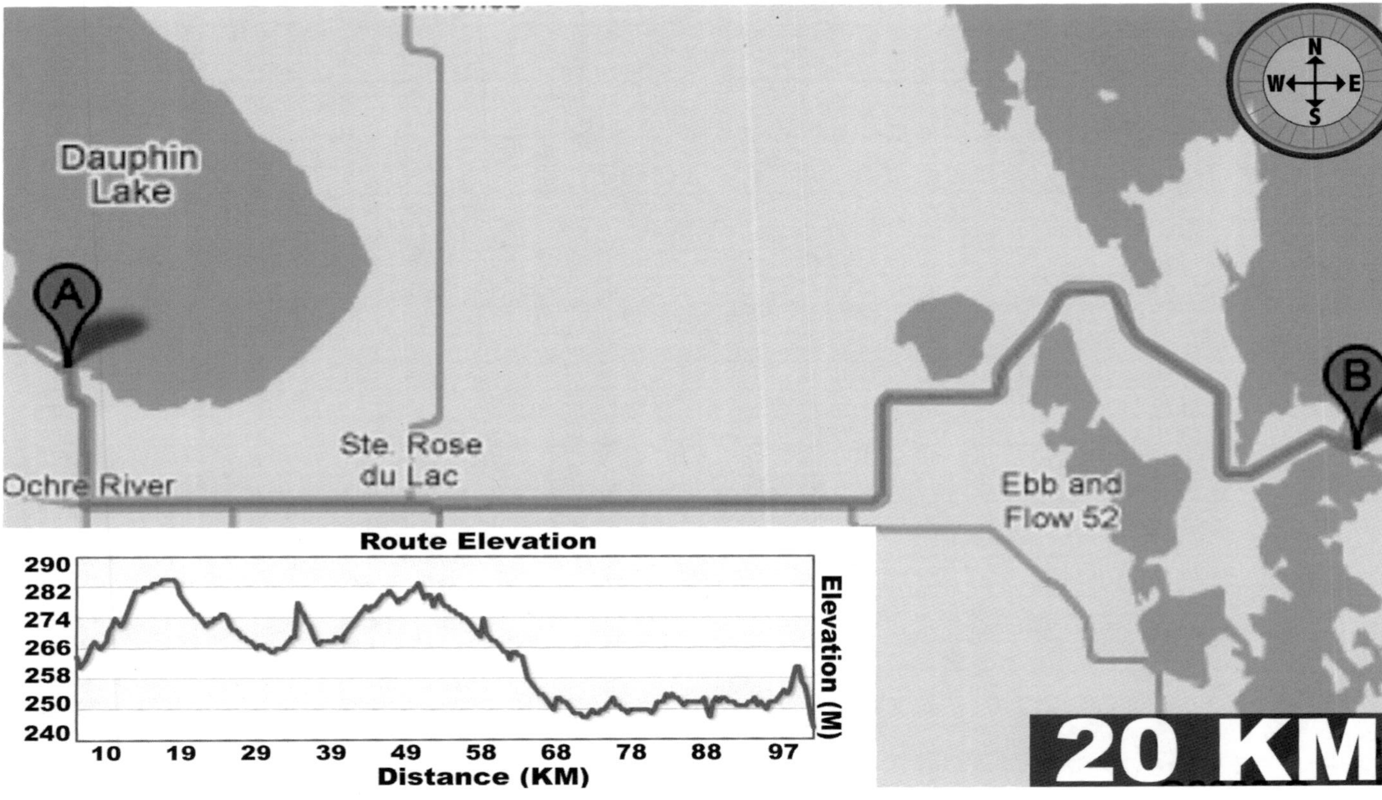
Dauphin Lake
A
Ste. Rose du Lac
Ochre River
Ebb and Flow 52
B
N
W
E
S
Route Elevation
290
282
274
266
258
250
240
10
19
29
39
49
58
68
78
88
97
Distance (KM)
Elevation (M)
20 KM

Narrows West Resort to Arborg and District Multicultural Heritage Village: (135.6)

The Interlake, defined as the area between Lake Manitoba and Lake Winnipeg is sparsely populated with humans and densely populated with wildlife. Expect quiet roads, friendly people and ample wetlands.

Arrive first in Eriksdale, population 911, home to quiet and affordable McEwen Memorial Campground. The campground has washrooms, a covered structure with a fireplace, but no showers. Restaurants and groceries are available in town.

The flat terrain, sparse distribution of people, abundance of wildlife and smooth highway will be some of the things you might discuss as you wind down at the campground in Arborg. All day, coniferous trees mix with the wetlands to form picturesque views.

In the early 1900s, mainly European immigrants settled this area. The populace continues to hold on to many traits of "the old country," especially in language and food. Their European roots make them sympathetic to cyclists, while their Manitoba friendliness ensure that they are great ambassadors to the area. The local dining specialty in the Interlake is the Perogie. This high-carbohydrate treat of a potato based filling wrapped in dough, boiled or fried and usually dipped in sour cream, is a must have for any hungry cyclist.

Enjoy a gentle descent into the Arborg and District Multicultural Heritage Village, which includes a quiet campground with hot showers. Outdoor displays depict what Arborg was like in years past.

Situated on the banks of the Icelandic River, Arborg, population 1 012, has a sporting goods store with some bike parts and other amenities to please the bike tourist including a bakery and a couple of restaurants. Also, don't miss the world's largest curling rock, one of Arborg's claims to fame.

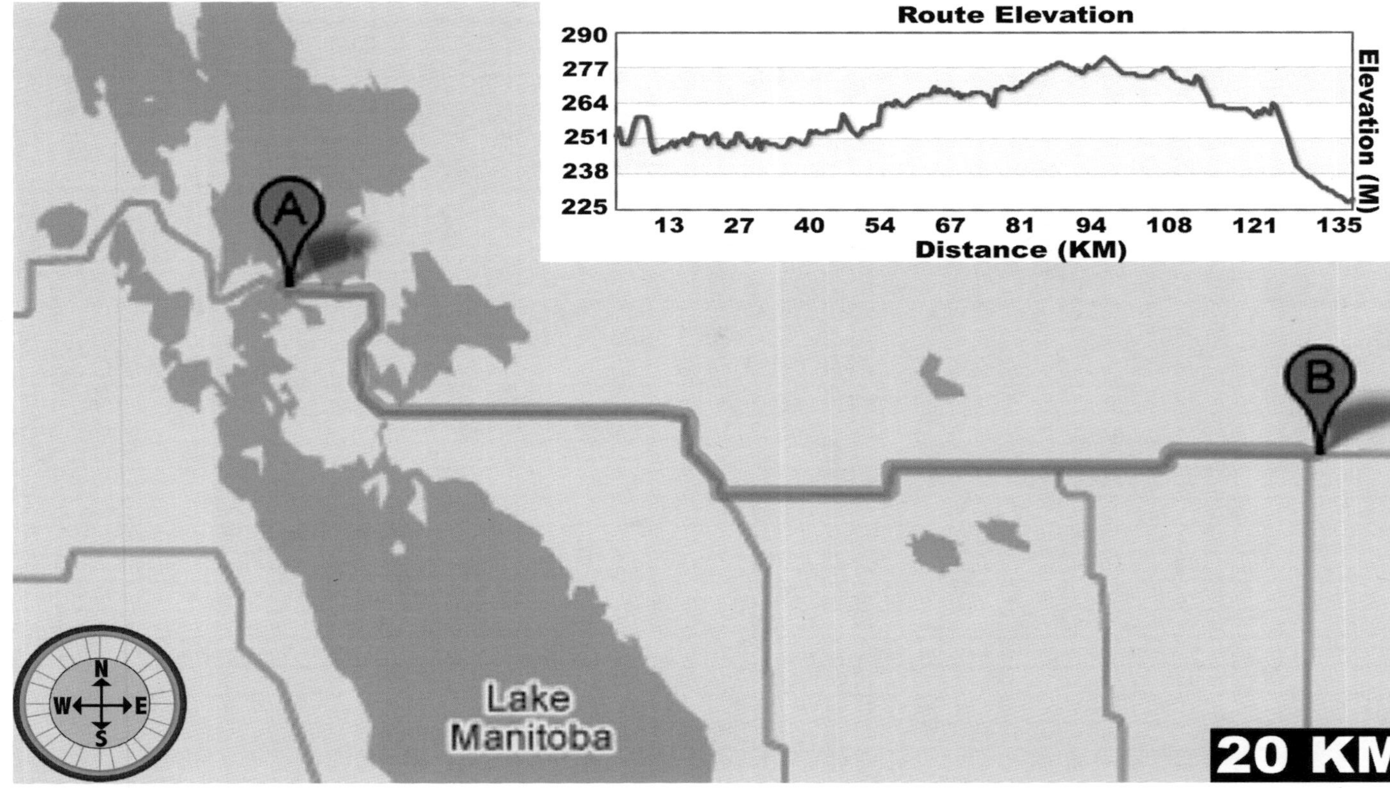

Route Elevation
290
277
264
251
238
225
13
27
40
54
67
81
94
108
121
135
Distance (KM)
Elevation (M)
A
B
N
W
E
S
Lake Manitoba
20 KM

Kilometre Log

0.0 Leave the Narrows West Resort Campground heading east on HWY 68.
23.4 Cycle through the town of Vogar.
35.0 Overton.
44.8 Oatfield.
57.4 HWY 68 turns into HWY 68 / HWY 6. Turn right here.
68.2 Eriksdale and McEwen Memorial Campground.
69.0 Turn left off of HWY 6 / HWY 68 onto Vimy Avenue / HWY 68.
106.3 Poplarfield and the intersection of HWY 68 / HWY 17. Take pictures of the over-sized deer, the Giant Buck.
134.7 Pass the main entrance to Arborg.
135.6 Turn left into the Arborg and District Multicultural Heritage Village.

Arborg and District Multicultural Heritage Village to Selkirk Municipal Campground: (105.3 K)

Today you will get your first glimpse of Lake Winnipeg, a notoriously beautiful and large lake. Canada's fifth largest lake has many limestone cliffs, the erosion of which is responsible for the pristine white sand beaches around the south part of the lake.

Many natural phenomena occur on Lake Winnipeg due to its shallow average depth and massive area. Northern winds push water into the south end of the lake and can cause waves of more than one metre in height. These giant waves are notoriously dangerous and can occur seemingly out of nowhere.

Road conditions will be good until you hit HWY 222 and start heading south. HWY 222 is narrow and usually lacking a shoulder, but vehicles will generally be traveling at a more casual pace than on most Manitoba highways.

This is cottage country, so expect traffic to be heavy Friday night and Sunday afternoon. Save yourself the hassle and try to avoid traveling during these times.

Make sure to stop just off the highway at Hnausa Beach Provincial Park. This provincial park has camping, washrooms and picnic tables and is a good spot to rest your legs and take a photo of this 418 kilometre-long lake.

Continue biking down HWY 222 until you reach Camp

Lake Winnipeg

Lake Winnipeg's health is currently being threatened due to an overloading of nitrogen and phosphate in the water. Compared to the volume of this relatively shallow body of water, Lake Manitoba has a massive watershed home to over five million people.

Just like humans, algae needs phosphorous to survive and grow. Unfortunately, humans are adding about 8,000 tonnes phosphorous annually to the lake while only 2,500 tonnes are expelled. The excess accumulates in the lake causing rapid algae growth, which threatens the health of the lake's ecosystems.

Although farms that surround the lake are partially responsible, the massive size of the lake's watershed mean that it is affected by the actions of people and industry hundreds of kilometres away.

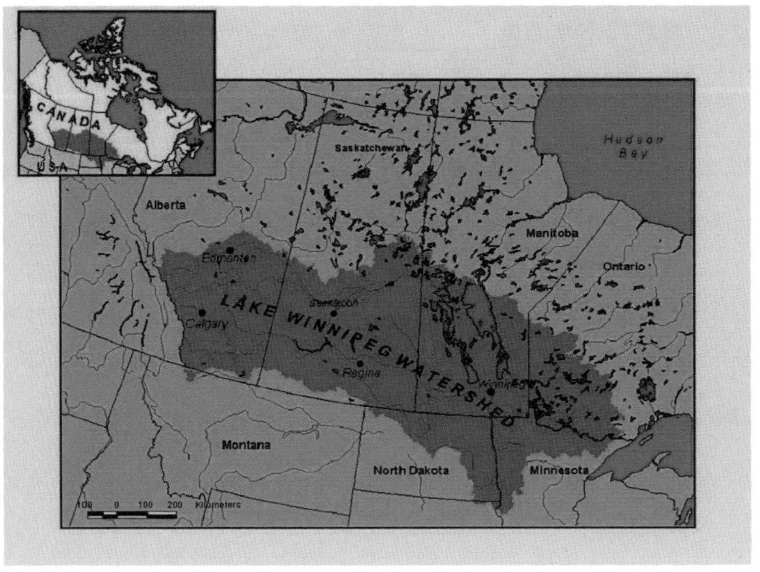

Morton Provincial Park on the shores of Lake Winnipeg. Named after Monsignor Thomas Morton, this provincial park was developed during the 1920s as a summer-camp for orphaned and under-privileged children. Camp Morton has shower facilities and Yurt rentals available.

Don't miss stopping at the city of Gimli. 5 797 local inhabitants enjoy this charming town that will make you feel as though you are in the Maritimes. Make sure to stroll around the large marina that houses commercial and recreational boats.

Whiskey fan? Well, even if you're not, you might be interested to know that Gimli is where world-famous Crown Royal Whiskey is distilled. Unfortunately, tours are not available.

Gimli's harbour is exceptional. Look to see fishermen in the area hauling in their catches, which are mostly white fish and pickerel.

The road from Gimli to Winnipeg Beach is densely occupied in the summer with tourists and seasonal businesses. Road conditions improve slightly after Gimli and even more after Winnipeg Beach.

Winnipeg Beach, in Winnipeg Beach Provincial Park, is a quaint lakeside resort town with a can't-miss water tower at the south end of its popular beach.

Selkirk, population 9 515, is a full service town with all amenities a bike tourist could need. The area is famous for the massive Channel Catfish that anglers pull out of the nearby Red River, some of which can weigh over fifty kilograms.

Make sure you leave time for the Manitoba Marine Museum, which aims to tell the nautical history of Lake Winnipeg and the Red River. The museum is located next to the Selkirk Municipal Campground, your scheduled stop for the evening. If you need bike parts check out Keystone Selkirk Source for Sports.

Kilometre Log

0.0 Head east on HWY 68 towards Lake Winnipeg.

13.3 Intersection of HWY 6 & HWY 68.

15.8 Intersection of HWY 68 & HWY 222. Turn right onto HWY 222.

23.8 Hnausa Beach Provincial Park.

37.2 Exit left to Camp Morton Provincial Park.

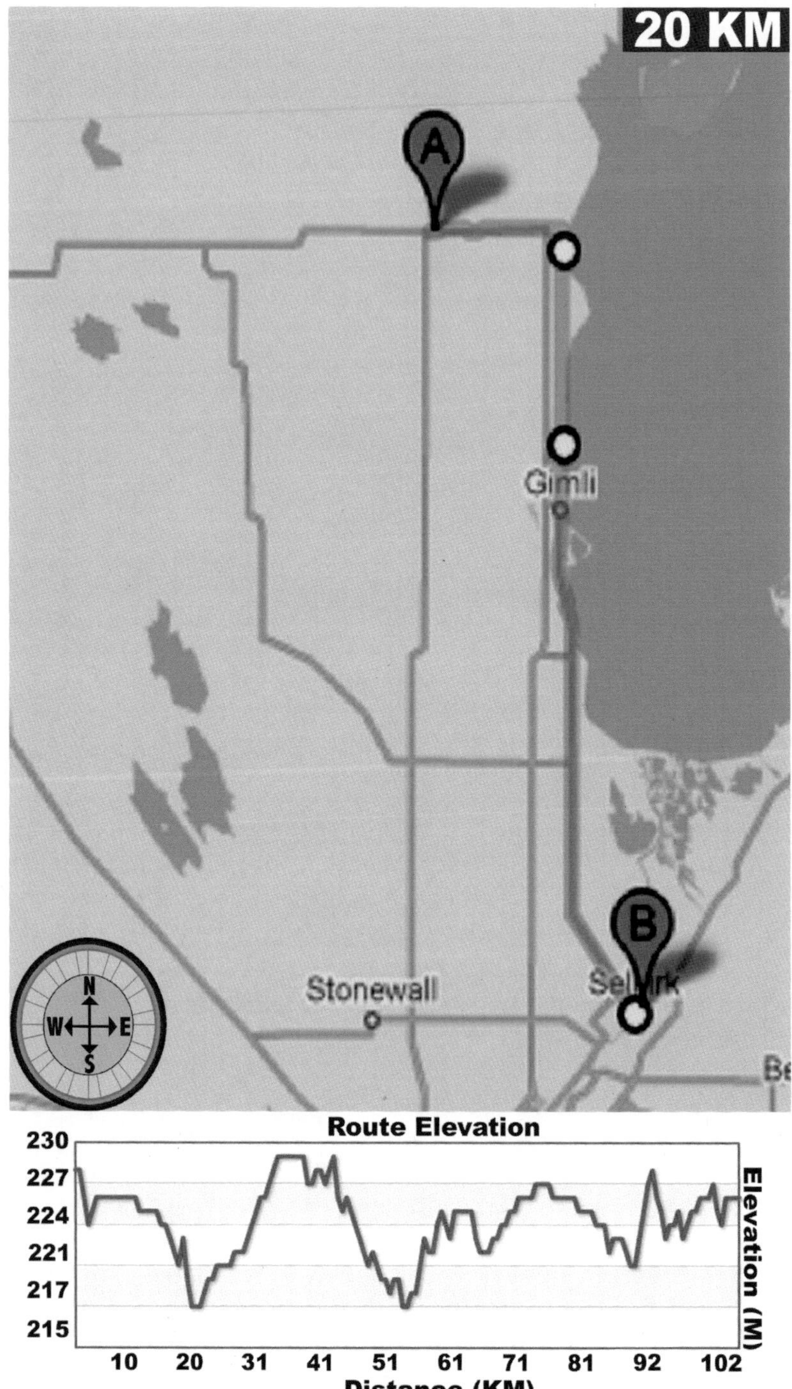
20 KM
A
Gimli
B
Stonewall
Selkirk
N
W
E
S
Route Elevation
230
227
224
221
217
215
10
20
31
41
51
61
71
81
92
102
Distance (KM)
Elevation (M)

45.7 Enter Gimli. HWY 222 becomes HWY 9.
60.2 Winnipeg Beach.
74.5 HWY 17 dead-ends into HWY 9.
83.2 Petersfield.
100.8 Enter Selkirk on Easton Drive / HWY 9A.
103.1 Turn left onto Manitoba Avenue.
103.8 Turn left onto Main Street.
104.5 Turn right on Queen Avenue.
105.3 Selkirk Municipal Campground.

Selkirk Municipal Campground to Caddy Lake Campground: (142.6 K)

35 kilometres south of Selkirk is the city of Winnipeg, Manitoba's provincial capital. I have by-passed Winnipeg because the road from the city to the Ontario border is dangerous and lacking a shoulder. With that being said, if you need something from Winnipeg before heading into the vast wilderness of Ontario, HWY 1 East is navigable. Avoid traveling this highway on Fridays when Winnipeggers are heading out to their cottages on the east side of the province.

If you choose to battle with HWY 1, ride your bike 143 kilometres from Winnipeg to the Falcon Lake Campground, just off HWY 1 before the Manitoba-Ontario border. Spend the evening there and join up with the *Canada by Bicycle* Route 11 kilometres to the east at West Hawk Lake.

Winnipeg lays at the convergence of the Assiniboine and Red Rivers. This area has a long and rich history as aboriginal people have been gathering at the meeting of these two rivers for thousands of years.

Monsieur Pierre LaVerendrye was the first person of European descent to arrive in this area, establishing Fort Rouge in 1738.

Winnipeg has a large, vibrant Francophone community centered on Saint Boniface in the southeast of the city.

Presently, Winnipeg is a multicultural city with two universities, many museums and a world-renowned orchestra.

Leave Selkirk and cross the Red River, which flows north to Lake Winnipeg and is designated as a Canadian Heritage River. It was a main trading route for Aboriginal and Voyageurs.

Pass by the outskirts of Beausejour, population 2 772, on the way to the west entrance of Whiteshell Provincial Park. The park lays on the western-edge of the Canadian Shield. The granite ridges that define many of the lakes and run along the sides of the road give the Whiteshell a rugged beauty. The 200+ lakes within Whiteshell Provincial Park are home to a variety of fish including world-class examples of northern pike, bass, walleye, lake and rainbow trout.

Make sure you stop at the entrance of the park and speak with the helpful staff. They will provide you with up to date maps and a wealth of knowledge about the area. Ask about petroforms, which are human-made patterns of rocks skillfully arranged on the ground.

There are many campgrounds sprinkled throughout the park. Most are close to the road and make good rest areas. Expect small stores to appear close to many of these campgrounds. This park is overflowing with wildlife. I narrowly avoided a slow speed collision with a white tailed deer and then had a fox walk right up to me, all in the same day.

Just before your arrival at your destination, Caddy Lake Campground, is The Lily Pond. It is a great place to take a rest and snap a photograph of the white and yellow lilies that cover the pond during summer months.

Many people spend their entire summer camped in this area. Don't be surprised if you find yourself, at the end of the night, swapping stories around a campfire.

Located next to the Caddy Lake Campground is a small resort. Ask the resort owners about renting a canoe to view the nearby Caddy Lake Rock Tunnels. Although groceries are available, selection is limited. Consider bringing supplies with you from a supermarket in Selkirk.

Kilometre Log

0.0	Leave Selkirk Municipal Campground heading southwest.
0.6	Turn left onto Eveline Street.
1.4	Turn left on HWY 204 and cross over the Red River.
4.2	Turn left off of HWY 204 onto HWY 509.
5.9	Intersection of HWY 509 & HWY 59. Turn right.
10.3	Cross HWY 44. Circle clockwise 270° to gain HWY 44.

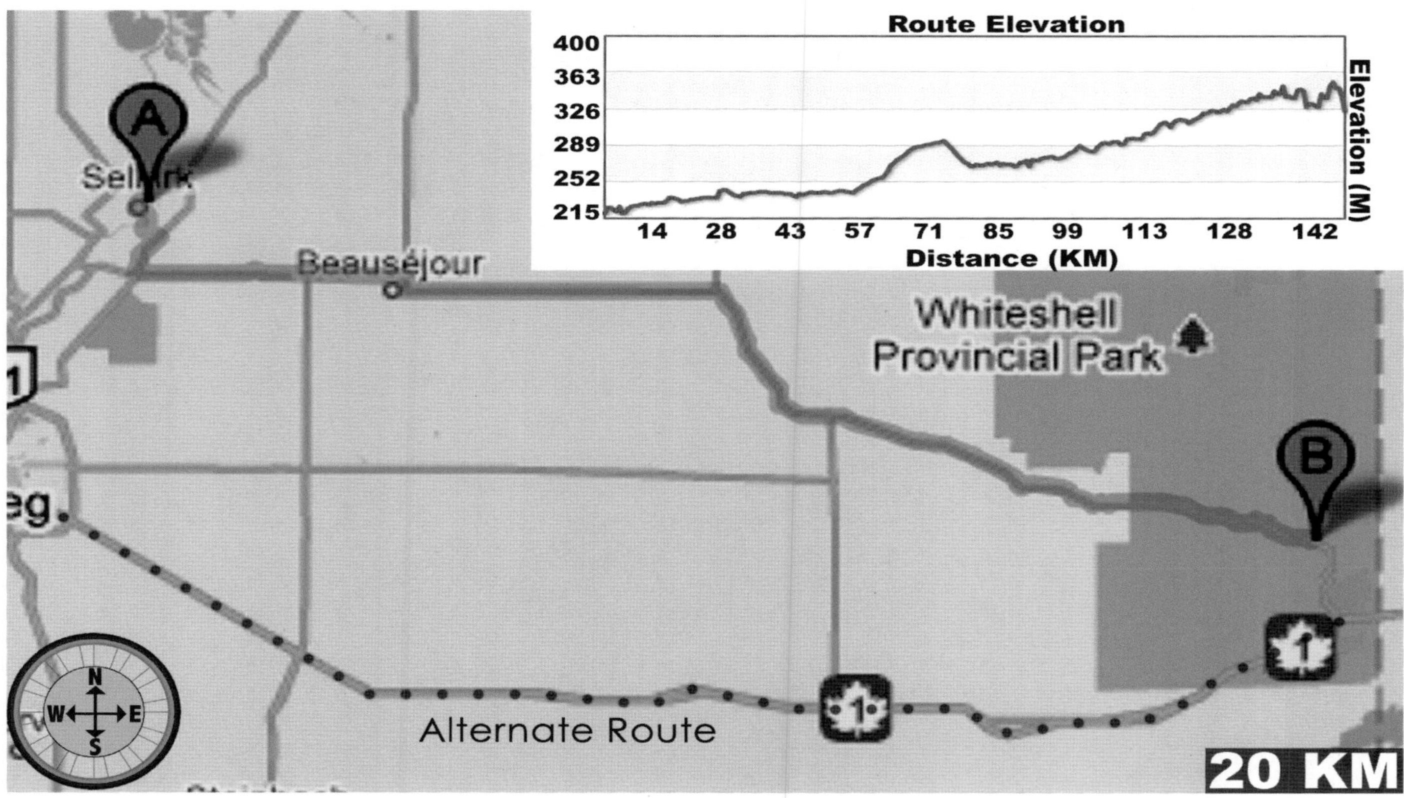

Route Elevation
400
363
326
289
252
215
Elevation (M)
14
28
43
57
71
85
99
113
128
142
Distance (KM)
A
Beauséjour
Whiteshell Provincial Park
B
N
W
E
S
Alternate Route
20 KM

36.4 Exit to Beausejour.
38.1 Intersection of HWY 12 & HWY 44. Turn right onto HWY 12.
39.6 Exit right to Beausejour. Turn left to remain on HWY 44.
54.4 Seddon's Corner. Intersection of HWY 214 & HWY 44.
70.0 Intersection of HWY 44 & HWY 11. Stay right on HWY 44.
84.2 Whitemouth.
89.9 Intersection of HWY 11 & HWY 44. Remain on HWY 44 heading east.
119.3 Rennie.
121.1 Intersection of HWY 44 & HWY 307.
122.9 Enter Whiteshell Provincial Park.
133.0 Bear Lake Picnic Site.
138.2 The Lily Pond.
142.2 Turn left toward Caddy Lake Campground.
142.6 Caddy Lake Campground.

Caddy Lake Campground to Kenora's Anicinabe RV Park & Campground: (68.5 K)

Leave Caddy Lake and cycle past West Hawk Lake. This lake is special because it was formed by a meteor slamming into the limestone. At 110 metres, it gets the nod as the province's deepest lake.

There is an excellent tourist office at the border of Manitoba and Ontario. Stop in and grab a map of Ontario and chat with the knowledgeable staff. www.ontariocamping.net provides a comprehensive list of campgrounds in Ontario.

From here to just before Ottawa you will be cycling through rocks, forest, lakes and more rocks. You can expect the road to be rolling constantly. Kenora to Ottawa is the most trying leg of the entire trip. Dense traffic and bugs will be your two major frustrations. Purchase a mosquito hat to cover your head while setting up your camp for the evening.

Climbing hills is a special skill that requires concentration and intensity. When climbing a hill, it is important that you keep your momentum and speed up for as long as possible. Try to get up on your pedals and pump your bicycle until you are exhausted, then sit down and put your bike in a lower gear.

The first town that you will reach upon entering Ontario

is Keewatin. Keewatin amalgamated with Kenora in 2000.

Kenora was originally named Rat Portage until town officials changed the name to a combination of Keewatin, the nearby town of Norman and Rat Portage. Kenora sits on the shore of Lake of the Woods, which is home to 14 552 islands and world-class walleye fishing. Shores of this lake connect Ontario, Manitoba and the state of Minnesota, USA. If you need bike repairs head downtown to Olympia Cycle.

Your destination for the evening is Anicinabe RV Park & Campground on the shores of Lake of the Woods. This is a city run campground with laundry facilities, internet and a small store.

Kilometre Log

0.0 Leave Caddy Lake Campground heading south towards HWY 44.
0.4 Turn left to head south on HWY 44.
6.1 Cycle past West Hawk Lake.
7.4 Intersection of HWY 44 & HWY 301. Stay left on HWY 44.
8.1 Turn right to remain on HWY 44.
10.9 Intersection of HWY 44 & HWY 1. Turn left onto HWY 1.
13.8 Leave Whiteshell Provincial Park and Manitoba. At the Manitoba-Ontario border HWY 1 turns into HWY 17. A large visitor centre is available here.
20.2 Intersection of HWY 17 & HWY 673.
40.6 Clearwater Bay.
52.0 HWY 17 splits to become HWY 17 & HWY 17A. Stay right on HWY 17.
59.1 Keewatin.
59.7 Cross a bridge over Lake of the Woods.
60.7 Cross a bridge over Lake of the Woods.
62.6 Cross a bridge over Lake of the Woods.
64.1 Enter Kenora on HWY 17 / Lakeview Drive.
64.6 Lakeview Drive / HWY 17 turns right and becomes Main Street S.
64.8 Turn left onto Second Street S.
65.8 Turn right onto 8th Avenue S / HWY 17.
66.6 Turn right onto Milikana Way.
67.7 Road dead-ends into Golf Course Road. Turn left.
68.5 Anicinabe Campground in Anicinabe Park.

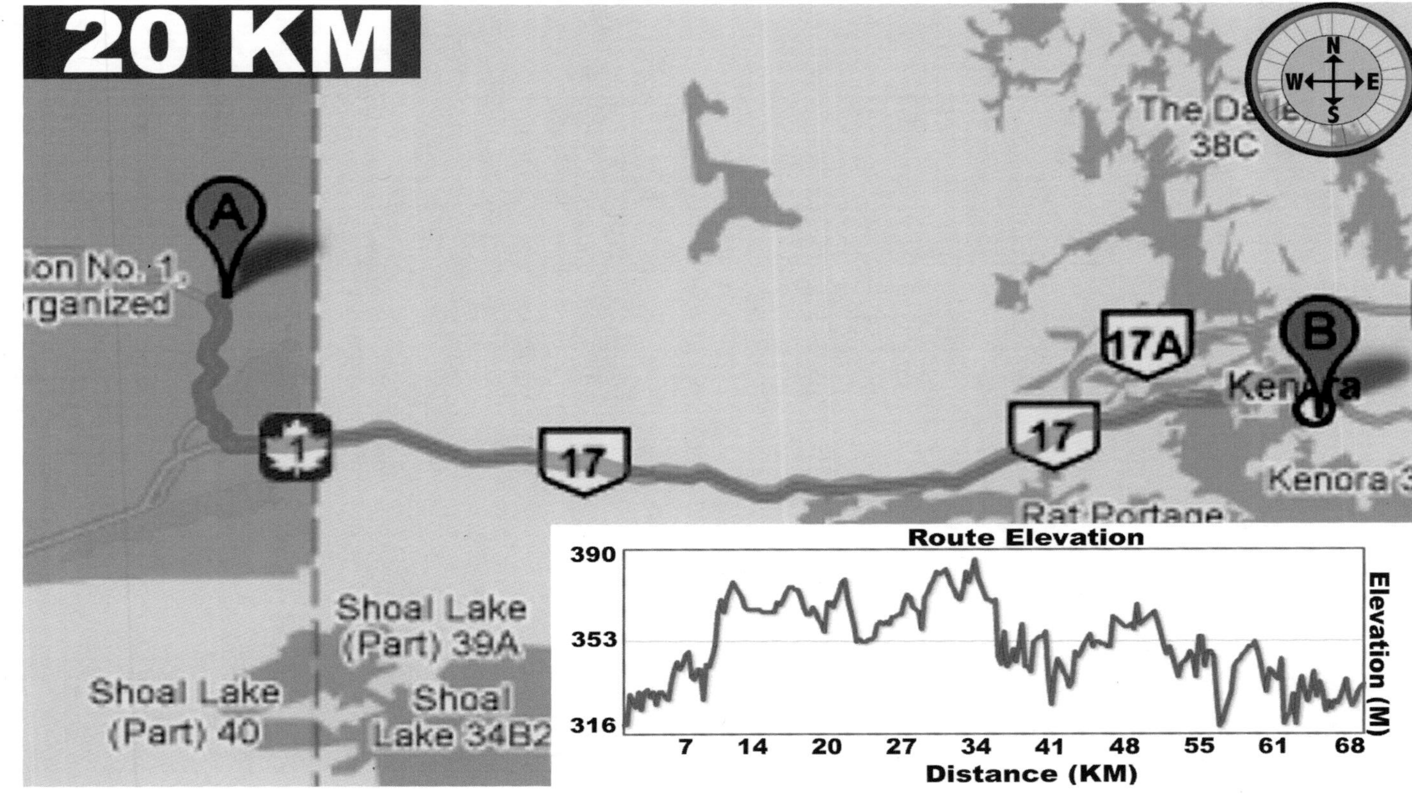
20 KM
A
B
1
17
17
17A
Shoal Lake (Part) 39A
Shoal Lake (Part) 40
Shoal Lake 34B2
Rat Portage
38C
N
E
S
W
Route Elevation
Elevation (M)
390
353
316
7
14
20
27
34
41
48
55
61
68
Distance (KM)

Province: Ontario
Population: 12 687 000
Area: 1 076 395 km^2
Industries: Manufacturing, hydro electricity, mining, agriculture, finance, forestry, tourism.
Highlights: Thunder Bay, Terry Fox Monument, Lake Superior, Kakabeka Falls, Ottawa, Parliament Hill.

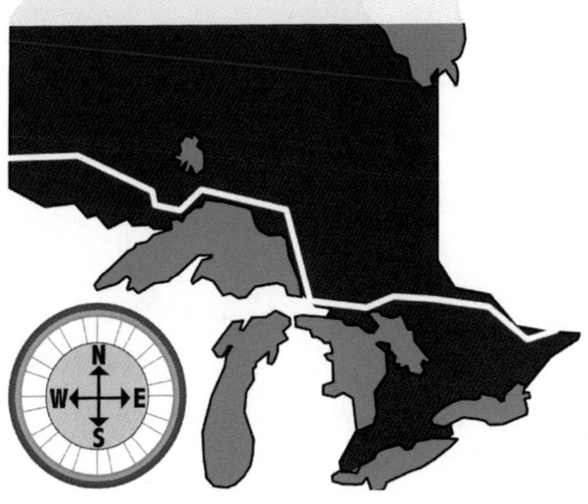

Anicinabe RV Park & Campground to Dryden's Northwestern Tent & RV Park: (137.9 K)

Stop and check out the plaque where the Last Spike was driven at Feist Lake connecting Thunder Bay to the Red River by rail in 1882.

Highway 17 cuts through striking walls of red granite in this area. Examples of the red rock can be found in Vermillion Bay, at the giant Inukshuk on the outskirts of town. Vermillion Bay, a small town next to Eagle Lake is a good place to take a rest and acquire food and beverage.

Expect to see many diverse examples of Inukshuks in the area. An Inukshuk is a rock or pile of rocks used as a landmark by Canada's Inuit. Placing Inukshuks on the land was necessitated by a need for a landmark on an otherwise barren land.

From Vermillion Bay head through Wabigoon towards your destination of Dryden Northwestern Tent & Trailer Park, on the city's west side. Dryden, population 8 195, is located on the shores of Wabigoon Lake. The primary industry in the area is pulp and paper. "Max the Giant Moose" is the town's mascot. Dryden is segmented by the highway and railroad. You can cross the railroad tracks at the west end of town and there is an underpass on the east side. If you want to cross over the tracks in the centre of town you must take an elevator to access the walkway above the railroad.

Nature's Inn RV Park & Marina is another campground located on the shores of Wabigoon Lake. If you need your bike fixed, head downtown and talk to the staff at Barrett Sporting Goods.

Kilometre Log

0.0 Leave Anicinabe Campground on Golf Course Road.
0.9 Turn right on Milikana Way.
1.9 Turn right off of Milkana Way onto HWY 17.
2.5 Leave Kenora.
2.8 Road splits. Stay right on HWY 17.
16.5 Intersection of HWY 17 & HWY 17A. Stay right on HWY 17.
20.6 Intersection of HWY 17 & HWY 71. Remain on HWY 17.
66.6 Winnange Lake Provincial Park.

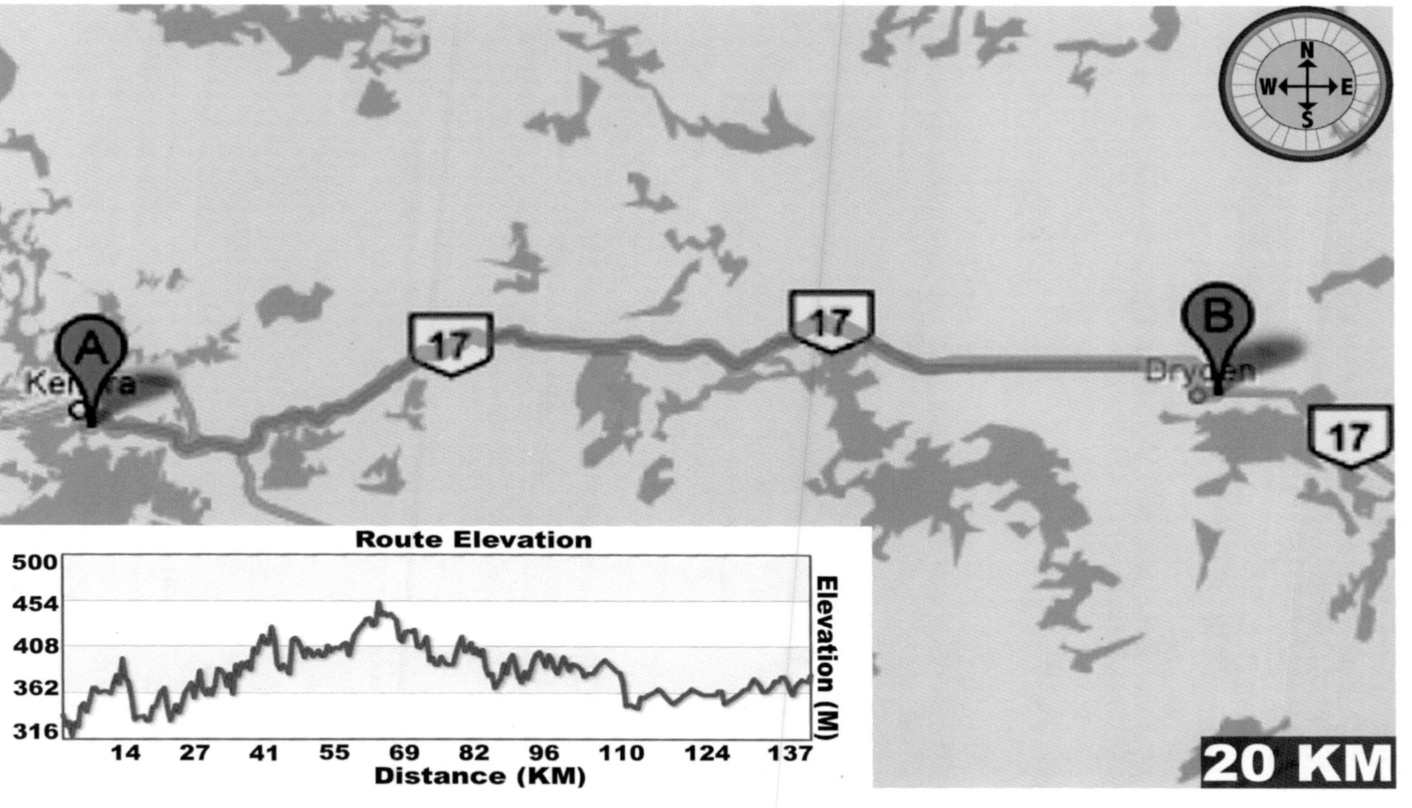
N
W
E
S
A
17
17
B
Dryden
17
Route Elevation
500
454
408
362
316
14
27
41
55
69
82
96
110
124
137
Distance (KM)
Elevation (M)
20 KM

92.8 Vermillion Bay.
94.7 Intersection of HWY 17 & HWY 105.
122.2 Oxdrift.
135.8 Enter Dryden on HWY 17 / Government Street.
137.9 Turn left into Northwestern Tent & Trailer Park.

Northwestern Tent & RV Park to Ignace's Davy Lake Campground: (106.5 K)

Today you will bike on a lonely road towards Ignace. Big rig traffic in this area can be quite intimidating to cyclists. Although these trucks are big and loud, the drivers are professionals and have usually driven this road many times. Expect to encounter more big rigs than commuter traffic in this area.

Aaron Provincial Park, on the shores of Thunder Lake, is a good place for a break or to spend the evening. Sandy beaches, playgrounds and a full service campground make this park a popular place during summer months. To book a site in an Ontario provincial park, call or visit their website.

After leaving Aaron Provincial Park you will bike between Thunder Lake on the north, and Wabigoon Lake on the south, towards the town of Wabigoon. There are a few small stores and restaurants close to the highway there.

Your destination for the evening is Davy Lake Campground in the heart of Ignace, population 1 431. The town is located just south of Sandbar Lake Provincial Park and boasts a grocery store, bank and a hardware store. Davy Lake Campground offers laundry, internet access and a small store.

Kilometre Log

0.0 Leave Dryden on Government Street heading east.
9.2 Thunder Lake is to your left.
14.2 Exit to Aaron Provincial Park
18.8 Wabigoon.
19.4 Pine Grove Camping and Motel.
28.7 Intersection of HWY 17 & HWY 72. Turn right to stay on HWY 17.
72.4 Intersection of HWY 17 & HWY 622.

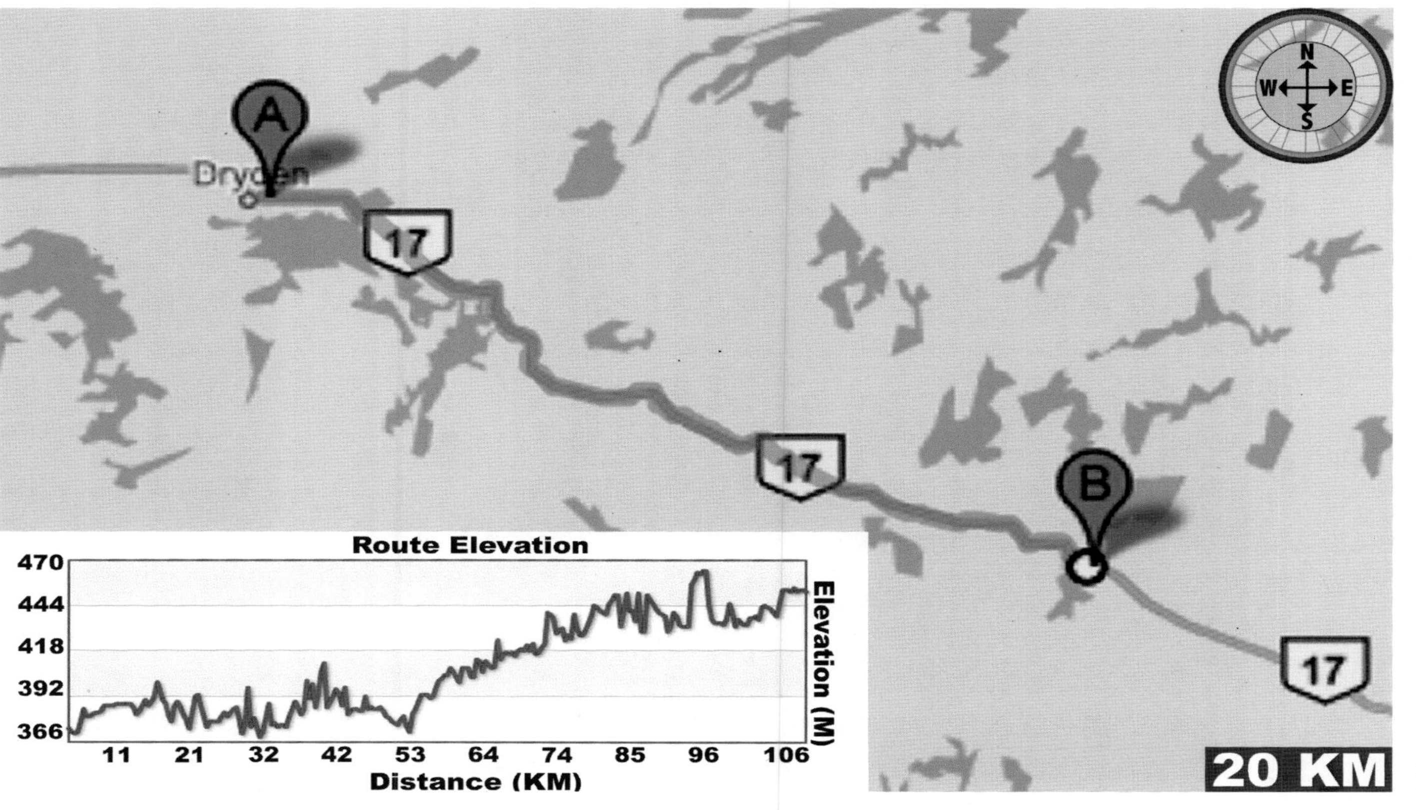
A
Dryden
B
17
17
17
N
W
E
S
Route Elevation
470
444
418
392
366
11
21
32
42
53
64
74
85
96
106
Distance (KM)
Elevation (M)
20 KM

104.8 Enter Ignace.
105.3 Turn right on West Street.
105.9 Turn left on Davy Lake Road.
106.5 Davy Lake Campground.

Davy Lake Campground to Savanne River Resort & Campground: (124.8 K)

Today is another lonely day on the road. You will want to stock up on food and water before leaving Ignace. From Ignace bike towards the small settlement of English River. There is a service station here with a few hotels. From English River there will be no place to get food or water until Upsala, so pack accordingly.

A highlight in your day will be crossing the continental divide. This unassuming ridgeline separates the watersheds of the St. Lawrence River and Hudson Bay.

Upsala is a small town centered on the highway. At the west end of town there is a general store with groceries and further down the road are two gas stations, both with restaurants. The first gas station (Canop) has a campground. Don't pass the second gas station without tasting a butter tart.

Leave Ignace and head towards your destination for the evening, Savanne River Resort & Campground. This small campground on the shore of the Savanne River has a small grocery store and canoe rentals.

Kilometre Log

0.0 Leave Ignace heading east on Davy Lake Road.
0.9 Davy Lake Road intersects with HWY 17. Turn right here.
57.9 English River.
59.7 Continental Divide. Time-zone changes to Eastern Standard here. Eastbound traffic turns their clocks forward one hour.
103.8 Upsala.
124.8 Savanne River Campground.

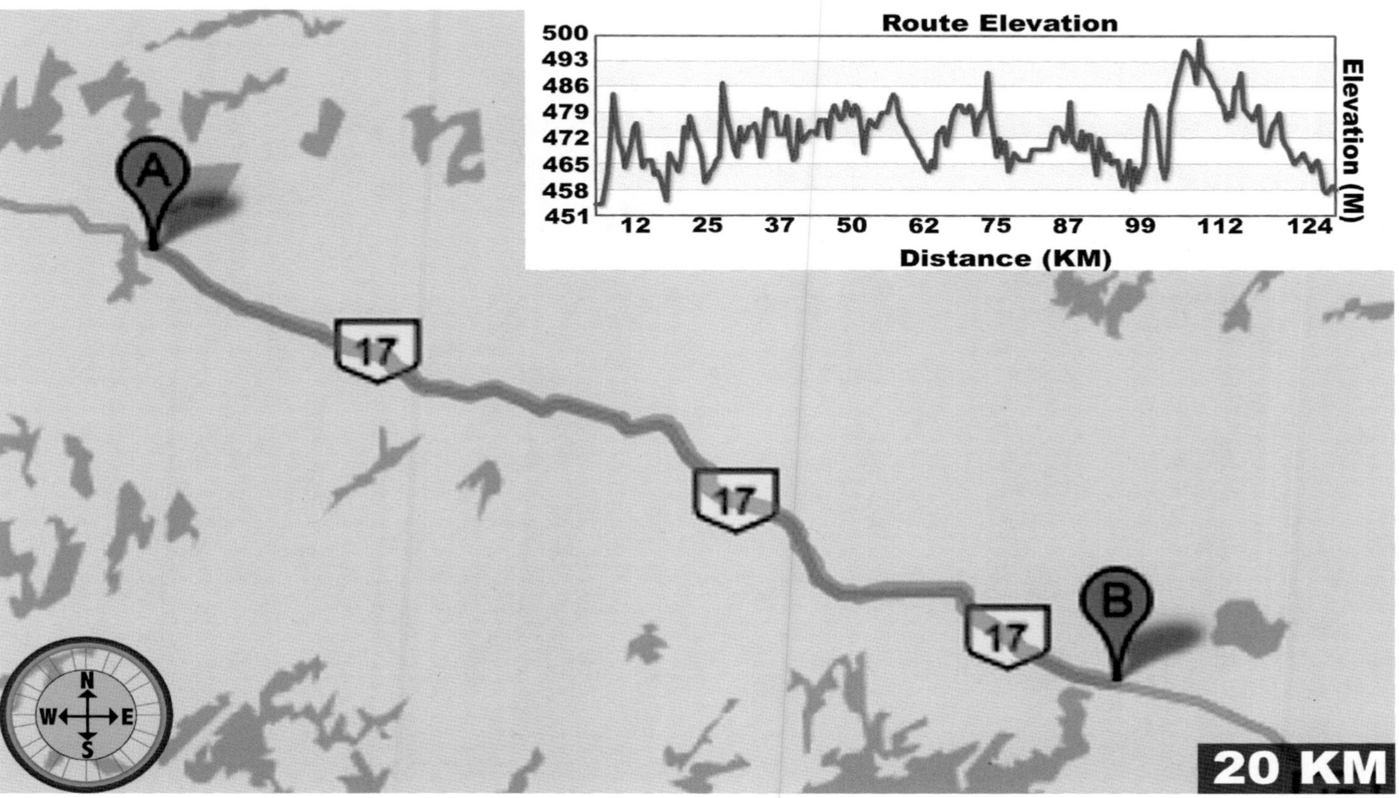
Route Elevation
Elevation (M)
500
493
486
479
472
465
458
451
12
25
37
50
62
75
87
99
112
124
Distance (KM)
A
17
17
17
B
N
W
E
S
20 KM

Aurora Borealis

If you aren't too tired at the end of day, stick your head outside of your tent after dark and look to the sky. You might see a stunning natural light show called aurora borealis. Also known as northern lights, the term aurora borealis was coined by French scientist Pierre Gassendi who combined the words Aurora, after the Roman goddess of dawn, and Boreas after the Roman god of the north wind. Aurora australis is the term used to describe auroras that occur at southern latitudes.

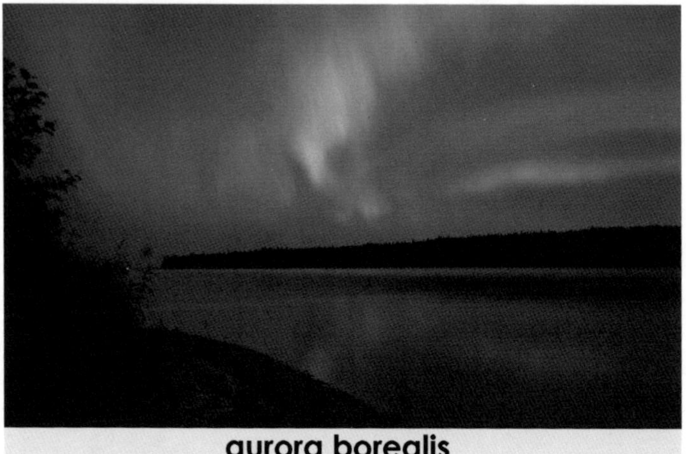

aurora borealis

The earth's atmosphere stretches hundreds of kilometres above the earth and contains mostly nitrogen and oxygen. The earth acts as a large magnet and pulls particles from the sun through the atmosphere. These particles striking the earth's atmosphere make the gasses glow and cause shimmering green lights across the dark sky.

Savanne River Resort to Thunder Bay's Trowbridge Falls Campground: (A 115.7 K B 136.1 K)

You can shave eighteen kilometres off your day by taking route A into the city. This route bypasses most of Thunder Bay and causes you to miss stunning Kakabeka Falls. Route B takes you to your campsite via Kakabeka Falls and downtown Thunder Bay. Both routes have similar topography.

The highlight of the ride from Savanne River to Ottawa is Kakabeka Falls, 30 kilometres west of Thunder Bay, in Kakabkea Provincial Park. The waterfall is part of the Kaministiquia River, which drops 40 metres into a gorge carved into the Precambrian shield.

Ojibwa legend states that when the daughter of an Ojibwa chief heard of an imminent attack from a Sioux tribe she pretended to be lost and purposely stumbled into the incoming tribe. She bargained for her life saying she would lead them to her camp in exchange for them not killing her. She was placed at the front of the canoe and led it over the falls sacrificing herself in order to save her community.

In 1970, the twin cities of Fort William and Port Arthur amalgamated to become Thunder Bay. Fort William was originally a fur trading post owned by the North West Company.

Port Arthur was named Prince Arthur's Landing in 1870. The Canadian government used the port to explore western Canada and build a road linking the great lakes to the Red River Colony and western Canada. Port Arthur makes up the north of the city while Fort William is to the south.

Amethyst, a violet quartz, is common in this area. Many stores in the downtown will sell you various examples of this rock that ancient Greeks believed could protect you from drunkenness.

Make sure to check out Fort William Historic Park, a reconstruction of the Northwest Company's fur trading post as it was in 1815. Explore fourty buildings spread over 225 acres and hear stories about the fur trade and its role in shaping Canada. Fort William Historic Park is located on the southwest side of Thunder Bay.

With your back to downtown look out towards the water and you will not need a great imagination to notice that the land formation in front of you resembles the sleeping body of a giant with its arms folded across his chest. The best views of this famous land mass come from the Terry Fox monument east of the city.

Go on an eating adventure in Thunder Bay. Check out the Persian, a Thunder Bay specialty, which is a cinnamon bun smothered in pink icing. Also, head to the Hoito Restaurant for a Finnish pancake to satisfy your hunger pangs.

Spend the evening at Thunder Bay's Trowbridge Falls Campground at one of the well-treed sites next to the Current River. The campground is located on the northeast side of town. Laundry facilities and a small store are available on site.

If you need bike repairs check out Fresh Air Experience.

Kilometre Log

0.0 Leave Savanne River Campground heading east on HWY 17.
54.7 Highway 17 merges with HWY 11 to become HWY 17/HWY 11.
75.5 Intersection of HWY 17 & HWY 102.

Route A

75.5 HWY 17 / 11 turns right. Remain headed straight on HWY 102 / Dawson Road.
101.8 Intersection of HWY 102 / Dawson Road & HWY 589.
108.5 HWY 102 / Dawson Road dead-ends into HWY 17 / HWY 11 / Thunder Bay Expressway. Turn left here.
114.8 Intersection of Thunder Bay Expressway / HWY 17 / HWY 11 and Hodder Avenue / HWY 17B / HWY 11B (S) and Copenhagen Road (N). Turn left here onto Copenhagen Road.
115.3 Turn left onto Trowbridge Road.
115.7 Enter Trowbridge Falls Campground.

Route B

75.5 Turn right and head south on HWY 17.
89.6 Kakabeka Falls Provincial Park. Remain on HWY 17.
90.4 Exit to Kakabeka Falls.
91.5 Exit Kakabeka Falls Provincial Park.
107.8 Intersection of HWY 17 / HWY 11 / Arthur Street & HWY 130.
114.8 Pass Thunder Bay International Airport on HWY 17 / Arthur Street W.

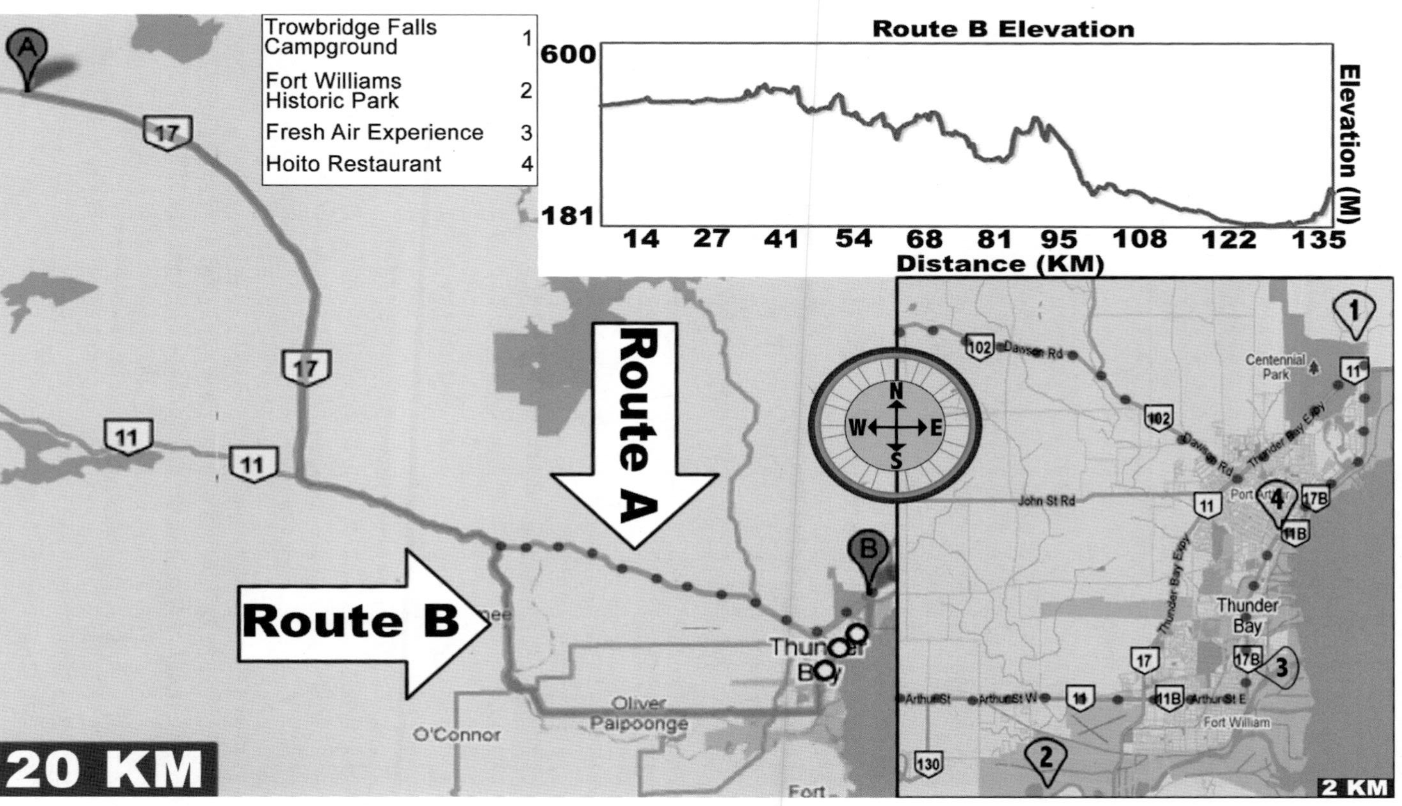
Trowbridge Falls Campground 1
Fort Williams Historic Park 2
Fresh Air Experience 3
Hoito Restaurant 4
Route B Elevation
600
181
Elevation (M)
14 27 41 54 68 81 95 108 122 135
Distance (KM)
Route A
Route B
N
W
E
S
Centennial Park
Thunder Bay
Port Arthur
Fort William
Dawson Rd
John St Rd
Thunder Bay Expy
Arthur St W
Arthur St E
Oliver Paipoonge
O'Connor
17
11
102
17B
11B
130
20 KM
2 KM

117.2 Intersection of HWY 17 / HWY 11 / Arthur Street W & Thunder Bay Expressway / HWY 17 (N) / HWY 61 (S). Arthur Street W turns into Arthur Street W / HWY 17B / HWY 11B.

118.7 Arthur Street W / HWY 17B / HWY 11B turns into Arthur Street E / HWY 17B / HWY 11B.

121.3 Arthur Street E / HWY 17B / HWY 11B intersects with May Street N. Turn left onto May Street N / HWY 17B / HWY 11B.

123.5 May Street North / HWY 17B / HWY 11B turns into Memorial Avenue / HWY 17B / HWY 11B.

126.8 Memorial Ave / HWY 17B / HWY 11B turns into Algoma Street S.

128.0 Algoma Street S turns into Algoma Street N.

130.8 Algoma Street N dead-ends into Lyon Boulevard W (W) / Gibson Avenue (E). Turn right onto Gibson Avenue.

131.2 Turn left onto Cumberland Street N / HWY 17B / HWY 11B.

132.0 Cumberland Street N / HWY 17B / HWY 11B turns into Hodder Avenue / HWY 17B / HWY 11B.

135.2 Hodder Avenue / HWY 17B / HWY 11B crosses Thunder Bay Expressway / HWY 17 / HWY 11 to become Copenhagen Road.

135.7 Turn left off of Copenhagen Road onto Trowbridge Road.

136.1 Trowbridge Falls Campground.

Trowbridge Falls Campground to Birchwood Campground: (86.6 K)

Make sure you stop at the Terry Fox Monument at the east end of the city. This 9-foot high statue of Terry Fox stands on a 45-ton granite base laid on a foundation of local amethyst. Terry fox is a Canadian hero because of his Marathon of Hope in which he attempted to run across Canada with one prosthetic leg. Terry continues to inspire people. The Terry Fox run is held annually on the first Sunday after Labour Day in Canada. The run is also held in countries all over the world, organized by Canadian Embassies. There is a good rest area at the statue site with washrooms and tourist information.

Today you will have the pleasure of biking next to Lake Superior, the third largest fresh water lake in the world. This massive body of water seriously influences weather and climate in the area. You will feel cool breezes off of the lake before you see it. Locals claim that water from Lake Superior is potable. The surface area of Lake Superior is 82 413 km^2 and it has an average depth of 147 metres.

On November 10, 1975, the SS Edmund Fitzgerald sank suddenly on Lake Superior without any distress signals. All 29 crew members perished. Legend states that Lake Superior seldom gives up its dead. Bacteria normally feed on a sunken decaying body creating gas that makes the body buoyant after about a week. The lake's cold water inhibits bacteria growth causing bodies to sink to the bottom and never resurface.

Today you will bike past the entrance to Ouimet Canyon Provincial Park. The park is home to a canyon over 100 metres deep. Snow often stays in the canyon into late spring allowing arctic flowers that are usually found 1 000 kilometres to the north to thrive. Near Ouimet Canyon Provincial Park is Eagle Canyon, which claims to have Canada's longest suspension bridge. Camping is also available. Unfortunately, the road to both Ouimet Canyon Provincial Park and Eagle Canyon is gravel, which is not always suitable for touring bikes. Assess the condition of the road and your desire to see the park before making your decision.

In Dorion there is a small store with an impressive wildlife mural covering the building. Limited groceries are available here.

Your destination for the evening is Birchwood RV & Tent Campground. The campground has wireless internet, laundry and a small store.

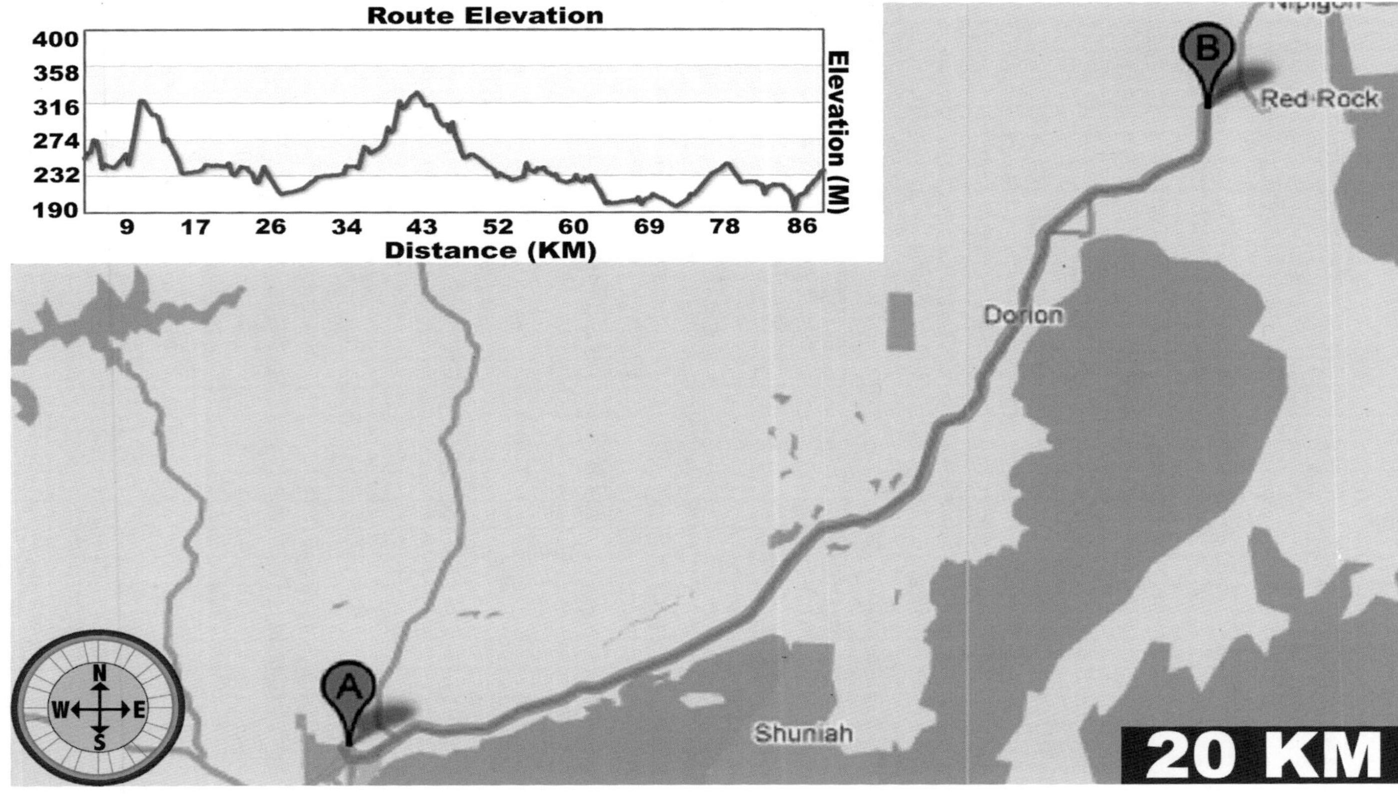
Route Elevation
400
358
316
274
232
190
9
17
26
34
43
52
60
69
78
86
Distance (KM)
Elevation (M)
B
Red Rock
Dorion
A
Shuniah
N
W
E
S
20 KM

Kilometre Log

0.0 Leave Trowbridge Falls Campground on Trowbridge Road.
0.4 Turn right onto Copenhagen Road.
0.9 Turn left onto HWY 17 / HWY 11 / Thunder Bay Expressway.
2.0 Exit left to Terry Fox Memorial and lookout.
5.6 Thunder Bay KOA campground.
37.4 Intersection of HWY 17 / HWY 11 & HWY 587.
40.1 Mirror Lake Campground.
46.1 Pearl. No services.
58.5 Exit to Ouimet Canyon Road.
64.1 Dorion.
67.5 Exit left on Wolf River Road to Wolf River Campground.
83.2 Cross over Black Sturgeon River on HWY 17 / HWY 11.
86.6 Exit left to Birchwood RV & Tent Campground.

Birchwood RV Tent & Campground to Rainbow Falls Provincial Park's Rossport Campground: (89.9 K)

Today you will have a challenging ride to just past the picturesque town of Rossport. During the second half of the day you can expect the rocky ledges that line the highway to turn to a vibrant colour of red. Also, the downhill at kilometre 75 is one of the fastest on the entire trip. Hang on tight and see how fast you can go!!

Many of the small towns in this area are served by Canadian Tire. In the summer these hardware stores carry a limited selection of bike parts.

Ride first into Nipigon, population 1 752. Nipigon is situated along the Nipigon River, which is home to Atlantic Salmon and world class trout fishing. Groceries are available here. Camping is available at Stillwater Park, on the east side of town.

In 2007, the Canadian government created the world's largest water reserve, called Lake Superior National Marine Conservation Area. The reserve covers 10 000 kilometres^2 of the lake's water and shoreline and protects it from industrial development. The reserve's western boundary is located at Thunder Cape at the tip of Sleeping Giant Provincial Park;

the west boundary is at Bottle Point east of Terrace Bay. This park helps provide high quality habitat to peregrine falcons, bears, wolves on the land and cold-water fish such as lake trout, walleye and whitefish.

Rossport, nestled on the shores of one of Lake Superior's most protected harbours, is a popular summer destination for tourists. Check out the marina, which was a significant stop for fur traders on route to Fort William. There is a great spot for a picnic on the east side of town between the highway and the lake. Although there are restaurants in Rossport, groceries are not available; you must carry them in from Nipigon.

Spend your evening just east of Rossport at the Rossport Campground in Rainbow Falls Provincial Park. Ask for a site with a view of Lake Superior. This campground is five kilometres west of Whitesand Lake Campground, also in the park. This park is named after the water that flows over rock ledges while cascading towards Lake Superior.

Kilometre Log

0.0 Leave Birchwood RV & Tent Campground heading northeast on HWY 17 / HWY 11.

3.2 Intersection of HWY 17 / HWY 11 & HWY 628.

13.1 Enter Nipigon on HWY 17 / HWY 11. Leave Nipigon on HWY 17.

15.0 Cross over the Nipigon River.

77.2 Pays Plat First Nation.

83.6 Exit to Rossport.

84.8 Exit to Rossport.

89.5 Turn right into Rossport Campground in Rainbow Falls Provincial Park.

89.9 Rossport Campground.

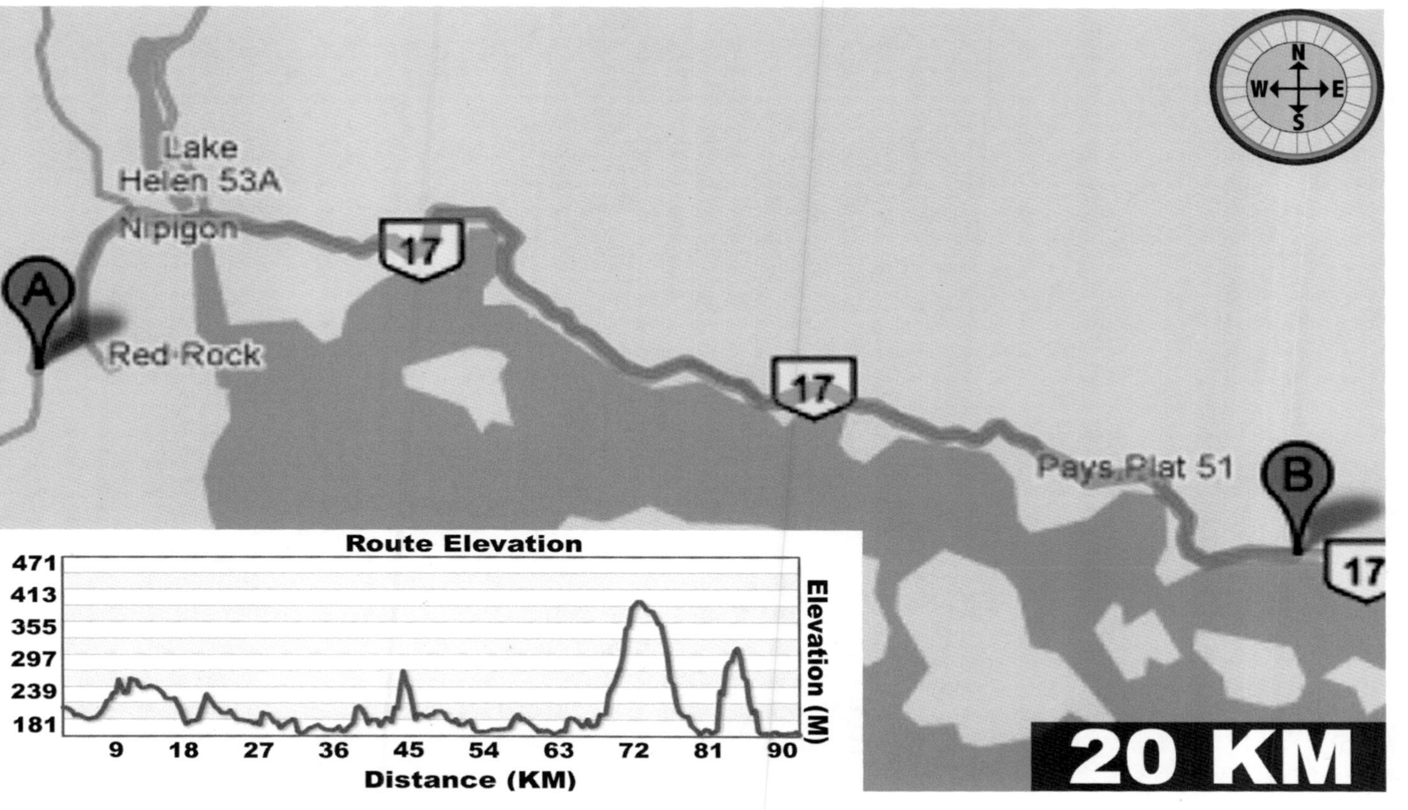

Lake Helen 53A
Nipigon
A
Red Rock
17
17
Pays Plat 51
B
17
N
W
E
S
Route Elevation
471
413
355
297
239
181
Elevation (M)
9
18
27
36
45
54
63
72
81
90
Distance (KM)
20 KM

Rossport Campground to Marathon's Penn Lake Park and Campground: (112.8 K)

Just past Rossport Campground, but still in Rainbow Falls Provincial Park is the Whitesand Lake Campground. This campground is near the cascading Rainbow Falls and has an extensive trail system.

Expect to see signs in this area for the Casque Isles Trail. This 52 kilometre long trail runs from Rossport along the shoreline of Lake Superior hopping from bay to bay until Aguasabon Falls & Gorge near Terrace Bay.

The viewing platforms for Aguasabon Falls are west of Terrace Bay and only a short bike down a paved road off of HWY 17. Watching the Aguasabon River plunge over 30 metres down the Aguasabon Gorge on route to Lake Superior is a must for anyone passing through the area.

Schreiber, population 901, is set on the shore of Lake Superior. Head downtown to check out the Downtown Railway and Heritage Festival Site to learn about the influence of the railway in this area. There is a tourist information booth adjacent to the festival site. Check out the Schrieber Public Library for internet access.

The next town you will pass through is Terrace Bay, population 1 625. Terrace Bay has a grocery store and is a good place to pick up supplies. Check out Terrace Bay Beach, a large sandy beach next to the Aguasabon Golf Course. On a clear day you can see the Slate Islands. Watch for the tourist information centre on the highway, which offers visitors a chance to check their e-mail at their free internet portal. Ask here about the Slate Islands and its 68 metre tall lighthouse.

Just west of Marathon is Neys Provincial Park which is host to a campground, one of Lake Superior's finest beaches and a rare herd of woodland caribou. The park is bound on the west by the shallow and sandy Little Pic River, which played an important role in the logging industry. Loggers would fall trees here and float them down Little Pic into Lake Superior where they would then be hauled to the Slate Islands for processing.

Your destination for the evening is Marathon's Penn Lake Park and Campground. Exit into Marathon from HWY 17 and plunge down a long hill. Marathon, population 3 863, has history as a resource town, first pulp and paper and then gold. There is a grocery store in town.

Spend the evening on the shores of Penn Lake at Penn Lake Campground. This lake is a warm alternative to frigid Lake Superior and a good place to have a swim. Laundry facilities are available and there is a small sheltered picnic site.

Kilometre Log

0.0	Leave Rossport Campground heading north towards HWY 17.
0.4	Turn right onto HWY 17.
3.7	Exit to Whitesand Lake Campground on your left.
15.0	Schreiber.
29.4	Terrace Bay.
79.3	Enter Neys Provincial Park.
82.5	Exit right into Neys Provincial Park.
82.9	Exit Neys Provincial Park.
105.8	Intersection of HWY 17 & Peninsula Road / HWY 626. Turn right.
109.3	Enter Marathon.
109.9	Turn left on Penn Lake Road. Remain on Penn Lake Road.
112.5	Turn left into Penn Lake Park.
112.8	Welcome to Penn Lake Campground.

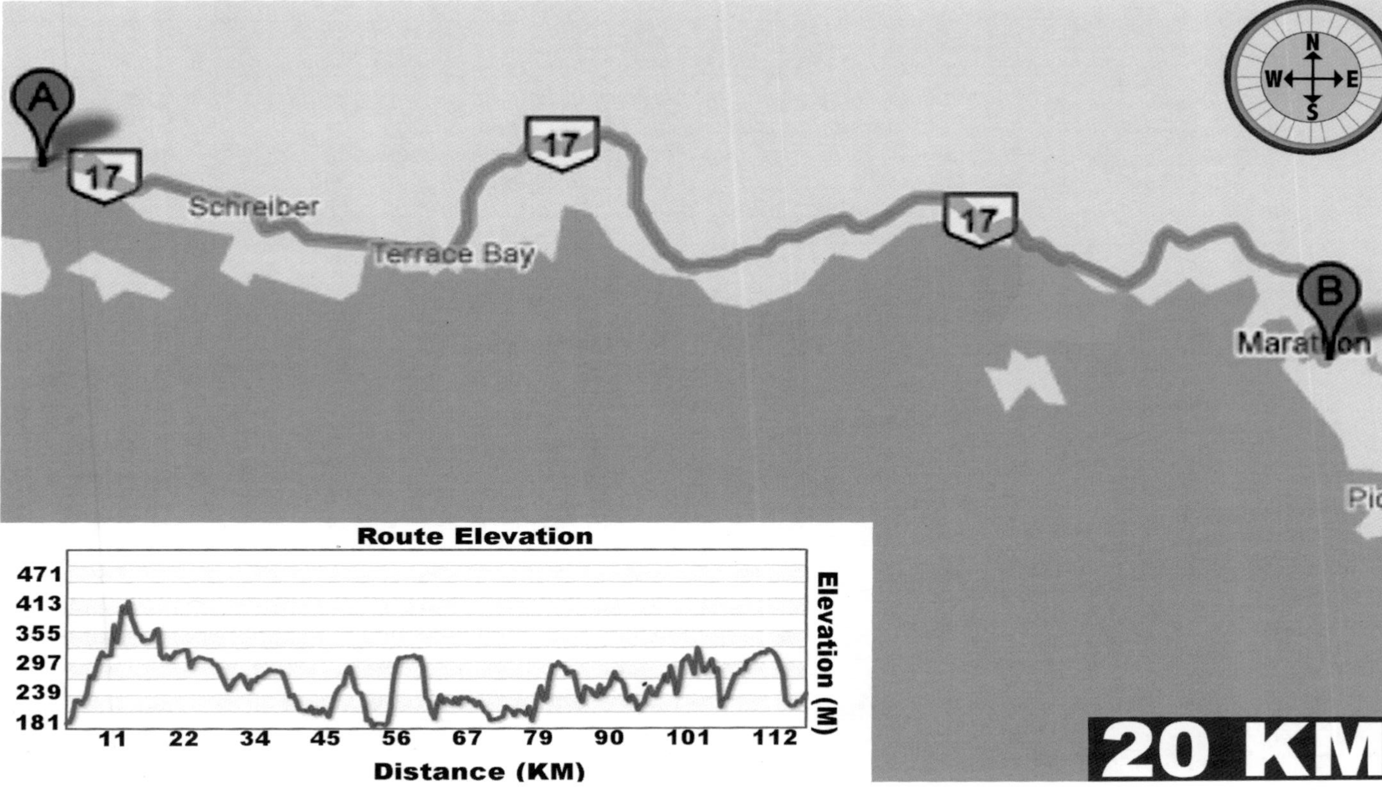

A
17
Schreiber
Terrace Bay
17
17
B
Marathon
Pic
N
W
E
S
Route Elevation
471
413
355
297
239
181
11
22
34
45
56
67
79
90
101
112
Distance (KM)
Elevation (M)
20 KM

Penn Lake Park and Campground to Obatanga Provincial Park: (132.7 K)

Watch for the red-bellied woodpecker in this area. They are identified by light gray face and underparts with black and white barred patterns on their back. Males have a red cap and females have a red patch on the back of their neck and one above the bill.

White Lake Provincial Park is a small provincial park that is a popular place for tourists because its lake is often warmer than Lake Superior. The park has a small campground, sandy beaches and is famous for orchids.

White River, population 841, is famous for being the birthplace of Winnie the Pooh. In 1914, troops from Winnipeg were being transported to eastern Canada for World War I. When the train stopped at White River, a lieutenant bought the small cub and named her Winnipeg for his hometown. The bear traveled with the brigade to Britain until they headed to battle in France. Winnie was sent to the London Zoo, where he became the inspiration of author A.A. Milne who penned the now world-famous Winnie the Pooh stories. White River has a giant statue of Winnie the Pooh on the side of the road. Check out the White River Heritage Museum and the Winnie the Pooh display. Stop in at North Superior Skate & Cycle for bike service.

Your destination for the evening is Obatanga Provincial Park. Listen for the distinctive call of the loon from any of 32 sparkling lakes located within the boundary of the park.

A major fire swept through this area in 1910 clearing old growth and allowing the forest to regenerate. Jack pine, whose seed-bearing cones only open in the heat of a blaze, are the first trees to return to a forest and are prominent in the park. Look for wild blueberries if you are visiting the park in August.

The campground office for Obatanga Provincial Park's campground is just off of the highway. Try to secure a site on the shore of Lake Burnfield where you can watch the sunset. Acquire groceries for the evening in White River.

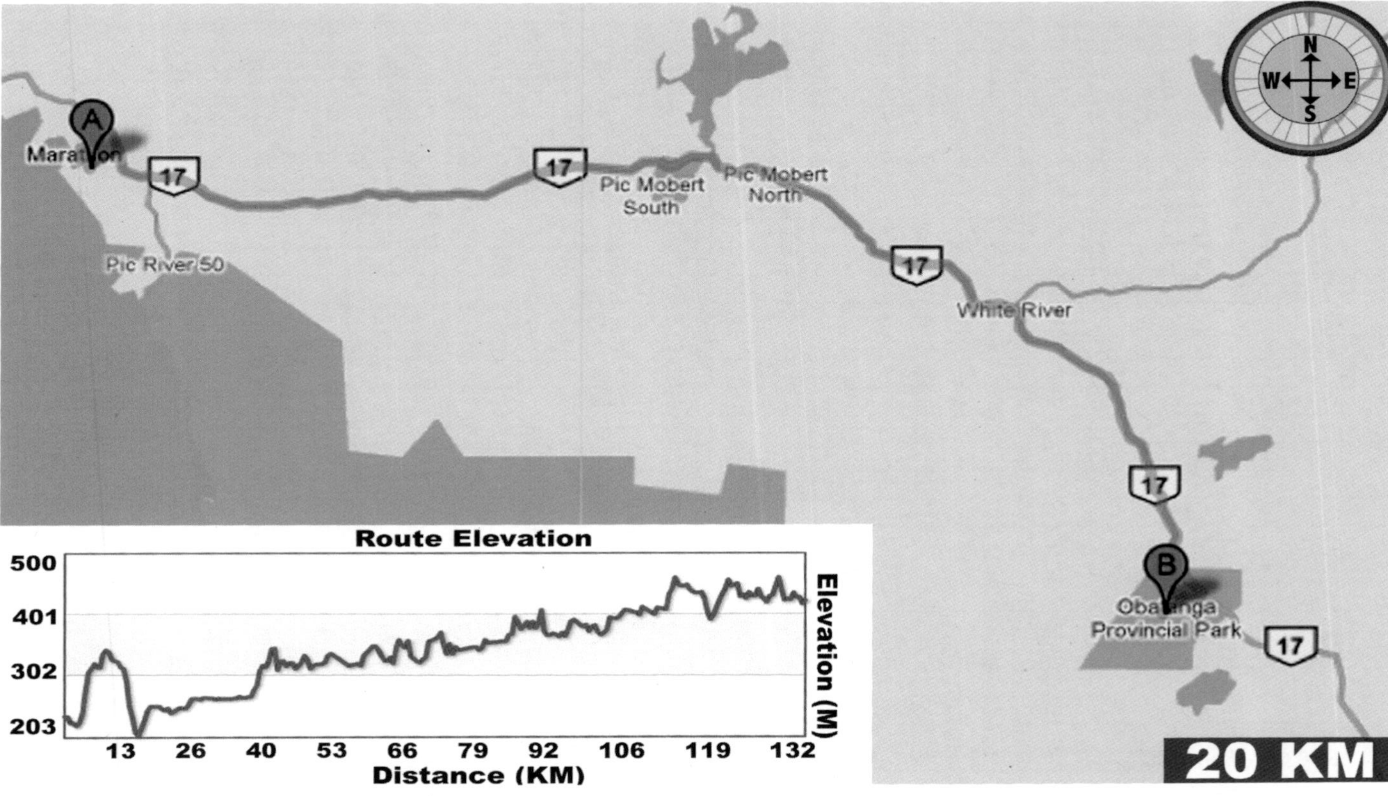
A
B
N
W
E
S
17
Pic River 50
Pic Mobert South
Pic Mobert North
White River
Provincial Park
20 KM
Route Elevation
500
401
302
203
13
26
40
53
66
79
92
106
119
132
Distance (KM)
Elevation (M)

Kilometre Log

0.0 Leave Penn Lake Park & Campground heading north towards Penn Lake Road.
0.3 Turn right onto Penn Lake Road.
1.9 Penn Lake Road dead-ends into Peninsula Road / HWY 626. Turn right here and climb to HWY 17.
5.8 Intersection of Peninsula road / HWY 626 & HWY 17. Turn right here.
12.5 Intersection of HWY 17 & HWY 627.
58.3 Enter White Lake Provincial Park.
62.2 Turn right to White Lake Provincial Park Campground.
62.8 Exit to White Lake Provincial Park.
63.6 Cross over White Lake Narrows on a bridge.
73.8 Cross over West White River.
95.2 White River.
96.3 Intersection of HWY 17 & HWY 631.
128.8 Enter Obatanga Provincial Park.
131.8 Turn right towards Obatanga Campground.
132.7 Obatanga Provincial Park Campground.

Obatanga Provincial Park Campground to Lake Superior Provincial Park's Agawa Bay Campground: (143.2 K)

Leave Obatanga Provincial Park and head towards Wawa. Wawa is off of the highway but you will probably need to enter the city to purchase supplies for the evening. The town's giant goose is visible from the highway and is located next to the tourist office, which is a good resource for information about viewing area waterfalls.

Mission Road intersects with HWY 17. Follow Mission Road into Wawa to find a grocery store.

Wawa, population 3 294, takes its name from "wewe," the Ojibwa word for wild goose. Wawa sits on the south shore of Wawa Lake. If you need to spend an evening here, check out Wawa RV Resort & Campground.

Lake Superior Provincial Park protects over 1600 kilometres^2 and is a popular destination for hiking, canoeing and kayaking. There are three campgrounds in the park; in the north is Rabbit Blanket Lake and in the south are both Agawa Bay and Crescent Lake.

There is a park office just south of Rabbit Blanket Lake

Campground and a tourist information site just north of Agawa Bay Campground. Both of these stations are accessible from HWY 17 and have friendly staff that will answer any questions you have. Crescent Lake Campground, near Agawa Bay Campground, is a tenting only campsite that lacks showers and electricity. The other campgrounds provide those amenities.

This provincial park is as inviting as any park on the entire trip. Rugged, rolling terrain makes the cycling challenging. You will be rewarded with views of the water that seem to go on forever giving you the feeling of being by an ocean.

Recommended stops in the park include Old Woman Bay and Catherine Cove. Stop at Old Woman Bay and watch waves roll in against three hundred foot cliffs. Catherine Cove is located in the centre of the park. Take a break and enjoy the stunning white sand beach. Here, water depth is low around the shore making the water a little warmer than typical Lake Superior temperatures.

Your destination for the evening is Agawa Bay Campground. The campground has laundry facilities and an outdoor theatre next to the visitor centre.

Kilometre Log

0.0 Leave Obatanga Provincial Park heading east towards HWY 17.
2.0 Turn right onto HWY 17.
5.0 Exit Obatanga Provincial Park.
17.1 Intersection of HWY 17 & HWY 519.
54.4 Cross over Magpie River.
54.8 Exit here to Wawa.
55.9 Intersection of HWY 17 & HWY 101.
70.4 Enter Lake Superior Provincial Park.
80.3 Old Woman Bay.
80.4 Old Woman River.
86.8 Rabbit Blanket Lake Campground.
126.1 Catherine Cove.
128.1 Cross over the Sand River.
140.0 Cross over the Agawa River.
143.2 Agawa Bay Campground.

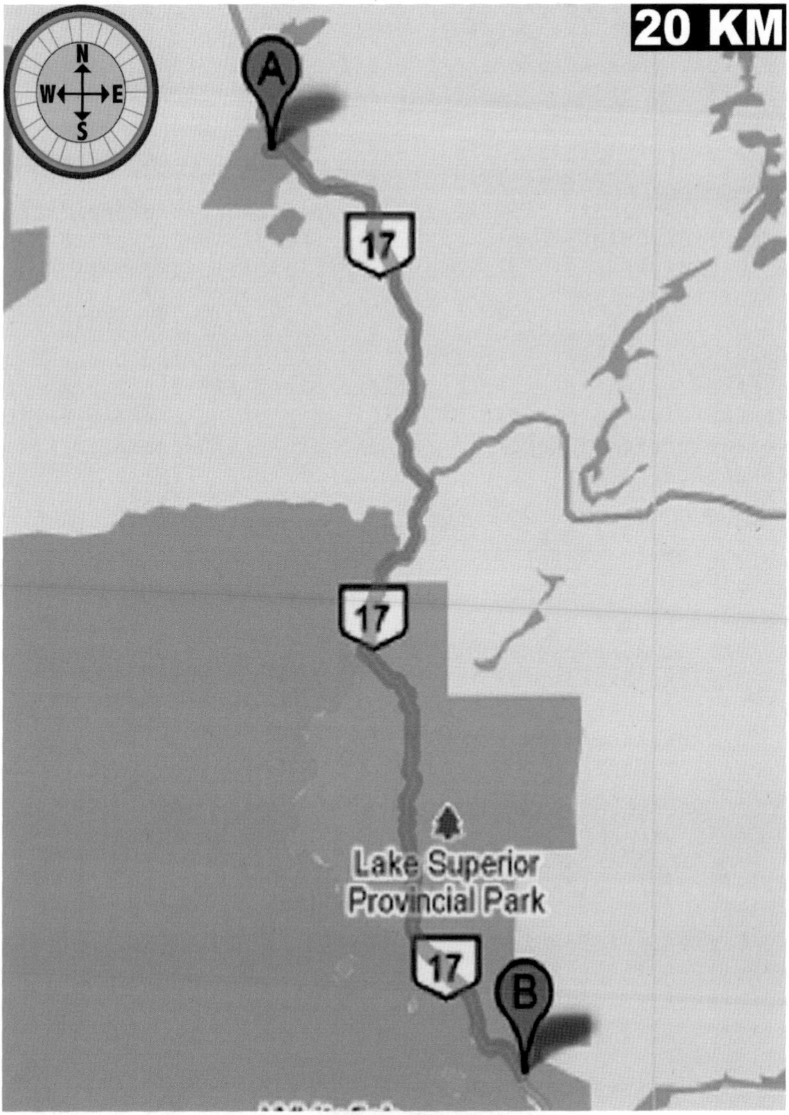

20 KM
N
W
E
S
A
17
17
Lake Superior
Provincial Park
17
B

Route Elevation
500
401
302
203
13
26
40
53
66
79
92
106
119
132
Distance (KM)
Elevation (M)

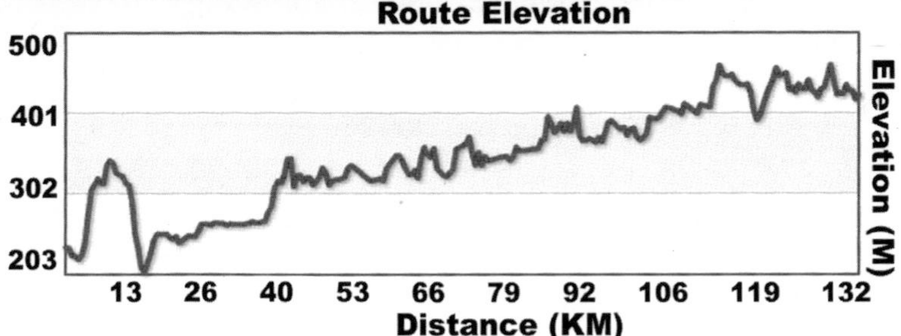

Agawa Bay Campground to Sault Ste. Marie's Velorution: (134.6 K)

Expect to see the word Algoma used frequently by business and government in this area. Although the origin of the word is disputed, many people believe that the word has been adopted by meshing "Algo," from Algonquin and "goma," from the aboriginal word meaning "sea." This translates into "Sea of the Algonquins."

As soon as you exit Lake Superior Provincial Park you will bike through the small town of Northgate. There is a small store here. Next you will enjoy a fast downhill into the settlement called Montréal River, which is centered on where the Montréal River empties into Lake Superior. There is a small campground just before you cross the bridge over Montréal River called Twilight Campground. This river generates hydro-electricity for residents in the area. Expect to see only a few gas stations before you arrive in Sault Ste. Marie.

Plan to stop at Pancake Bay Provincial Park and enjoy the wide, sheltered, sandy bay. From a viewing platform you can see the spot where the Edmund Fitzgerald sank during a storm in November, 1975. Camping is available here. Pancake Bay gets its name because Voyageurs used to stop here while en-route from Fort William to Montréal. They would have just enough flour to make pancakes before arriving in Sault Ste. Marie and restocking their supplies.
Just past Pancake Bay is Batchawana Bay Provincial Park. This park is a popular place for families to picnic. Camping is not available.

Your destination for the evening is Velorution Bike Shop in Sault Ste. Marie. Although I have visited a lot of great bike shops in Canada, Velorution is undoubtedly the best in the nation. Next to the store is a small campground, where bike tourists can camp for free. Attached to their shop is a shower and washroom that you can access via a coded lock on the door. You can get any work you need done on your bike in the morning while you are packing up your tent before heading down the road. Call ahead to let staff know you are coming and to get the password for the shower area in case you arrive after store hours. Velorution is located on the north side of Sault Ste. Marie very close to HWY 17, so you will not have to head into downtown.

Sault Ste. Marie, population 74 948, is located on the St. Mary's River, which separates Ontario from Michigan. You can cross the river into Michigan on the International Bridge into the town of Sault Ste. Marie, Michigan. Sault means "waterfall" or "rapids" in pre-17th century French translating the name of this city to "St. Mary's Falls." This area was traditionally used by the Ojibwa as a place to catch whitefish.

The major industries in Sault Ste. Marie are steel-making and forestry.

Visit the Sault Ste. Marie Canal National Historic Site where in 1895, this canal formed the last link between the St. Lawrence River and Lake Superior. At the time it was the world's longest lock and the first to operate with electric power.

Groceries and services are available near Velorution.

Kilometre Log

0.0 Leave Agawa Bay campground heading south on HWY 17.
8.3 Exit to Crescent Lake Campground.
9.3 Exit Lake Superior Provincial Park.
17.4 Montréal River.
18.4 Twilight Campground.
18.6 Cross over Montréal River.
60.4 Pancake Bay Provincial Park.
70.7 Batchawana Bay Provincial Park.
73.7 Cross over Carp River.
81.8 Chippewa Falls. View a cascading waterfall here.
111.4 Blueberry Motel & RV Park.
120.8 Intersection of HWY 17 & HWY 556.
128.2 Enter Sault Ste. Marie on HWY 17 / Great Northern Road.
134.1 Intersection of HWY 17 / Great Northern Road & Second Line E / HWY 550 (W) And HWY 17 / Second Line E (E). Turn left here.
134.5 Intersection of Second Line E / HWY 17 & Old Garden River Road. Turn left here.
134.6 Enter Velorution.

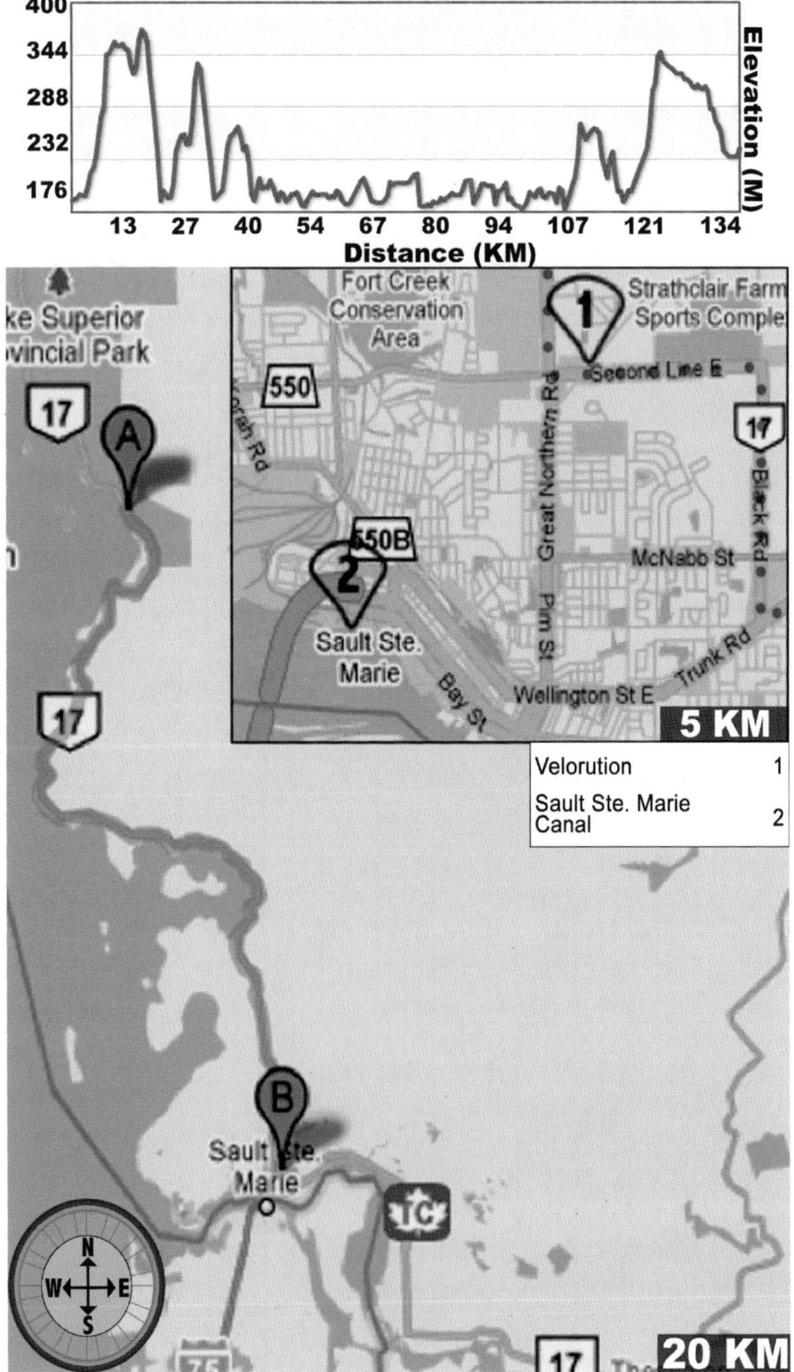

Route Elevation
400
344
288
232
176
Elevation (M)
13 27 40 54 67 80 94 107 121 134
Distance (KM)
ke Superior
vincial Park
17
A
17
B
Sault Ste.
Marie
TC
17
20 KM
Fort Creek
Conservation
Area
Strathclair Farm
Sports Comple
550
Second Line E
17
Black Rd
550B
McNabb St
Great Northern Rd
Pim St
Sault Ste.
Marie
Bay St
Wellington St E
Trunk Rd
5 KM
Velorution 1
Sault Ste. Marie Canal 2
N
W
E
S

Velorution to Blind River's MacIver's Motel and Campground: (133.2 K)

Expect a distinct change in both weather and geography as you cycle away from Sault Ste. Marie. The land will be less rocky than around Lake Superior. Pack sufficient food and water as this is another lonely stretch of highway.

Pass through Desbarats and head towards Bruce Mines, population 627. The town is located on the shores of the north channel of Lake Huron. Bruce Mines was named after James Bruce, Governor General of Canada in 1846, when a copper mine was founded in the area.

Today, Bruce Mines is a popular tourist destination with a nice marina. Groceries and restaurants are available here. Check out the restored Simpson Mine Shaft, which demonstrates how copper was mined in the 1800s. If you want to spend the evening here check out Bruce Mines Campground & RV Park, located within city limits.

Thessalon, population 1 312, is a popular retirement town located on the shores of the Thessalon River. Thessalon has a long history in the lumber industry.

Iron Bridge is a small town with a few small stores that is famous for the sturgeon fishing in the nearby Mississagi River. Iron Bridge received its name in 1886, when a steel bridge was constructed to replace the existing wooden one over the Mississagi. In 1949, a concrete bridge replaced its namesake bridge.

From Iron Bridge follow the Mississagi River towards Blind River. Your destination is MacIver's Motel & Campground, just west of Blind River on the left side of the road. Groceries are available just down the road in Blind River.

Blind River, population 3 780, is named after the nearby Blind River, which got its name when Fur Traders could not see the mouth of the river while paddling through the North Channel. Blind River has a long history in first the forest and later the uranium industry. Check out the Timber Village Museum next to the Travel Centre on the east side of town.

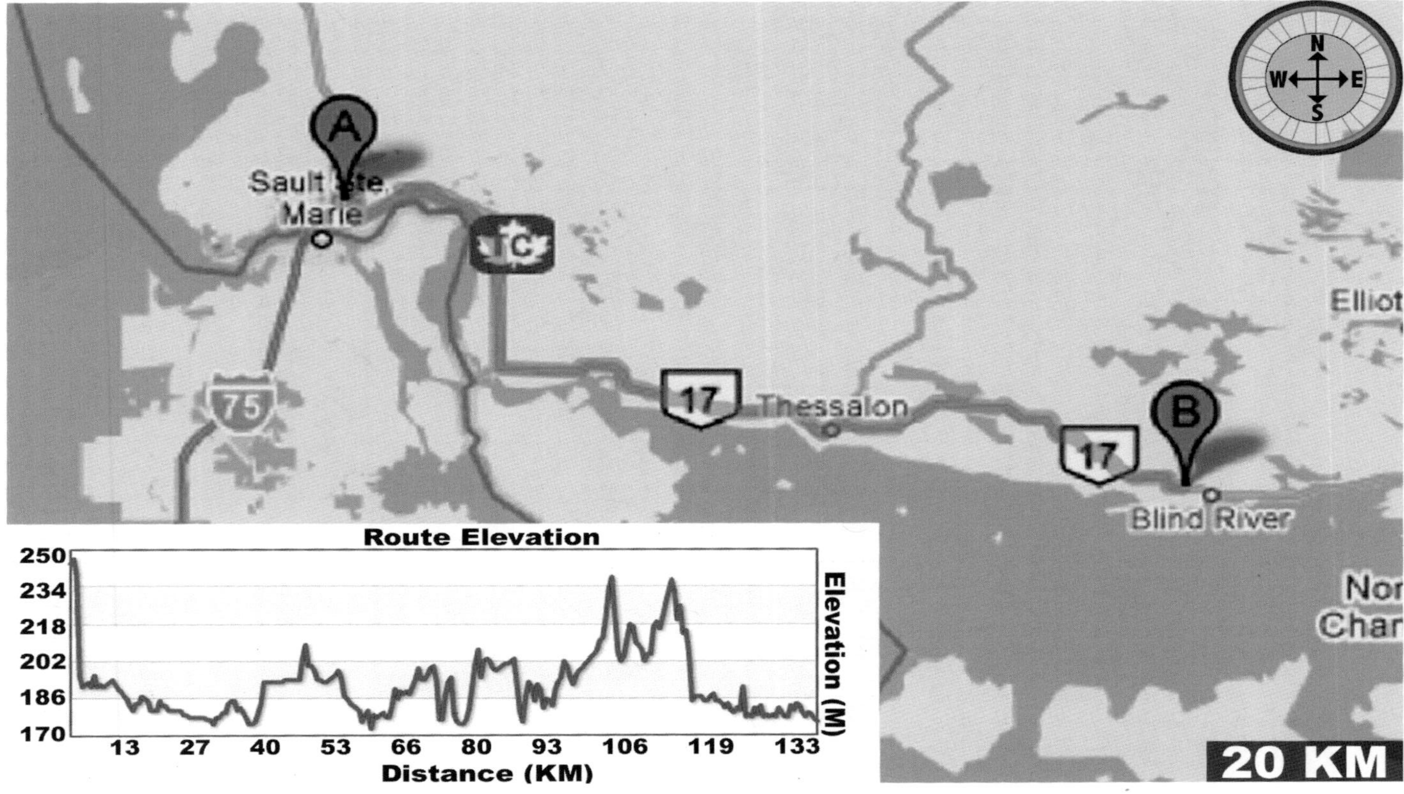

A
Sault Ste. Marie
TC
75
17
Thessalon
17
B
Blind River
Elliot
Nor
Char
N
W
E
S
Route Elevation
250
234
218
202
186
170
13 27 40 53 66 80 93 106 119 133
Distance (KM)
Elevation (M)
20 KM

Kilometre Log

0.0 Leave Velorution heading south on Old Garden River Road towards HWY 17 / Second Line E.
0.1 Turn left onto HWY 17 / Second Line E heading east.
2.0 HWY 17 / Second Line E turns right and becomes HWY 17 / Black Road. Turn right here.
4.6 Intersection of HWY 17 / Black Road and HWY 17 / Trunk Road. Turn left.
9.7 HWY 17 takes a 90° left turn here. Continue cycling straight on HWY 17B.
10.8 Cross over a small creek.
15.8 Cross over a small creek.
24.3 Echo Bay.
30.6 HWY 17B merges with HWY 17.
46.7 Intersection of HWY 17 & HWY 548.
53.0 Desbarats.
64.8 Bruce Mines.
85.0 Thessalon.
109.1 Clear Lake Camp.
112.2 Iron Bridge. Cross over Mississagi River.
133.2 Turn left into MacIver's Motel & Campground.

MacIver's Motel and Campground to Sudbury's Carol's Campsite & RV Park: (173.9)

Today's ride is an extremely long one. By this time I am assuming that you are in fabulous shape and getting excited about reaching Ottawa and Québec. If biking 174 kilometres does not appeal to you, spend the evening in Espanola. There is a campground and affordable hotels available.

Leave your campground and head through Blind River. Continue biking towards Spragge and then Serpent River.

Espanola, population 5 314, is a good spot for a rest on your way to Sudbury. The name Espanola is attributed to a story about an Ojibwa tribe raiding a village far to the south and returning with a white woman who spoke Spanish. She married a chief and taught her children to speak her language. When French Voyageurs came to the area they heard some of the people speaking Spanish and remarked, "Espagnole." It was later anglicized to become Espanola. The name was also given to the river in the area. Espanola is largely a forestry town. Camping is available in Espanola at Lake Aspey Resort, just south of town.

Sudbury, population 157 857, is the largest city in northern Ontario. During construction of the Canadian Pacific Railway in 1883, blasting and excavation revealed large deposits of nickel in this area. These nickel deposits have largely influenced how Sudbury has developed as a city. As a resource town, the city has ridden cyclical demand for its products and has been through many boom and bust cycles.

The mineral extraction that has occurred in this area has not happened without ill effects to the area's ecosystems. Air pollution and urban sprawl wreaked havoc on nearby lakes, vegetation and wildlife. In the 1970s the city and industry began to clean their act up as best they could. Part of this effort includes the Inco Superstack, the 380 metre chimney that rises above the Inco Copper Cliff Smelter. The chimney is the second tallest freestanding structure in Canada.

Don't be surprised to hear French being spoken in Sudbury. Approximately 30 percent of the population is francophone. Laurentian University is bilingual and College Boreal is exclusively francophone. With 330 lakes within its boundaries, Sudbury boasts more lakes than any other municipality in Canada.

If you have time, make sure to visit Science North, an interactive science museum on the shore of Lake Ramsey. Also, check out The Giant Nickel, next to Dynamic Earth, a science exhibition and multimedia show that exhibits the unique geology and rich mining heritage of the area.

The most efficient way to enter Sudbury is on HWY 55. Exit onto this highway on the west side of Sudbury at Whitefish. Return to HWY 17 and cycle on the south shore of Kelly Lake. On the way to the campground you will have an opportunity to purchase groceries on Regent Street. Your destination for the evening is Carol's Campsite & RV Park.

Kilometre Log

0.0	Leave MacIver's Motel & Campground heading east on HWY 17.
4.6	Enter Blind River on HWY 17 / Causley Street.
5.9	Cross over Blind River.
30.2	Spragge.
34.2	Spragge KOA Campground.
36.4	Intersection of HWY 17 & HWY 108 and Serpent River.
41.3	Cross over Serpent River.
54.8	Spanish. Services available.
76.3	Spanish River. Cross over the Spanish River.
101.2	Intersection of HWY 17 & HWY 6. Turn right here to visit Espanola.
116.9	Nairn Centre.
136.3	HWY 17 changes to double lane at the intersection of HWY 55 & HWY 17. Turn right here onto HWY 55.
139.2	Whitefish.
140.1	Graham Centennial Park & Campground.
148.4	Naughton.
156.5	Intersection of HWY 55 & HWY 17. Stay right to gain HWY 17 East.
159.8	Cycle beside Kelly Lake.
164.6	HWY 17 & Long Lake Road. Turn left here.
166.7	Intersection of Long Lake Road & Regent Street. Turn right here. Grocery stores are located here on Regent Avenue
170.3	Regent Street passes HWY 17 and becomes HWY 69 S. Remain on HWY 69 S.
173.8	Turn left into Carol's RV Park & Campground on the south shore of Richard Lake.
173.9	Carol's Campsite and RV Park.

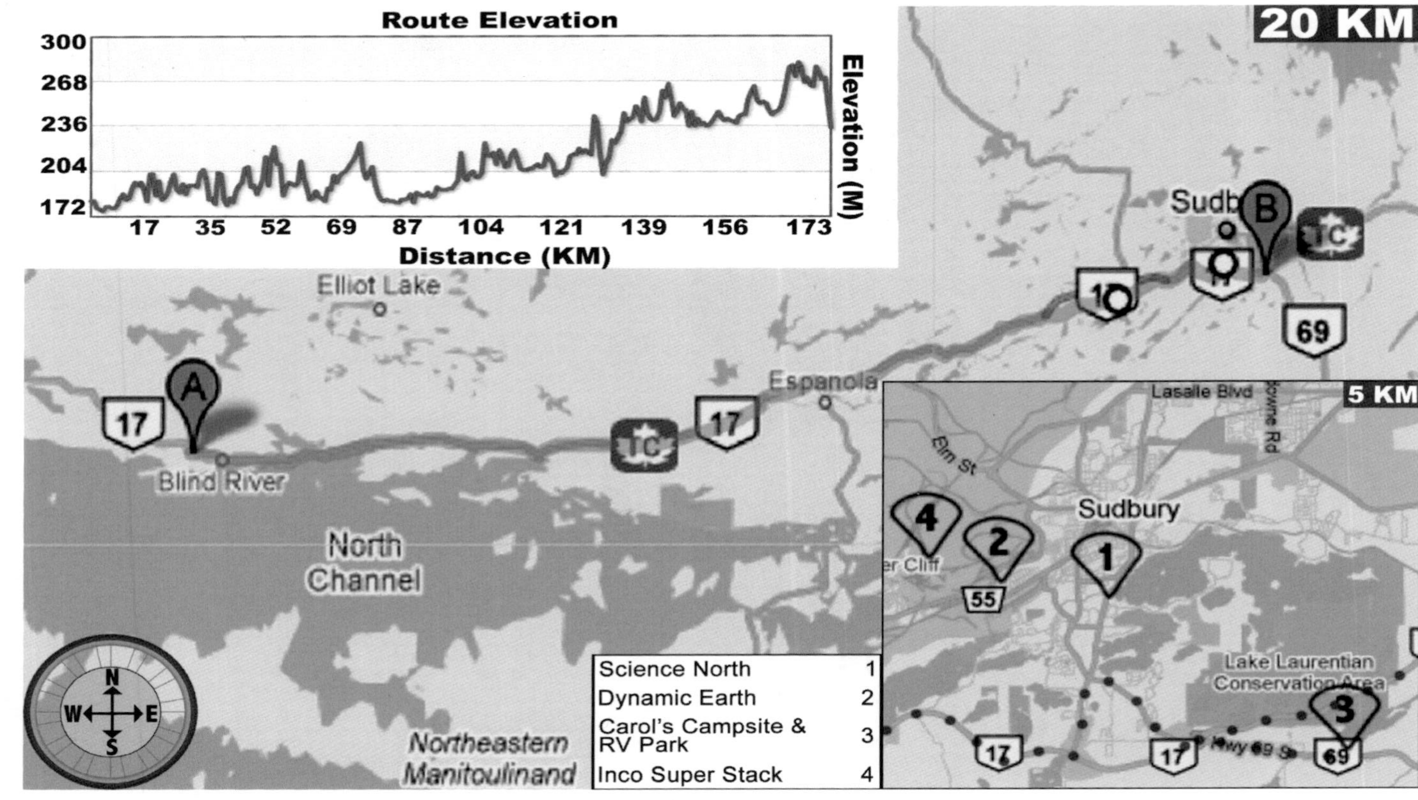
Route Elevation
300
268
236
204
172
17
35
52
69
87
104
121
139
156
173
Distance (KM)
Elevation (M)
20 KM
Elliot Lake
Blind River
17
A
TC
Espanola
North Channel
Northeastern Manitoulinand
Sudb
B
69
N
W
E
S
Science North 1
Dynamic Earth 2
Carol's Campsite & RV Park 3
Inco Super Stack 4
5 KM
Lasalle Blvd
Elm St
Sudbury
55
Lake Laurentian Conservation Area
Hwy 69 S

Carol's Campsite & RV Park to North Bay's Franklin Campground: (138.4 K)

From Sudbury to Ottawa, you can expect population, traffic and francophone density to increase.

Nipissing Lake is located between the Ottawa River and Georgian Bay, which is part of Lake Huron. Nipissing means "big lake" in Algonquin. The lake is unique because it is host to islands that are part of an eroded volcanic pipe. Volcanic pipes are formed by violent eruptions in an unusually deep volcano. Lava flows towards the surface like an uncorked Champagne bottle and then hardens to create an island.

Sturgeon Falls, population 6 383, is a tranquil town next to the Sturgeon River. It was here that I was spoken to in French for the first time as I headed east, in a grocery store. The downtown's streets are paved in tindle stone, giving it a European feel. At present, 80% of the residents of Sturgeon Falls identify themselves as francophone. If you are looking for a good place to go for a swim, head to the corner of King & Ethel. If you want to spend the evening nearby, take a right turn on Dutrisac Road on the east end of town and head to Dutrisac Cottages, 3 kilometres south of HWY 17.

North Bay is located between Lake Nipissing and Trout Lake. It straddles the Ottawa River Watershed to the west and the Great Lakes Basin to the east. The city is also located at the intersection of HWY 11 and HWY 17.

Approaching North Bay, expect to see a sign on the highway stating that bikes are not allowed on the road. Locals tell me that people bike on the road and that the rule is not enforced.

If you need work done on your bicycle head to Cycle Works.

North Bay is home to Nipissing University and Canadore College, combining for a total of 7 000 full-time students. Tourism, transportation and CFB North Bay play a prominent role in the city's economy.

Some attractions in North Bay include the Community Museum & Heritage Centre in the downtown area. Also, near the intersection of Seymour Street and HWY 17 / HWY 11 is the Dionne Quintuplets Museum, where you can learn about the five identical international superstars in their original farmhouse.

Because North Bay is located on a watershed divide, it was necessary for Fur Traders to portage between Trout Lake and Lake Nipissing. Today it is possible to follow some of the same paths that Voyageurs lugged their heavy canoes over. Many men died under the strain of their load and are buried in the area.

In 1961, workers were digging in Champlain Park on the banks of the La Vase River when they discovered artifacts from the past indicating that this area was the location of Fort Laronde, a historic fur trading post.

Your destination for the evening is the Franklin Motel & Trailer Park. This popular campground is located near the shore of Lake Nipissing and has an outdoor pool. Champlain Tent & Trailer Park is located 3 kilometres further south of this campground on the shore of Lake Nipissing.

Kilometre Log

0.0 Leave Carol's Campsite & RV Park biking west on HWY 69 S.

3.6 Exit left and circle 270° clockwise to gain HWY 17 heading east.

5.6 Stay on HWY 17 and cycle through Lake Laurentian Conservation Area.

14.9 HWY 17 turns 90° to your right. Turn right to remain on HWY 17.

22.9 Pass through Wahnapitae and cross over the Wanhapitae River.

54.2 Intersection of HWY 17 & HWY 535.

57.4 Cross over the Veuve River.

62.9 Warren and the intersection of HWY 17 & HWY 539.

76.6 Intersection of HWY 17 & HWY 575 (N)

77.5 Intersection of HWY 17 & HWY 64 (S) and the town of Verner. HWY 17 & HWY 64 merge.

92.7 Sturgeon Falls. Downtown, HWY 64 / HWY 17 becomes HWY 17.

107.2 Little Sturgeon River empties into Lake Nipissing here.

124.9 Enter North Bay on HWY 17.

130.2 At the intersection of HWY 17 & Algonquin Avenue, HWY 17 becomes HWY 17 / HWY 11.

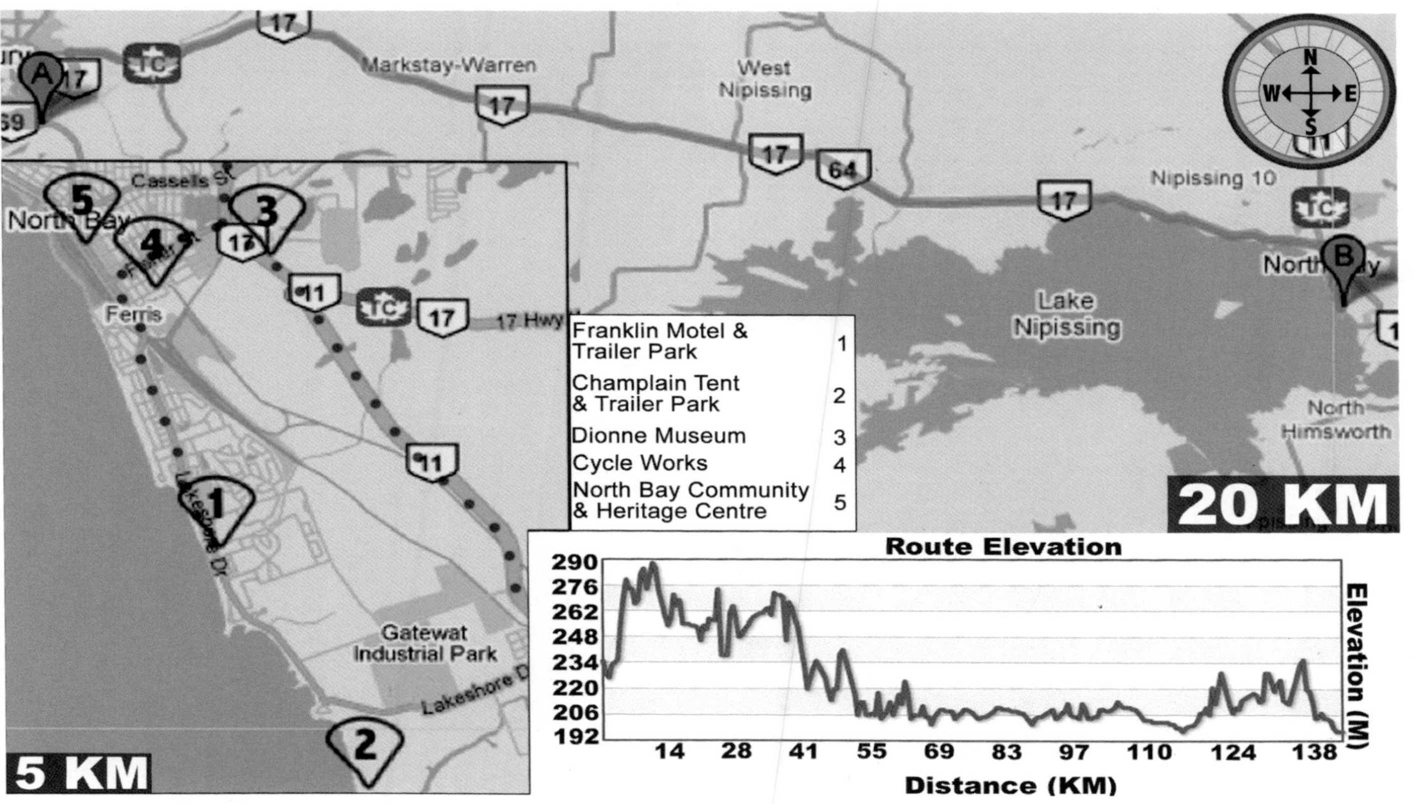

Markstay-Warren
West Nipissing
Nipissing 10
Lake Nipissing
North Himsworth
Cassels St
North Bay
Ferris
17 Hwy
Gatewat Industrial Park
Lakeshore Dr
20 KM
5 KM
Franklin Motel & Trailer Park 1
Champlain Tent & Trailer Park 2
Dionne Museum 3
Cycle Works 4
North Bay Community & Heritage Centre 5
Route Elevation
Elevation (M)
290
276
262
248
234
220
206
192
14
28
41
55
69
83
97
110
124
138
Distance (KM)

132.2 Cycle between Thompson Park on your right and Northgate Shopping Centre on your left.
132.7 Intersection of HWY 17 / HWY 11 & Fisher Street. Turn right here.
134.2 Intersection of Fisher Street and Main Street E. Turn left.
135.2 Cross over railroad tracks. Main Street E becomes Lakeshore Drive here.
138.4 Franklin Motel & Trailer Park.

Franklin Campground to Driftwood Provincial Park Campground: (139.7 K)

After you leave North Bay you will cycle on HWY 17 along the southern edge of Samuel du Champlain Provincial Park. This park is named after the 17th century explorer and celebrates the Voyageurs who tackled portages and rapids here. In the park you can view a replica birch bark freighter in the heritage centre or hike to lookouts to enjoy panoramic views of the area. Mattawa River flows through the park towards Mattawa where it joins the Ottawa River. Two campgrounds with 215 sites are located in the park.

After Samuel du Champlain Park you will bike towards Mattawa, which means "meeting of the waters" in Ojibwa. Traditionally, Mattawa was an important transportation intersection for people traveling from Montréal. They would leave the Ottawa River here and travel on the Mattawa River towards Lake Nipissing. Look for large wooden statues of historical figures in this area. Camping is available in Mattawa at Sid Turcotte Park.

From Mattawa you will follow the Ottawa River, which defines the border of Ontario and Québec for much of its length, all the way into Ottawa. The Ottawa River's source is Lake Capimitchigama in the Laurentian Mountains of central Québec; it terminates into Lake of Two Mountains and St. Lawrence River in Montréal. The Ottawa River played a prominent role in the Algonquin peoples lives as well as in the timber industry. Today, the river's use as a cargo route has been eclipsed by railway. However, the river now generates hydro-electricity for the area.

There is a small general store near the entrance of Driftwood Provincial Park, but I recommend getting your supplies for the evening in Mattawa.

Driftwood Provincial Park has 80 campsites, most of which offer a view of the Ottawa River and the Laurentian Hills beyond. There is a sandy beach nearby and laundry facilities are available.

Kilometre Log

0.0 Leave Franklin Motel and head north on Lakeshore Drive.
3.2 Cross over railway tracks. Lakeshore Drive becomes Main Street E.
3.7 From Main Street E turn right onto Fisher Street.
5.2 Fisher Street dead-ends into HWY 17 / HWY 11. Turn right onto HWY 17 / HWY 11 and head east.
6.3 HWY 17 and HWY 11 split. Stay right and circle 270° clockwise to access HWY 17 heading east.
17.3 Intersection of HWY 17 & HWY 94.
38.3 Rutherglen.
49.8 Enter Samuel de Champlain Provincial Park.
54.7 Exit Samuel de Champlain Provincial Park.
58.8 Taggart Lake Campground.
63.9 Enter Mattawa on HWY 17 / John Street.
65.1 John Street / HWY 17 becomes McConnell Street / HWY 17.
65.7 Turn right off of HWY 17 / McConnell Street onto HWY 17 / Valois Drive.
117.9 Bissett Creek.
134.1 Morning Mist Resort & Campground.
134.6 Stonecliffe. Small general store here.
139.7 Driftwood Provincial Park.

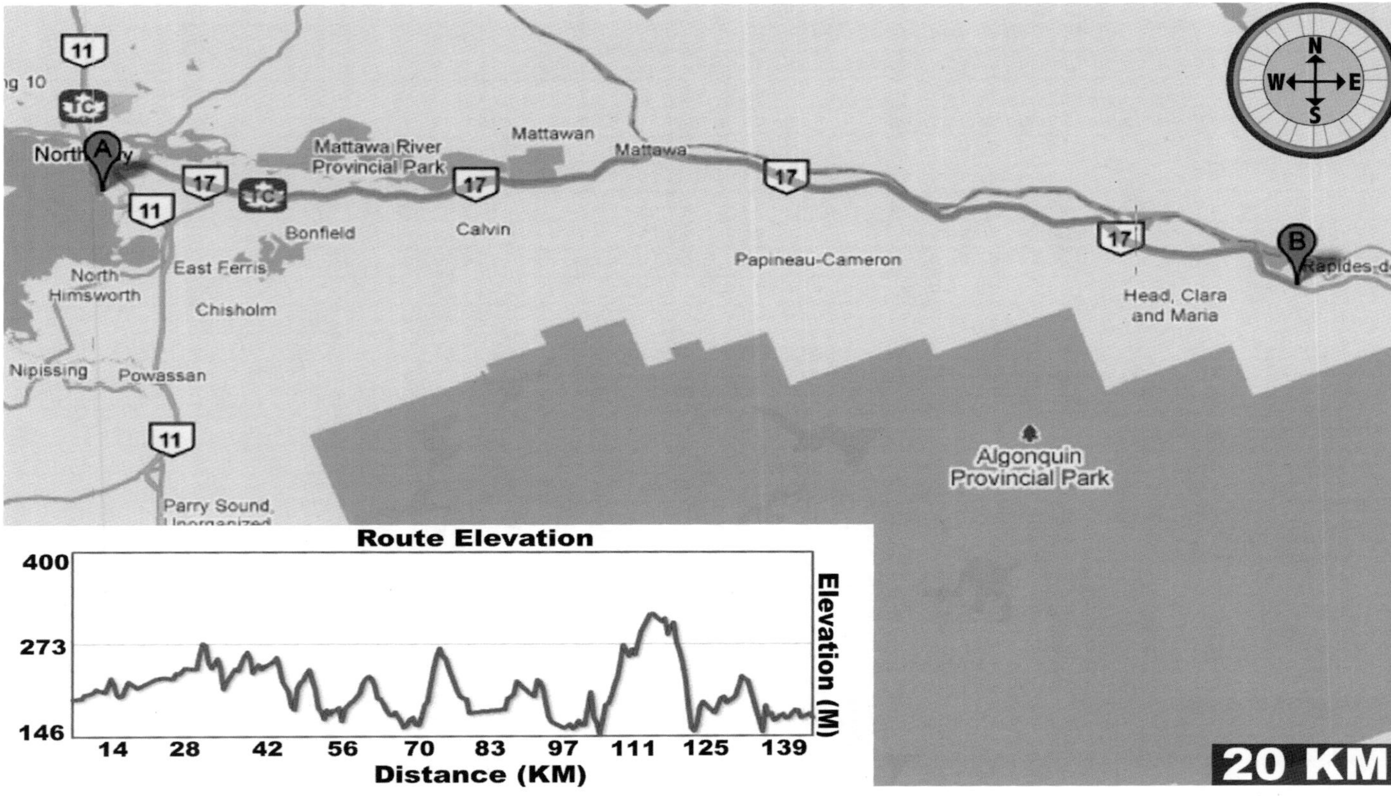

11
ng 10
TC
North Bay
A
17
11
TC
Mattawa River
Provincial Park
Bonfield
17
Calvin
Mattawan
Mattawa
17
Papineau-Cameron
17
Head, Clara
and Maria
B
Rapides-de
N
W
E
S
North
Himsworth
East Ferris
Chisholm
Nipissing
Powassan
11
Parry Sound,
Algonquin
Provincial Park
Route Elevation
400
273
146
14
28
42
56
70
83
97
111
125
139
Distance (KM)
Elevation (M)
20 KM

Driftwood Provincial Park to Cobden's Veteran's Memorial Campground: (106.8 K)

Bike first through the town of Deep River. Deep River was a planned community that began in 1944, as part of the Manhattan Project to house employees of the nearby Chalk River Nuclear Research Laboratory. If you have some spare time, check out the Canadian Clock Museum on James Street.

From Deep River you will cycle towards Chalk River, a small town famous for being home to Chalk River Laboratories, which is a site of research and development to support and advance nuclear technology.

HWY 17 takes you past the exits to both Pembroke and Petawawa. They are both off of the highway and offer no services. Petawawa is home to the military base CFB Petawawa so don't be surprised if you see troops out on the road. Pembroke is located at the confluence of the Muskrat and Ottawa Rivers and is largely a farming and timber town.

Your destination for the evening is Cobden Veteran's Memorial Campground, located on the edge of Muskrat Lake in downtown Cobden, population 992. The campground is located within Veteran's Memorial Park and is home to a popular sandy beach. Groceries are available in Cobden.

Kilometre Log

0.0 Leave Birchwood Provincial Park Campground heading east on HWY 17.
2.4 Mackey.
10.3 Rolphton.
28.8 Deep River.
30.9 Ryan's Campsite & Gifts.
38.3 Enter Chalk River on HWY 17.
54.7 First exit to Petawawa.
72.9 Exit to Pembroke.
78.7 Intersection of HWY 17 & HWY 41.
90.7 Cross over Muskrat River.
105.9 Enter Cobden on HWY 17.
106.5 Turn left off of HWY 17 onto Astrolabe Road.
106.8 Enter Cobden Veteran's Park and Campground.

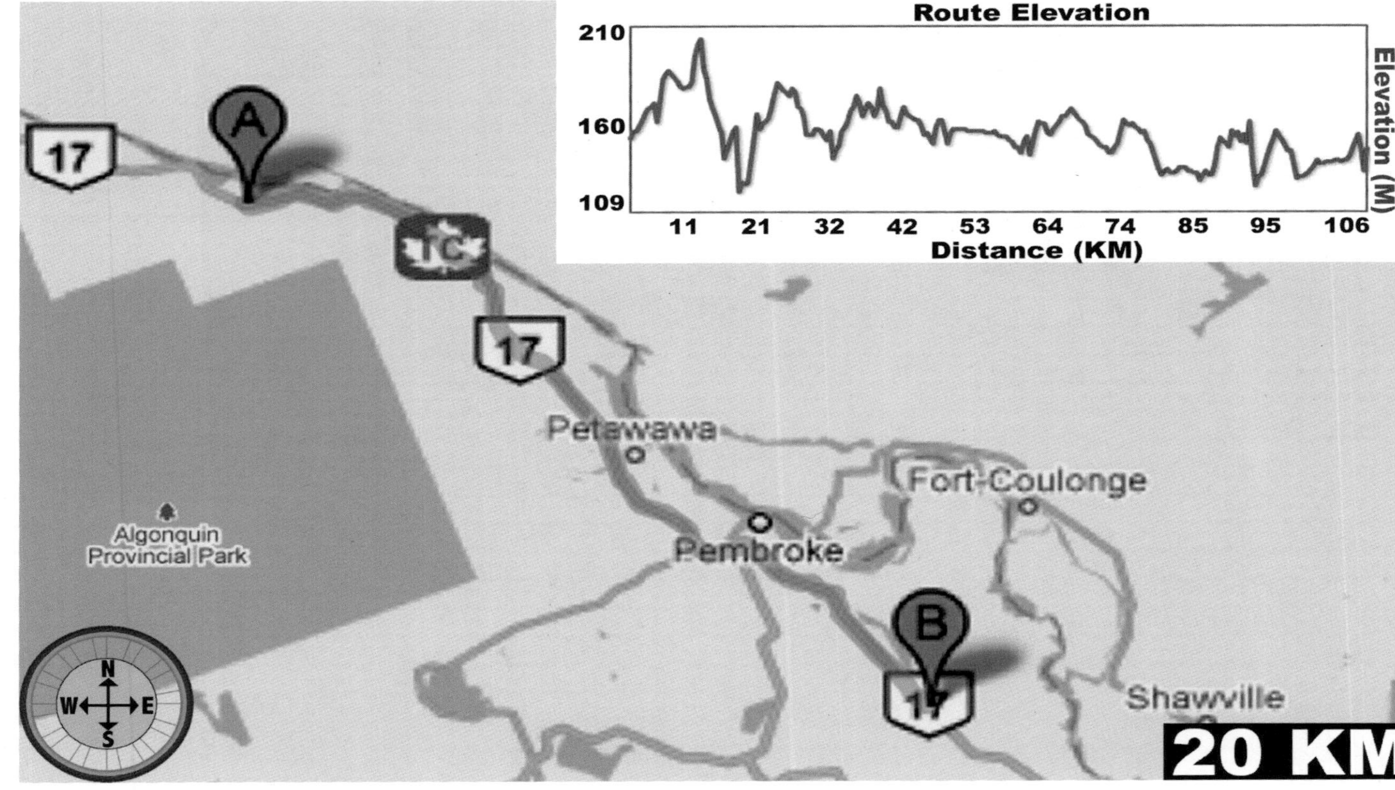

Route Elevation
210
160
109
11
21
32
42
53
64
74
85
95
106
Distance (KM)
Elevation (M)
17
A
17
Algonquin
Provincial Park
Petawawa
Pembroke
Fort-Coulonge
B
17
Shawville
N
W
E
S
20 KM

Veteran's Memorial Campground to Ottawa's Parliament Hill: (121.1 K)

Today you will leave the buggy confines of rural northern Ontario and cycle into Ottawa, Canada's national capital.

In Ontario, cyclists are not permitted on any HWY in the 400 series. At Arnprior, HWY 17 changes to 417, meaning you will have to detour. Arnprior is located at the mouth of the Madawaska River, where it enters into the Ottawa River.

As you bike into Ottawa you will cycle through the Greenbelt, which is a ring of parkland that circles Ottawa. Real estate development in the green belt is strictly controlled. The original plan for the land was to prevent urban sprawl and provide green space for future generations. The Greenbelt was proposed by Jacques Greber in 1950, and was intended to circumscribe an area large enough for 500 000 people. Presently, Ottawa has a population of 812 129, far exceeding the population Greber planned for.

The Ottawa River's Rideau Canal connects Ottawa to Kingston, 202 kilometres away. The Duke of Wellington was an ardent proponent of this project and appointed Lieutenant-Colonel John By to oversee the task. When By arrived in Canada he set up shop near the mouth of the Rideau River and the area became known as Bytown. The canal was opened in 1832, and is still in use today. The construction of Rideau Canal was proposed after the War of 1812, between the United States and the British Empire. The canal is now a UNESCO World Heritage Site, operated by Parks Canada. A bike path runs along the side of the canal through Ottawa.

In 1855, Bytown was given the name Ottawa after the resident Odawa First Nations People. In 1857, Queen Victoria was asked to choose a common capital for the Province of Canada. Surprisingly, she chose Ottawa which was at the time a logging town. It was far from Upper Canada's major centres of Québec City and Montréal and distant from Lower Canada's major centres of Kingston and Toronto. This made Ottawa a compromise between the two sections of Canada. Also, Ottawa was surrounded by dense forest making it hard to attack over land, while the Ottawa River and Rideau Canal eased transport to both the east and west. In 1858, the Queen officially named Ottawa the capital of Canada.

No visit to Ottawa would be complete without exploring Parliament Hill. Stroll around the grounds of this architectural beauty or take a guided tour. Originally, Parliament Hill was the site of a military base in the 18th and early 19th centuries, developed after being named the capital by Queen Elizabeth.

There are five main buildings on Capital Hill. The Centre Block contains the Senate and Commons chambers. It was built between 1916 and 1927 to replace the original building which was destroyed in a fire in 1916. In front of this building is the Peace Tower, which stands in honour of the men and women who sacrificed their lives in World War I. This freestanding tower is made of Nepean sandstone and measures 92.2 metres from base to the top of the bronze flagpole.

Behind Centre Block is the Library of Parliament, which overlooks the craggy bluffs of the Ottawa River. The East Block was built in two stages; the main section was constructed in the mid-1800s, and in 1910, a wing was added to the rear. The building was originally designed to provide space for lowly government employees, not legislators, as this building is less ornate than the rest. The West Block opened in 1865, and was designed using Gothic Revival Style. Today it houses Ministers, Members of Parliament, committee rooms and the Confederation Room.

Ottawa is also host to many museums including the Bytown Museum, Canadian War Museum, National Gallery of Canada, Currency Museum of the Bank of Canada and the Canadian Museum of Contemporary Photography.

Camping in Ottawa is limited. The most convenient place to spend the evening is in the green belt at Ottawa Municipal Campground. This campground is over 20 kilometres from Parliament Hill and downtown Ottawa. I have included an alternate route to the Ottawa Municipal Campground to accompany the route to Parliament Hill.

Ottawa's Barefoot Hostel and Hostelling International's Ottawa Jail Hostel come highly recommended and both are close to Parliament Hill.

Kilometre Log

0.0	Exit Veteran's Memorial Campground on Astrolabe Road heading south towards HWY 17.
0.1	Turn left onto HWY 17 and exit Cobden.
22.6	Horton.
47.3	Approach Arnprior and turn left at the intersection of HWY 17 & Pine Grove Road (W) / Division Street S (E) onto Division Street S.
49.9	Follow Division Street S to the intersection of River Road (W) / Elgin Street W (E). Turn right here onto Elgin Street.
50.8	Turn slightly left off of Elgin Street W onto Madawaska Street.
51.3	Cross over the Madawaska River. Madawaska Street becomes Madawaska Boulevard.
57.6	Madawaska Boulevard / HWY 17 intersects with Galetta Side Road. Turn left here.
60.8	Cross over a small creek in Galetta.
73.4	Remain on Galetta Side Road until it dead-ends into Dunrobin Road / HWY 9. Turn right here.
93.0	Dunrobin Road / HWY 9 dead-ends into March Road / HWY 49. Turn left onto March Road / HWY 49.

If heading downtown, skip italicized side route to Ottawa Municipal Campground:

101.1 From March Road turn left onto Corkstown Road.

103.9 Exit left into Ottawa Municipal Campground.

If you spend the evening in Ottawa Municipal Campground, re-trace your route until you meet up with March Road and then follow the route to Parliament Hill.

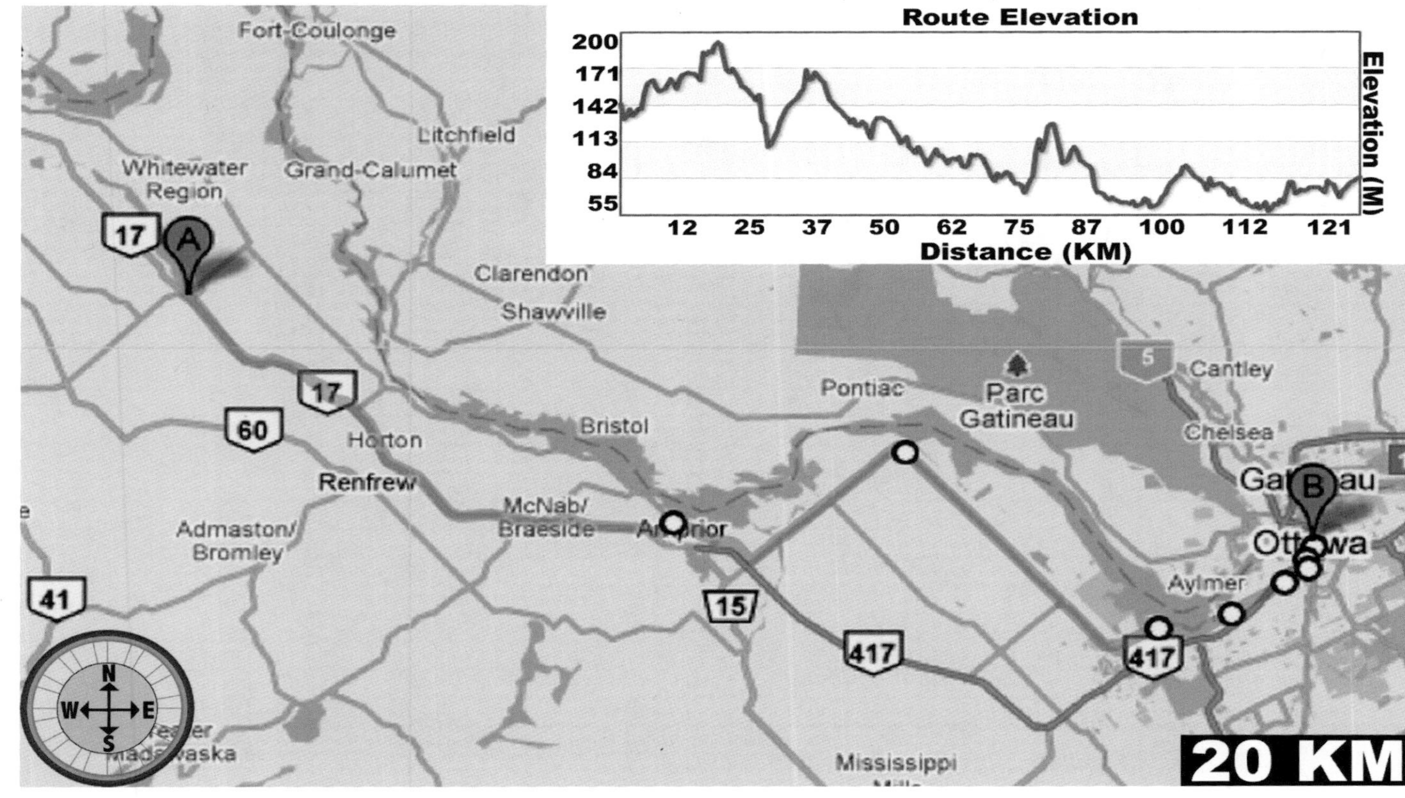

Fort-Coulonge
Litchfield
Whitewater Region
Grand-Calumet
Clarendon
Shawville
Bristol
Horton
Renfrew
McNab/ Braeside
Admaston/ Bromley
Pontiac
Parc Gatineau
Cantley
Chelsea
Aylmer
Mississippi
17
60
41
15
417
5
A
B
N
W
E
S
Route Elevation
200
171
142
113
84
55
Elevation (M)
12
25
37
50
62
75
87
100
112
121
Distance (KM)
20 KM

To Parliament Hill

98.6 Turn left off of March Road / HWY 49 onto Carling Avenue / HWY 38.

106.6 Bike Past Andrew Haydon Park and Beltown Park, both on your left.

113.3 Carling Avenue / HWY 38 crosses HWY 417.

117.5 Carling Avenue / HWY 38 dead-ends into Bronson Avenue. Turn left on Bronson Avenue.

119.1 Turn right off of Bronson Avenue onto Laurier Avenue W.

120.7 Turn left on Metcalfe Street.

121.1 Welcome to Parliament Hill.

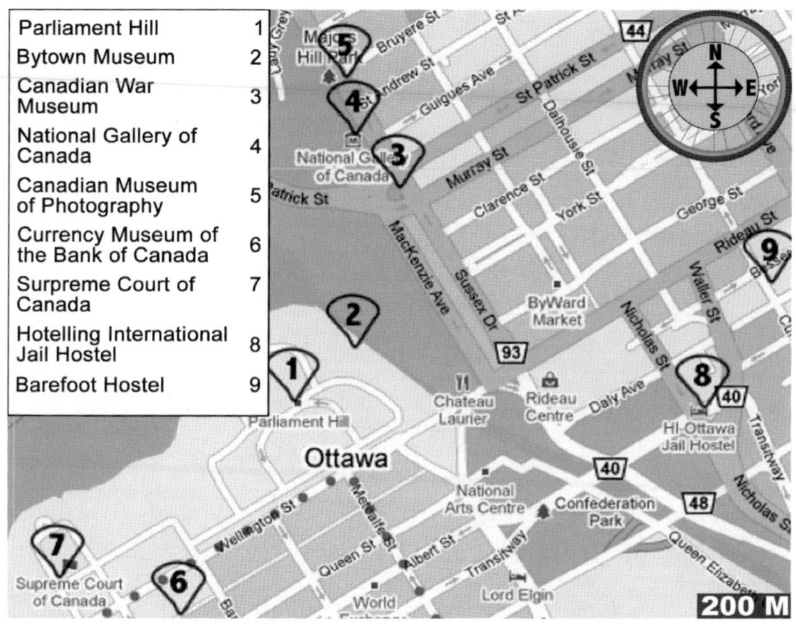

Parliament Hill to Camping Municipal Brownsburg-Chatham: (120.6 K)

The road that runs in front of Parliament Hill is Wellington Street. Looking at the front of Parliament Hill, you want to head left, (west) on Wellington Street and cross the Ottawa River into Gatineau on Portage Bridge North.

Today you will leave Ottawa and head towards Montréal along the Ottawa River. The Ottawa River Valley is flat and fertile, making for enjoyable cycling. Expect there to be many "traversière" (ferry) crossings as you bike down the north side of this famous river. Crossings usually occur regularly, 24 hours a day, and cost a few dollars for cyclists. Always wait for vehicle traffic to exit until you bike up the road away from the ferry.

Cross the Ottawa River from downtown Ottawa into Gatineau, Québec, population 242 124. Gatineau is the third largest city in Québec. Annual tourist events in Gatineau include an international fireworks competition as well as a hot air balloon festival every September Long Weekend.

The Canadian Museum of Civilization, the most visited museum in Canada, is located directly across the river from Parliament Hill. The museum's purpose is to collect, study and preserve objects that tell the human history of Canada and the cultural diversity of its people.

The first town that you will cycle through is Thurso, population 2 299, which is a small pulp and paper town famous for being the home of hockey superstar Guy LaFleur.

Papineauville, population 2 167, is another small town that offers cyclists a chance to eat and rehydrate.

Next, cycle through Montebello, which is world famous for the Château Montebello Resort, the largest log structure ever built. Your destination for the evening is Brownsburg-Chatham Municipal Campground on the north shore of the Ottawa River.

Kilometre Log

0.0	With Parliament Hill on your right, head west on Wellington Street.
1.3	Turn slightly right off of Wellington Street onto Ottawa River Parkway and cross the Portage Bridge.
1.9	Cross the Ottawa River and enter Gatineau, Québec on Boulevard Maisonneuve.
3.5	Boulevard Maisonneuve turns into Boulevard Fournier as you cross over the busy Autoroute de la Gatineau.
3.8	Cycle over Gatineau River.
5.0	Bike through Lake Leamy Ecological Park.
5.8	Cross over Gatineau River again. After crossing the bridge, Boulevard Fournier becomes Boulevard Gréber. Stay on this road until it intersects with HWY 148 / Boulevard Maloney.
8.3	Boulevard Gréber intersects with HWY 148 / Boulevard Maloney O. Turn right here. Remain on HWY 148 for the next one hundred kilometres.
12.2	Boulevard Maloney O / HWY 148 turns into Boulevard Maloney E / HWY 148.
14.6	Pass by Beauchamp Lake Park.
18.2	Pass by McLaurin Bay Park.
23.3	Boulevard Maloney E / HWY 148 becomes Chemin De Montréal O / HWY 148 here.
31.9	Turn right on Rue Notre Dame / HWY 148.
32.2	Turn left onto Chemin De Montréal E / HWY 148.
46.8	Enter Thurso on HWY 148 / Rue Victoria.
58.0	Plaisance.
65.9	Enter Papineauville on Rue Papineau / HWY 148.
72.2	Montebello.
78.4	Fassett.
88.9	Pointe-au-Chêne.
95.1	Calumet.
101.0	Turn right off of HWY 148 onto Rue Maple / HWY 344.
103.1	Turn left off of Rue Maple / HWY 344 onto Rue Principale / HWY 344.
109.1	Rue Principale / HWY 344 turns into Route Des Outaouais / HWY 344.
120.6	Enter Camping Municipal Brownsburg-Chatham.

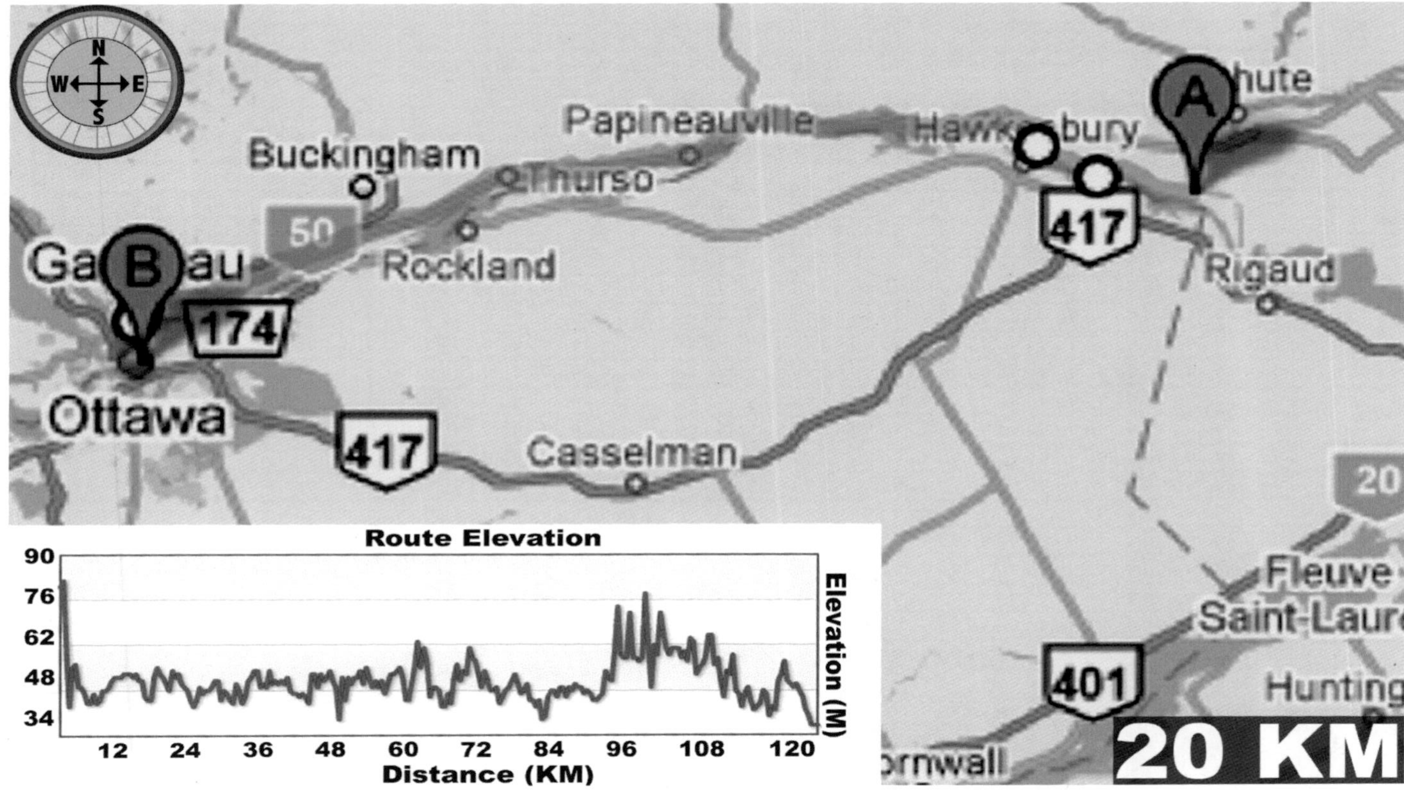

N
W
E
S
Papineauville
Buckingham
Thurso
Rockland
B
A
50
174
417
417
Ottawa
Casselman
Rigaud
20
401
20 KM
Route Elevation
90
76
62
48
34
12 24 36 48 60 72 84 96 108 120
Distance (KM)
Elevation (M)

Province:	Québec
Population:	7 782 561
Area:	1 542 056 km^2
Industries:	Agriculture, forestry, pulp & paper, aerospace, technology.
Highlights:	Québec City, Montréal, Plains of Abraham, Québecois culture, St. Lawrence River Valley, poutine.

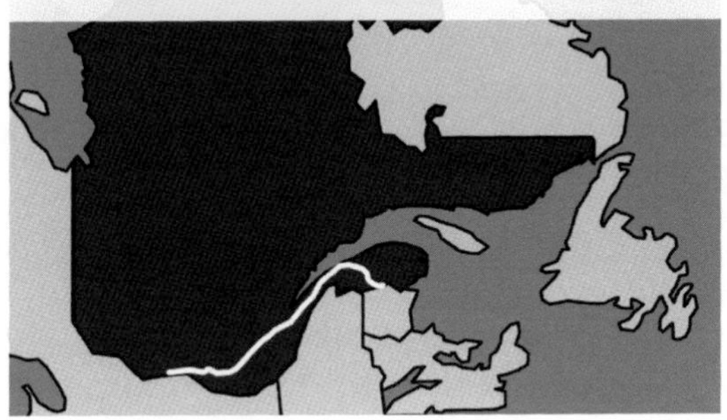

Camping Municipal Brownsburg-Chatham to Montréal's Parque LaFontaine: (88.8 K)

The Fleur-de-lis adorns the Québec national flag. The flag takes its white cross from the ancient royal flags of France. The white fleur-de-lis are taken from a banner honouring the Virgin Mary that was carried by General Louis-Joseph de Montcalm when he and his troops arrived at present day New York.

The act regarding the flag and emblems of Québec dictates that the Québec flag take precedence over any other flag or emblem. To avoid confusion, the flag is often flown alone without the Canadian Flag.

In 1995, the government of Québec announced a partnership with Vélo Québec in which they constructed La Route Verte, a 4 000-kilometre bike trail linking all parts of Québec. Québecers claim it as the best bike route in the world, and it may very well be. During your trip through Québec you will see signs indicating La Route Verte, however, you will not cycle on this path exclusively as it often zigs and zags, making it inefficient to follow all of the time. If you are staying at a hotel or campground and see a sticker that reads "Bienvenue Cyclists," they will have a pump and tools on location as well as information about repair centres and tourist information offices.

Montréal, population 1 620 593, sits on an island in the middle of the St. Lawrence River and takes its name from Mont-Royal, the triple-peaked hill in the heart of the city. Montréal is the second largest French-speaking city in the world, next to Paris, France.

Archaeological evidence indicates that aboriginal people had occupied the area for 2 000 years before French explorer Jacques Cartier claimed the area for France in 1535.

Montréal is Canada's cultural capital, as it lays at the confluence of French and English traditions. During summer months, downtown Montréal is a beehive of activity while Montréalers celebrate the many festivals including the Just for Laughs Comedy Festival, Montréal International Jazz Festival and the Montréal World Film Festival.

Montréal is a good place to be a cyclist. Over 500 kilometres of trails snake through the city. In 1999, Bicycling Magazine named Montréal as the most bike friendly city in North America. There is an abundance of bike shops in Montréal to get your steed ready to hit the road. Mile-End Bike Garage is a cooperative bike shop that aims to put bike repair within everyone's reach.

Mark Twain commented on Montréal by saying, "This is the first time I was ever in a city where you couldn't throw a brick without breaking a church window." The city boasts four stunning Catholic basilicas including Mary, Queen of the World Cathedral, Notre-Dame Basilica, St. Patrick's Basilica and Saint Joseph's Oratory, which is Canada's largest church.

The closest campground to downtown Montréal is Montréal South KOA, but it is far away from the action of Montréal. I will lead you to Parque Lafontaine and you can find a place to stay from there. Hostelling International Montréal is a good choice.

Kilometre Log

0.0 Leave Brownsburg-Chatham cycling east on HWY 344 / Route des Outaouais.

0.4 Turn left onto Montée Saint-Phillippe.

4.6 Montée Saint-Phillippe intersects with HWY 148 Route Du Canton. Turn right.

6.7 HWY 148 curves to the left.

7.5 Exit right off of HWY 148 onto HWY 50 / Autoroute Maurice-Richard.

9.2 Pass over Rivière du Nord.

12.8 Exit right off of HWY 50 / Autoroute Maurice-Richard onto HWY 148.

24.8 Enter Saint-Hermas. Take a left turn to remain on HWY 148.

31.1 Turn right onto Route Arthur-Sauvé / HWY 148.

51.5 Enter Saint-Eustache on Boulevard Arthur-Sauvé and cross HWY 640. Stay on HWY 148 / Boulevard Arthur-Sauvé.

53.8 Cross over Rivière des Mille Îles. Remain on Boulevard Arthur-Sauvé.

55.9 Turn left off of Boulevard Arthur-Sauvé / HWY 148 onto Boulevard Dagenais O.

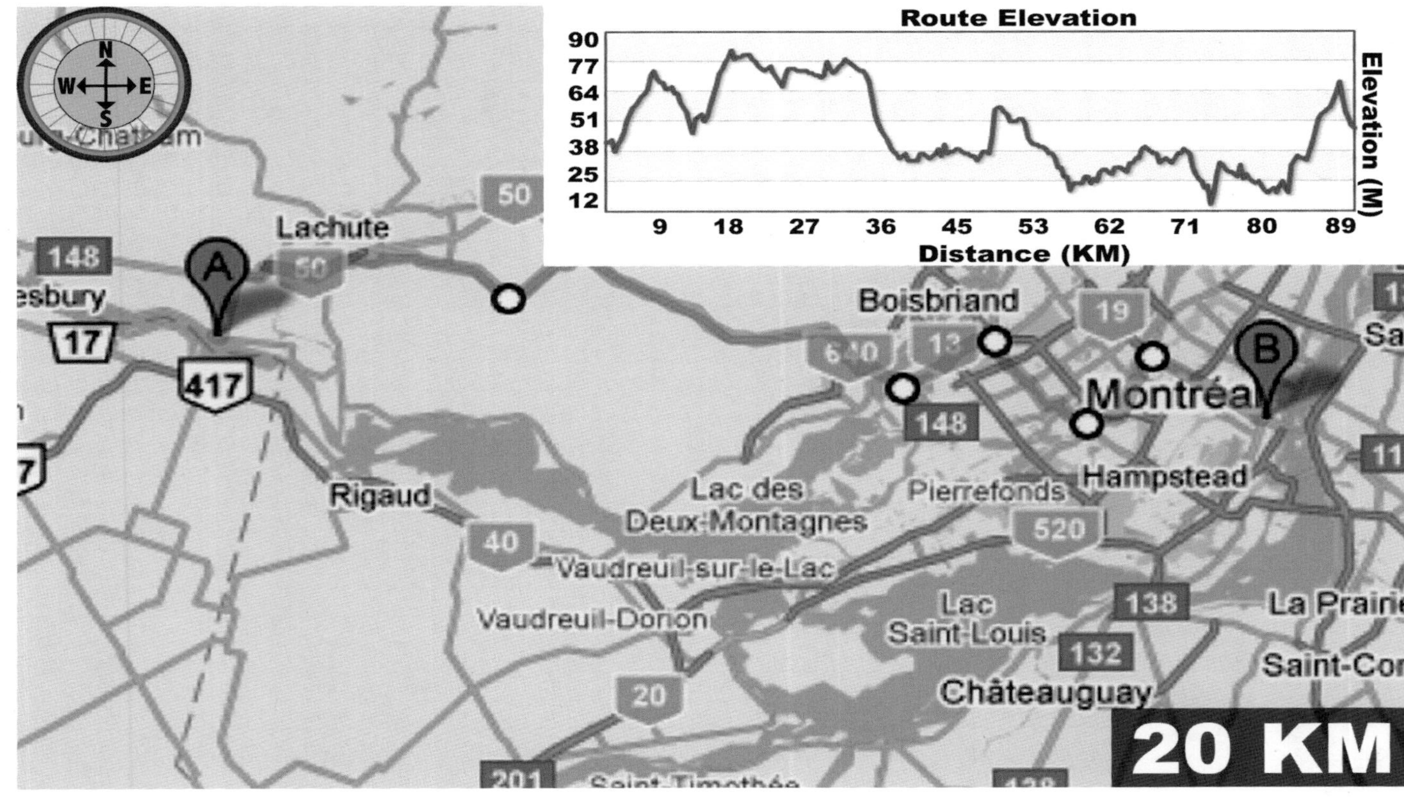
N
W
E
S
Route Elevation
90
77
64
51
38
25
12
9
18
27
36
45
53
62
71
80
89
Distance (KM)
Elevation (M)
50
Lachute
148
A
50
17
417
Boisbriand
19
640
13
B
Montréal
148
Rigaud
Lac des
Deux-Montagnes
Pierrefonds
Hampstead
520
40
Vaudreuil-sur-le-Lac
Vaudreuil-Dorion
Lac
Saint-Louis
138
La Prairie
132
Châteauguay
20
20 KM

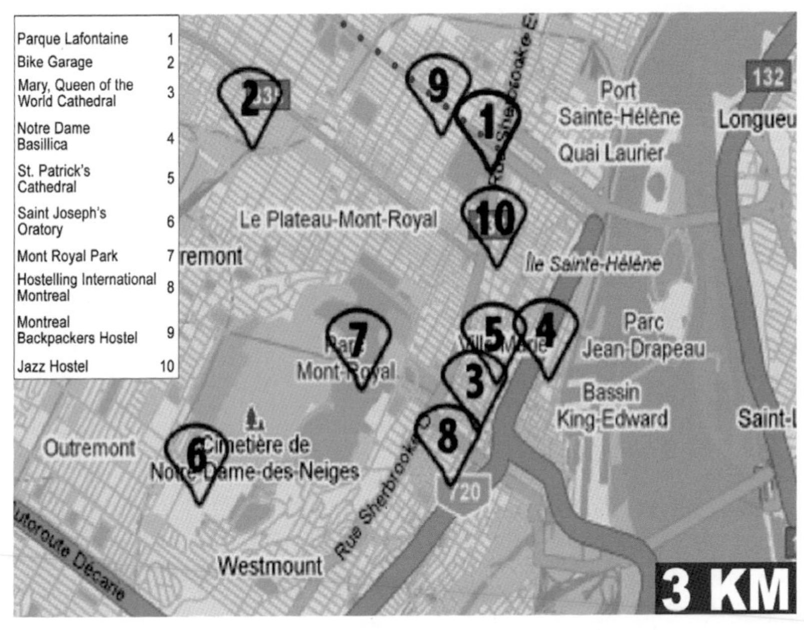
Parque Lafontaine 1
Bike Garage 2
Mary, Queen of the World Cathedral 3
Notre Dame Basillica 4
St. Patrick's Cathedral 5
Saint Joseph's Oratory 6
Mont Royal Park 7
Hostelling International Montreal 8
Montreal Backpackers Hostel 9
Jazz Hostel 10
Port Sainte-Hélène
Longueu
Quai Laurier
Le Plateau-Mont-Royal
Île Sainte-Hélène
Parc Jean-Drapeau
Bassin King-Edward
Outremont
Cimetière de Notre-Dame-des-Neiges
Rue Sherbrooke
Westmount
Autoroute Décarie
132
720
3 KM

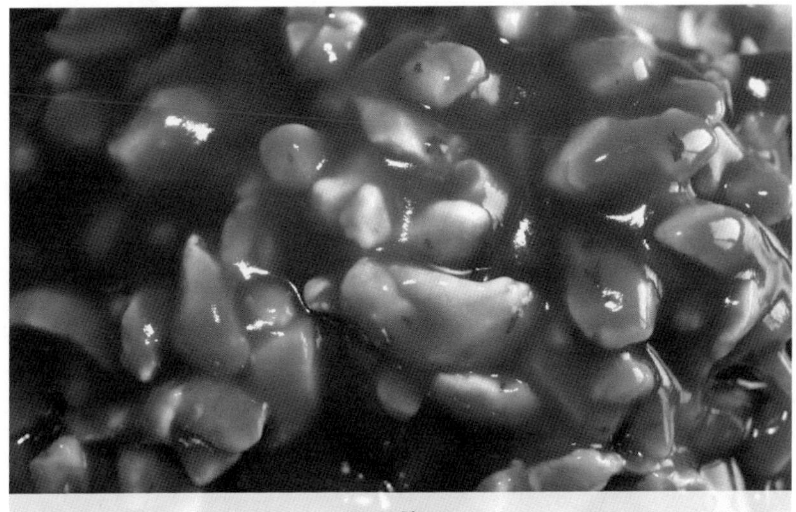

Poutine

59.8 Cross HWY 13 / Autoroute Chomedey.
63.1 Turn right off of Boulevard Dagenais O onto Boulevard Curé-Labelle / HWY 117.
65.1 Cross over HWY 440 / Autoroute Laval.
70.3 After Boulevard Curé-Labelle turns to the left, turn right onto Boulevard Chomedey / HWY 117.
70.5 Cross over Rivière des Prairies. Boulevard Chomedey / HWY 117 becomes Boulevard Laurentien / HWY 117.
73.1 Turn left onto Boulevard Henri-Bourassa O.
75.4 Boulevard Henri-Bourassa O crosses Autoroute des Laurentides / HWY 15.
80.3 Turn right off of Boulevard Henri-Bourassa onto Avenue Papineau.
83.0 Cross HWY 40 on Avenue Papineau.
88.8 Parque Lafontaine.

Parque LaFontaine to Camping et Marina Louiseville: (104.9 K)

Today you will cycle out of Montréal and bike along the St. Lawrence River. It starts narrow and widens as it opens into the Atlantic Ocean. You will enjoy your time spent near this historic river.

The St. Lawrence River connects the Great Lakes with the Atlantic Ocean and forms part of the international boundary between Ontario and New York State. This river was first explored by Europeans in 1535 by Jacques Cartier with help from Iroquoian chief Donnacona's two sons. Originally, the Lachine Rapids in Montréal made the river navigable only to Montréal. In 1825, the Lachine Canal opened which allowed ships to pass the rapids.

From 1942 to 1944, the St. Lawrence was a war zone between Germany and Canada.

The St. Lawrence Seaway opened in 1959. This series of locks allows ocean-going freighters to travel into the Great Lakes.

HWY 138 runs parallel to the giant river and will be your path into Québec City. Locals refer to it only as Québec, so drop the word "city" to sound like a seasoned veteran. In Montréal, many people speak freely in either language, but bilingualism is less prominent as you head east. When you ask people if they speak English they will often tell you no, but in reality have quite a good grasp of the language. Talk slowly and clearly in these situations and they will most likely understand you.

The banks of the St. Lawrence are populated with small towns on both sides. Expect every town in Québec to have an impressive church. Also, look for "Dépanneur," which means convenience store in French. Also, "Caisse Croûte," which translates to "broken crust" or "break the bread," is a small restaurant that specializes in poutine, but will probably serve sandwiches and other small meals. A Caisse Croûte is quick and affordable, perfect for a bike tour lunch.

Today you will start biking on Chemin du Roy, which translates into "King's Highway" in English. This road was completed in 1737, connecting Québec City to Repentigny, east of Montréal. At time of completion the road was the longest north of the Rio Grande River.

Get your supplies for the evening in the Berthierville. Mention Jacques Villeneuve and watch the locals face light up. Jacques grew up in Berthierville.

As you approach the small town of Maskinonge, watch in the distance for a prominent church steeple that beacons you towards it. Also, Louiseville has a giant church with blue doors, impressive even by Québec standards.

Your destination for the evening is Camping et Marina Louiseville.

Kilometre Log

0.0 With Parque Lafontaine to your left cycle north on Rue Sherbrooke E / HWY 138.

8.3 On Rue Sherbrooke E / HWY 138 cycle over Autoroute Louis-H-Fontaine.

21.9 Cross over Rivière des Mille Îles and Île Bourdon. Rue Sherbrooke E / HWY 138 turns into Rue Notre Dame / HWY 138.

38.8 Saint-Sulpice.

41.7 Camping Marquis.

48.3 Enter Lavaltrie on HWY Rue Notre Dame / HWY 138.

52.0 Rue Notre Dame / HWY 138 becomes Côte Grande O / HWY 138.

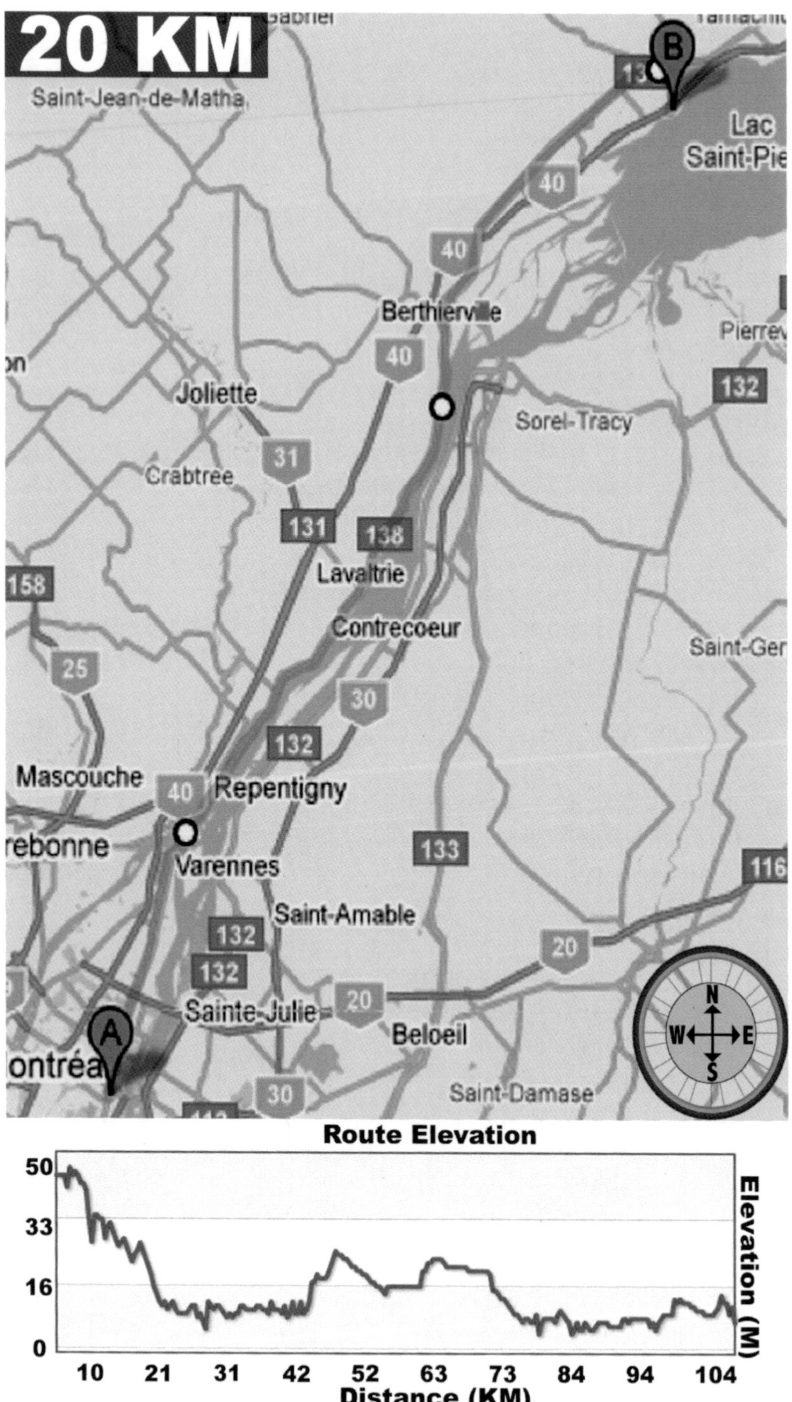
20 KM
Saint-Jean-de-Matha
B
Lac
40
40
Berthierville
40
Joliette
Sorel-Tracy
132
31
Crabtree
131
138
Lavaltrie
158
Contrecoeur
25
30
132
Mascouche
40
Repentigny
Varennes
133
Saint-Amable
132
132
20
20
Sainte-Julie
A
Beloeil
30
Saint-Damase
N
W
E
S
Route Elevation
50
33
16
0
10
21
31
42
52
63
73
84
94
104
Distance (KM)
Elevation (M)

72.2 Enter Berthierville on Rue Notre Dame / HWY 138.
79.4 HWY 138 crosses HWY 40.
94.0 Maskinongé.
99.3 Enter Louiseville on HWY 138 / Boulevard Saint-Laurent O.
101.2 Turn right on 2E Avenue.
107.9 Cross HWY 40. 2E Avenue becomes Rang du Lac-Saint-Pierre O.
104.3 Turn left on Rang du Lac-Saint-Pierre E.
104.9 Camping et Marina Louiseville.

Camping et Marina Louiseville to Portneuf's Camping Panoramique: (110.1 K)

Highway signs indicate that Trois Rivières, population 121 666, is much closer than you would expect. That is because these signs are indicating the distance to Trois Rivières-Ouest, which is far from downtown Trois Rivières.

Trois Rivières, translating to "three rivers," in English, is located at the confluence of the Saint-Maurice and Saint Lawrence Rivers. The reason that the city is named Trois Rivières is because Rivière Saint-Maurice has three mouths into the St. Lawrence. Trois Rivières is known as the National Poetry Capital of Québec; there are plaques displaying poetic verses in many parts of the city.

In this area on June 8, 1776, during the American Revolutionary War, the British defeated an attempt by the Americans to advance up the Saint Lawrence River valley. This fight is known as the Battle of Trois Rivières.

In 1908, the majority of the city was burnt to the ground in a massive fire. Only a few of the buildings remained. This gave the city a chance to re-design itself and the downtown today has a charming feel to it. If you are looking to camp close to here check out Camping Rochelle, north of town.

Spend some time exploring Trois Rivières. If you need bike repairs, head to Laferte Bicycles.

Your destination for the evening is Camping Panoramique on the west edge of Portneuf, population 3 086. This town lays at the convergence of the Portneuf and St. Lawrence Rivers.

Kilometre Log

0.0 Leave Camping et Marina Louiseville biking northeast on Rang Du Lac-Saint-Pierre E.
0.7 Rang du Lac-Saint-Pierre dead-ends into Rang du Lac-Saint-Pierre O. Turn right here.
1.2 Pass under HWY 40 / Autoroute de la Rive-Nord. Rang du Lac-Saint-Pierre O Changes to 2E Avenue.
4.3 Turn right off of 2E Avenue onto HWY 138 / Boulevard Saint-Laurent E.
13.6 Enter Yamachiche on HWY 138 / Rue Sainte-Anne.
22.4 HWY 138 crosses HWY 40.
24.3 Enter Pointe-du-Lac on HWY 138 / Rue Notre Dame O / HWY 138.
35.0 Cross HWY 55 and enter Trois Rivières . Rue Notre Dame O becomes Boulevard Gene-H-Kruger / HWY 138.
37.9 Traffic circle. Turn right and cycle 2 blocks east on Boulevard de la Commune towards Rue Notre Dame Centre.
38.1 Boulevard De la Commune dead-ends into Rue Notre Dame Centre.
39.6 Turn left off of Rue Notre Dame Centre / HWY 138 onto Rue Laviolette / HWY 138.
40.7 Turn right off of HWY 138 / Rue Laviolette onto Boulevard du Saint-Maurice.
41.6 Cross over Rivière Saint-Maurice.
42.5 After crossing Rivière Saint-Maurice, Boulevard du Sainte Maurice / HWY 138 becomes Rue Fusey / HWY 138.
43.4 Turn right off of Rue Fusey / HWY 138 onto Rue Saint-Laurent / HWY 138.
44.3 Turn left off of Rue Saint-Laurent / HWY 138 onto Boulevard Sainte-Madeleine.
46.6 Sainte Marthe-du-Cap. Boulevard Sainte-Madeline / HWY 138 becomes Rue Notre Dame E / HWY 138 here.
57.7 Camping Royal.
60.3 Champlain.
70.9 Enter Batiscan on HWY 138.
73.2 Cross over Rivière Batiscan. Don't be afraid to walk your bike over this flat-inducing bridge.

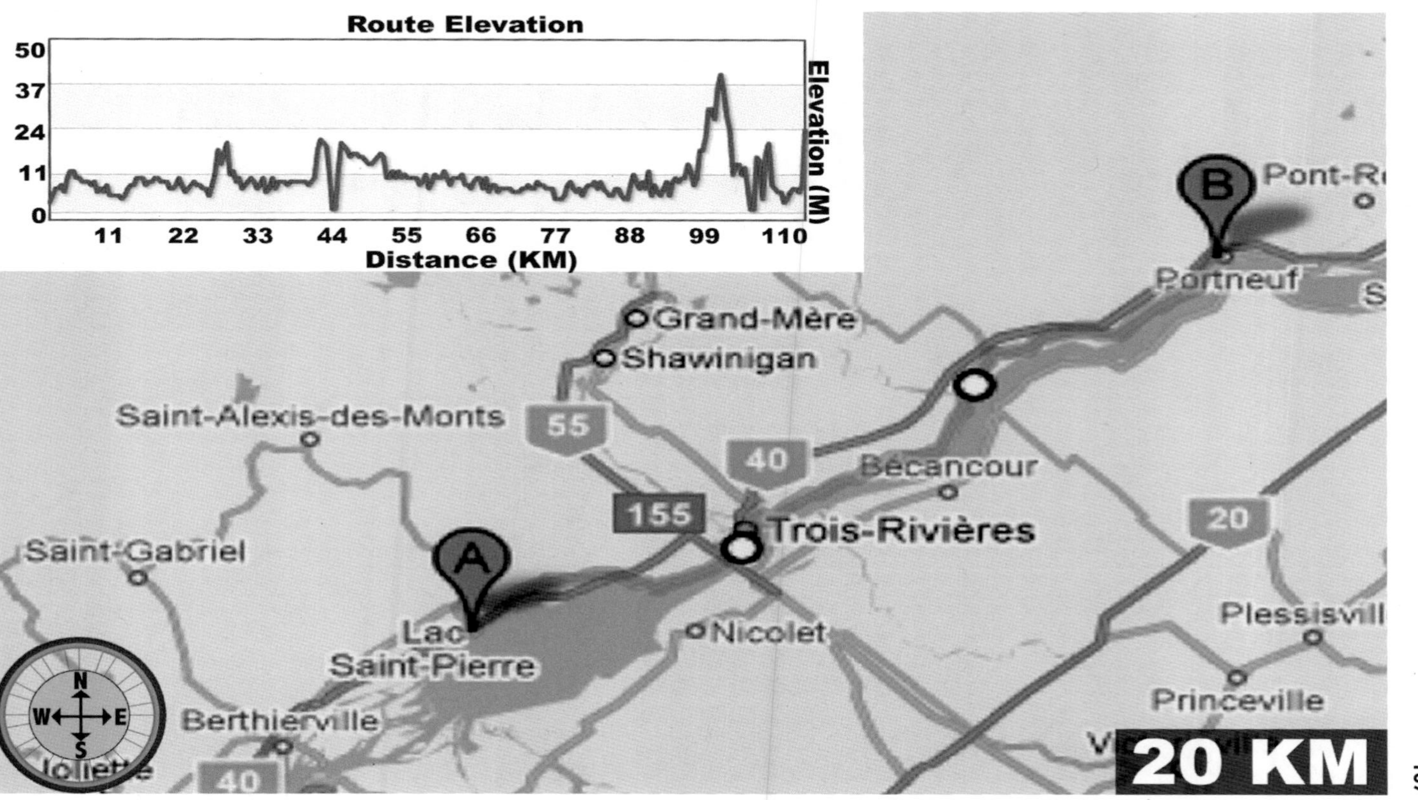
Route Elevation
Elevation (M)
50
37
24
11
0
11
22
33
44
55
66
77
88
99
110
Distance (KM)
B
Portneuf
Grand-Mère
Shawinigan
Saint-Alexis-des-Monts
55
40
Bécancour
155
Trois-Rivières
20
Saint-Gabriel
A
Lac
Saint-Pierre
Nicolet
Plessisvill
Princeville
N
W
E
S
Berthierville
40
20 KM

79.4 Cross over the Sainte-Anne River and view Sainte-Anne-de-la-Pérade's stunning church.
95.2 Enter Grondines on HWY 138.
104.8 Enter Deschambault on HWY 138.
109.6 On the west side of Portneuf turn left on Route Du Côteau des Roches.
110.1 Turn left into Camping Panoramique

Camping Panoramique to Québec City's Auberge Internationale de Québec: (62.4 K)

Enjoy a short ride into Québec City, which is located at a narrowing of the St. Lawrence River. In Algonquin, Kebec means "where the river narrows." The city was founded by Samuel de Champlain in 1608. The ramparts that surround old Québec are the only remaining fortified city walls north of Mexico. This fortified area is a UNESCO World Heritage Site.

Close to downtown are the Plains of Abraham, a historic site within Battlefields Park. Originally, it was grazing land but became famous as the site of the Battle of the Plains of Abraham on September 13, 1759. Under a veil of darkness, British soldiers, under the command of General Wolfe, climbed the steep cliff towards the plains, where they surprised and defeated the French.

General Wolfe, as well as French commander Marquis de Montcalm, died in the battle that left control of Québec City to the British. This allowed the Brits to take control of Canada the following year which distinctively shaped the way Canada grew as a country.

Québec City is the capital of Québec. Check out the Parliament Building, which is most spectacular when lit up in the evening.

Québec City's skyline is dominated by the Château Frontenac, which was built for the Canadian Pacific Railway company. It opened in 1893, and is a sister hotel to Banff Springs and Château Lake Louise. Québec City is a charming place to visit and is one of my top three spots to visit in the country. The city's beauty will rival any others but the most impressive part to me was how relaxed and mellow the people were. It is a world-class tourist destination with a small town feel.

Québec City is known internationally for its Summer Festival or Festival d'été. This annual festival began in 1968. It presents hundreds of musical shows in various venues over 11 days at the beginning of July.

There are two campgrounds within ten kilometres of downtown Québec City, but I recommend the hostel Auberge Internationale de Québec. It is located in the heart of Old Québec, allowing you to spend more time exploring this beautiful city without commuting back and forth to a campsite. The hostel has a courtyard where you can lock up your bikes as well as an industrial kitchen that is as nice as any hostel on the globe. Make sure to call ahead to reserve a room as the hostel can fill up quickly especially on weekends and during July and August. If there is no vacancy try Planete Backpackers.

Kilometre Log

0.0 Leave Portneuf heading southeast on Route Du Côteau des Roches towards HWY 138 / 2E Avenue.
0.6 Turn left onto 2E Avenue / HWY 138.
12.1 Enter the industrial town Donnacona, population 5 564.
14.3 Cross the Jacques-Cartier River.
24.1 Intersection of HWY 138 & HWY 365.
26.0 Neuville.
36.9 Saint-Augustin-de-Desmaures.
41.5 Cross HWY 40 on HWY 138.
44.7 Pass the Québec City Airport on HWY 138 / Boulevard Wilfred-Hamel.
51.2 Pass under Autoroute Henri IV on HWY 138 / Boulevard Wilfred-Hamel.
52.2 Bike past Parc Duberger-Les Saules on HWY 138 / Boulevard Wilfrid-Hamel.
54.1 Cross Autoroute Robert-Bourassa.
55.7 Just before St. Charles River turn right onto Avenue Saint-Sacrement.
57.0 Avenue St. Sacrement turns into Avenue Holland.
58.3 Turn left off of Avenue Holland onto Rue Grande Allée O / HWY 175.
61.1 Rue Grande Allée O / HWY 175 becomes Rue Grande Allée E as you bike past Parque des Champs de Bataille.

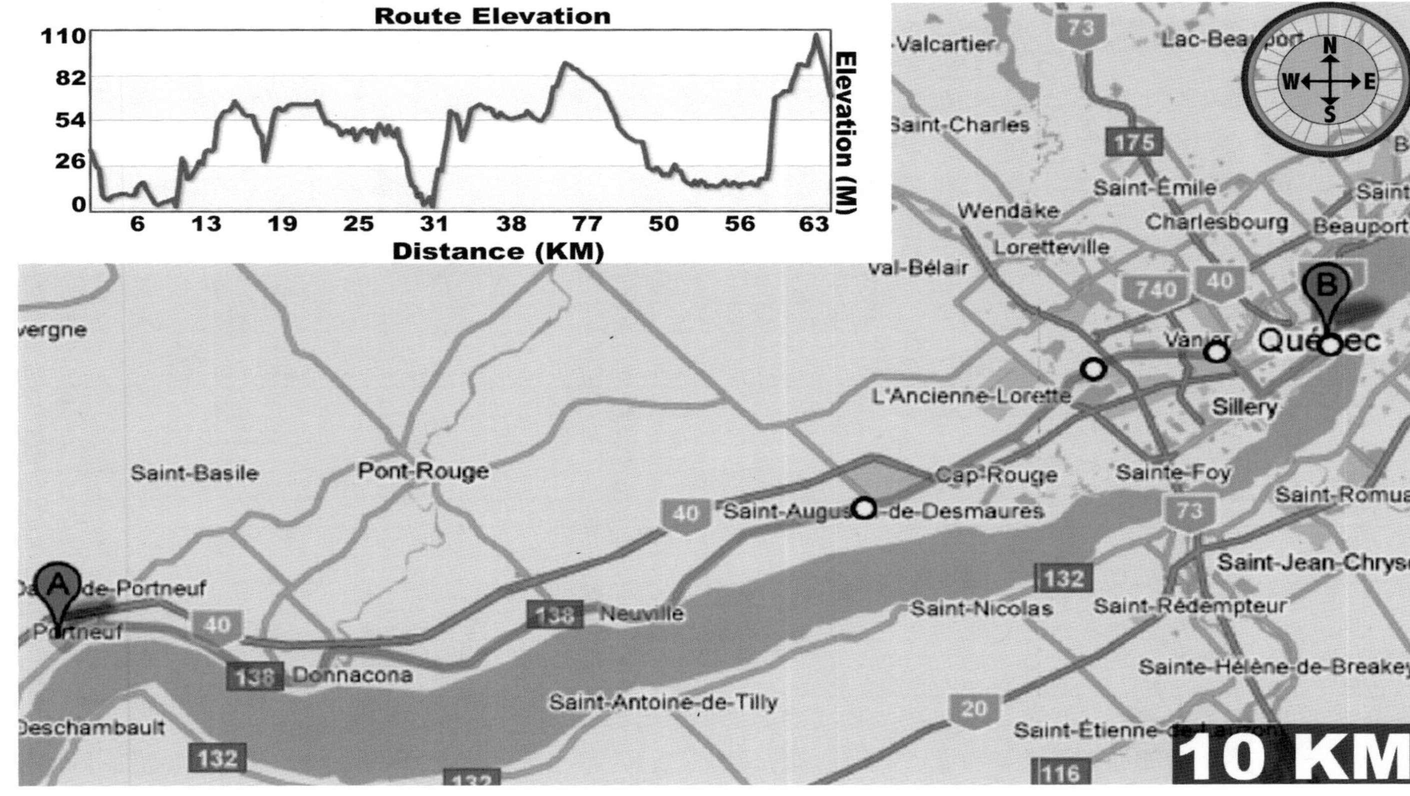

Route Elevation
110
82
54
26
0
6
13
19
25
31
38
77
50
56
63
Distance (KM)
Elevation (M)
Valcartier
Lac-Beauport
Saint-Charles
Saint-Émile
Wendake
Charlesbourg
Beauport
Loretteville
Val-Bélair
Vanier
L'Ancienne-Lorette
Sillery
Saint-Basile
Pont-Rouge
Cap-Rouge
Sainte-Foy
Saint-Augus
-de-Desmaures
de-Portneuf
Neuville
Saint-Nicolas
Saint-Rédempteur
Donnacona
Saint-Antoine-de-Tilly
Sainte-Hélène-de-Breakey
Deschambault
A
B
N
S
E
W
73
175
740
40
138
132
20
116
10 KM

61.8 Rue Grande Allée E becomes Rue St-Louis here. Continue straight on Rue St.-Louis.

62.1 Turn left on Rue Ste.-Ursule.

62.4 At the corner of Rue Ste.-Ursule and Rue Dauphine is your destination, Auberge Internationale de Québec.

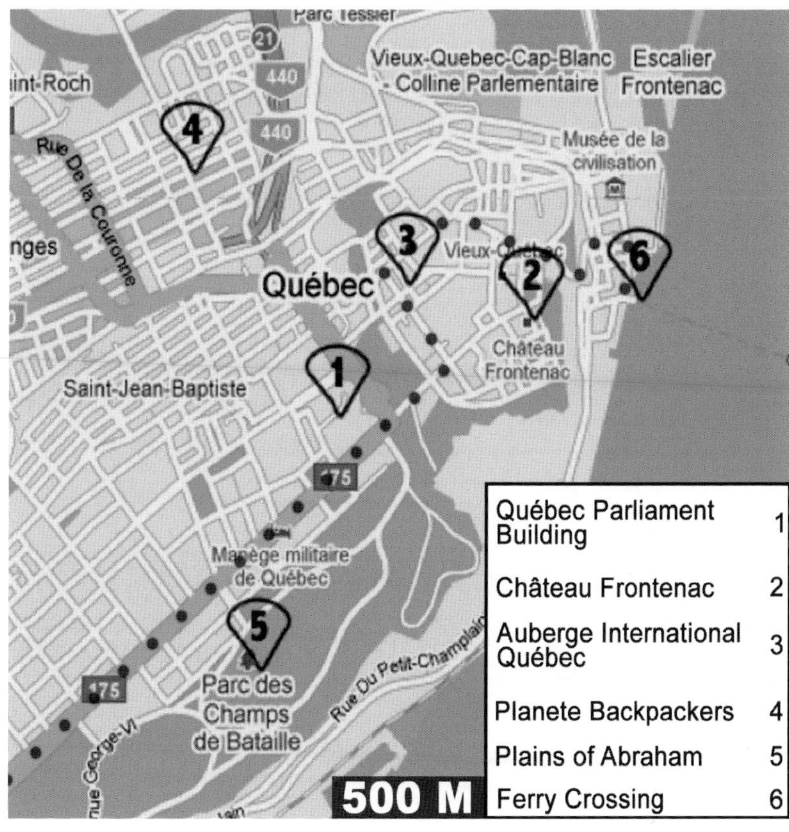

Auberge Internationale de Québec to Camping Municipal du Rocher Panet: (80.6 K)

Leave Québec City and ferry across the St. Lawrence into the town of Levis. Have your camera ready as the ferry ride provides a great opportunity for photos.

From the ferry dock you will bike along the St. Lawrence before meeting up with HWY 138 on the east side of Levis. The ride along 132 to L'Islet will take you through small picturesque towns that all have spectacular churches and friendly people. You will bike on HWY 132 until reaching the New Brunswick border in Miramichi.

Montmagny, population 11 654, is a good place to get groceries before you arrive at the campground in L'Islet. The town is Canada's Snow Goose Capital and home to the International Accordion Festival every September. If you need bike work done here, check out Intersport.

Across from L'Islet is L'Isle Aux Grues (goose island). The main industry on the island is dairy farming. The people of the island produce some of the finest cheese in the world including their most famous brand, "Riopelle de l'Isle." This type of cheese is named after Jean-Paul Riopelle, a renowned Québecois artist and painter.

Your destination for the evening is Camping Municipal Du Rocher Panet in L'Islet. The municipal campground is a nice spot to spend the evening. The campground has internet as well as laundry facilities. Next door to the campground is Tibo Bicyk, a high-quality bike shop with knowledgeable staff.

Kilometre Log

0.0 From Auberge Internationale de Québec head northwest on Rue Ste-Ursule.

0.1 Turn right on Rue St-Jean.

0.4 Rue St-Jean ends. Take a slight right on Côte de la Fabrique.

0.6 Turn right onto Rue des Jardins.

0.65 Turn left onto Rue de Buade.

0.8 Turn left onto Rue Port-Dauphin.

0.85 Turn right onto Côte de la Montagne.

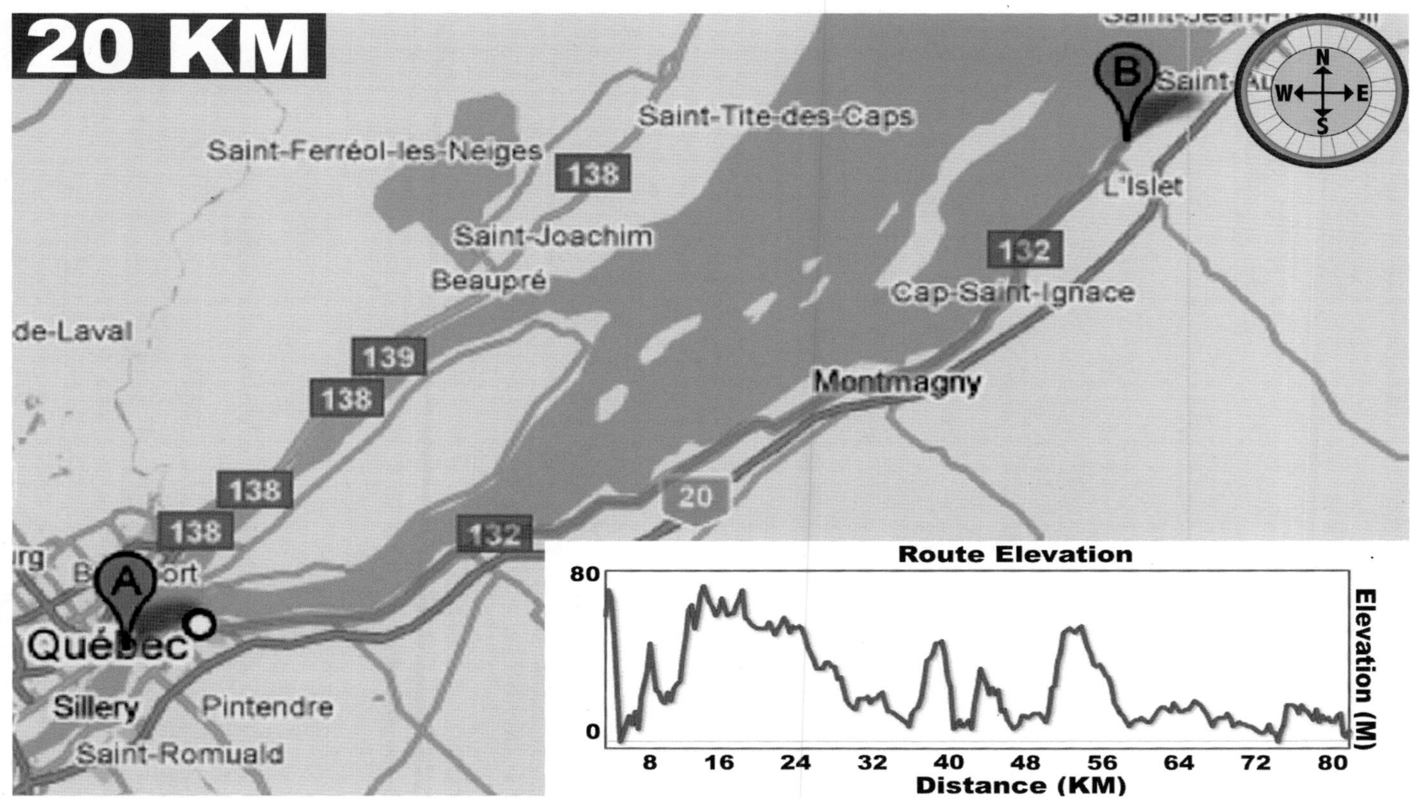

20 KM
N
W
E
S
Saint-Tite-des-Caps
Saint-Ferréol-les-Neiges
138
Saint-Joachim
Beaupré
L'Islet
132
Cap-Saint-Ignace
de-Laval
139
138
Montmagny
138
138
20
132
Québec
Sillery
Pintendre
Saint-Romuald
Route Elevation
Elevation (M)
80
0
8
16
24
32
40
48
56
64
72
80
Distance (KM)

1.2 Stay on Côte de la Montagne as it twists and turns before it dead-ends into Rue Dalhousie. Turn right here.
1.4 Québec-Levis Ferry.
1.6 Bike away from the ferry and take an immediate left on Rue Saint-Laurent.
3.0 Rue Saint-Laurent takes a slight right turn and becomes Rue Saint-Joseph. Remain on Saint-Joseph until intersecting with HWY 132.
3.5 Rue Saint-Joseph takes a slight left turn and remains Rue Saint-Joseph.
8.8 Stay left as Rue Saint-Joseph merges with HWY 132 / Boulevard de la Rive-Sud.
15.3 Enter Beaumont. On Route Du Fleuve / HWY 132.
18.6 Camping Carol.
26.1 Saint-Michel-de-Bellechasse.
33.7 Saint Vallier.
42.0 Berthier sur-Mer.
57.7 Montmagny.
66.9 Cap-Saint-Ignace.
79.0 Intersection of HWY 132 / Chemin des Pionniers O & HWY 285.
80.0 Maritime Museum du Québec.
80.5 Turn left off of HWY 132 / Chemin des Pionniers E onto Route Du Quai.
80.6 Camping Municipal Du Rocher Panet.

Camping Municipal du Rocher Panet to Rivière du Loup's Camping du Quai: (110.3 K)

From L'Islet, continue cycling east on the banks of the St. Lawrence River. Agriculture will become more prominent as the ground becomes more fertile. Apples and corn are the crops of choice for farmers in this area.

First bike through Saint-Jean-Port-Joli, population 3 372, which is home to many artisans that produce woodcarvings and sculptures.

Next you will cycle through La Pocatière, population 4 575, an agricultural town that is home to Musée François-Pilote, which highlights the Québecois agriculture history. The town is also home to Collège de Sainte-Anne-de-la-Pocatière.

The Appalachian mountains start to make themselves present on the north shore of the river at this point. As you cycle further east you can expect them to become more prominent on the south side as well. They will not make a considerable impact on your cycling as the road hugs the river and remains quite flat. Late in the afternoon, the setting sun silhouettes the north-shore mountains, giving them an ominous monocolour appearance.

The St. Lawrence River continues to widen as you bike south and many large islands become visible. The river approaches 20 kilometres in width around Rivière-du-Loup.

Rivière-du-Loup, population 18 586, is named for the nearby river, which translates to "Wolf's River" in English. There is a ferry available in town that crosses the St. Lawrence River to Saint-Simeon on the north shore. Evidence of the culture of Rivière-du-Loup is easily recognizable. Expect to see art blended into parks and buildings all over the city. If you have time, check out the Musée du Bas Saint Laurent, which explains many interesting facts about what goes on both on top of and below the mighty St. Lawrence River. If you need a roof over your head, check out Rivière du Loup International Hostel. For bike repairs, head to Hobby Cycle.

Your destination for the evening is Camping du Quai. It is located adjacent to the ferry so follow the traversière signs to locate the campground. The campground has laundry facilities and wireless internet access.

Kilometre Log

0.0 Leave Camping Municipal du Rocher Panet heading southeast towards HWY 132 / Chemin Des Pionniers on Route Du Quai.

0.1 Turn left on HWY 132 / Chemin Des Pionniers E.

5.2 Chemin Des Pionniers E / HWY 132 becomes Avenue De Gaspé O / HWY 132 here.

12.4 Enter Saint-Jean-Port-Joli on HWY 132 / Avenue De Gaspé O.

19.2 HWY 132 / Avenue De Gaspé E becomes Route De la Seigneurie / HWY 132.

29.7 Cross HWY 20.

38.5 La Pocatière.

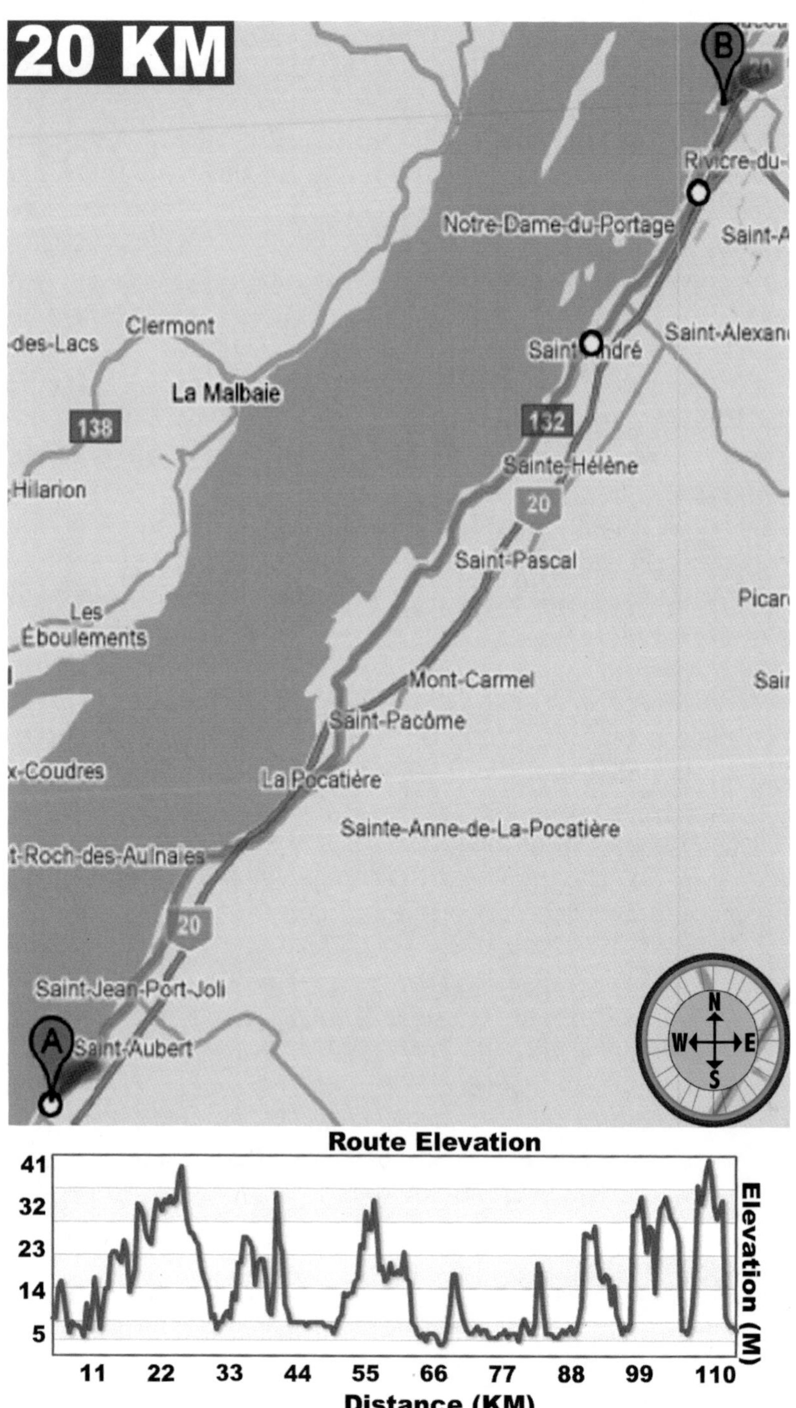

20 KM
B
A
Rivicre-du-
Notre-Dame-du-Portage
Saint-A
Clermont
-des-Lacs
Saint-André
Saint-Alexan
La Malbaie
138
132
Sainte-Hélène
Hilarion
20
Saint-Pascal
Picar
Les
Éboulements
Mont-Carmel
Sai
Saint-Pacôme
x-Coudres
La Pocatière
Sainte-Anne-de-La-Pocatière
t-Roch-des-Aulnaies
20
Saint-Jean-Port-Joli
Saint-Aubert
N
W
E
S
Route Elevation
41
32
23
14
5
11
22
33
44
55
66
77
88
99
110
Distance (KM)
Elevation (M)

43.8 Cross over HWY 20 / Autoroute Jean-Lesage.
46.4 Cross over Rivière Ouelle. Turn left after crossing the river for Camping Rivière Ouelle.
67.4 Kamouraska.
103.9 Cross HWY 20 staying left to enter Rivière du Loup on HWY 132 / Rue Fraser.
107.6 Turn left off Rue Fraser HWY 132 onto Côte Saint Jacques / HWY 132.
108.1 Cross over Rivière du Loup. HWY 132 / Côte Saint-Jacques becomes HWY 132 / Boulevard Cartier here and turns to the left. Remain on HWY 132 / Boulevard Cartier.
109.1 Cross HWY 20 on HWY 132 / Boulevard Cartier.
109.6 After crossing a small stream take an immediate left on Rue De l'Ancrage.
110.3 Turn right to enter Camping du Quai.

Camping du Quai to Rimouski's Camping de L'Anse: (99.3 K)

After leaving Rivière du Loup you will bike through the small town of L'Isle-Verte. The town is named after the nearby Ile Verte which is accessible by ferry from L'Isle-Verte. Tourists visit the area to purchase fish from local fisherman and to view Québec's oldest lighthouse, which was built in 1809.

The next town that you will visit is Trois-Pistoles, population 3 500. There is a ferry in town that crosses the St. Lawrence to the north shore. The town of Trois-Pistoles claims to be the most francophone city in the province. As such, it is home to Western University's Annual French Immersion Program. The town is named after a silver goblet that was lost in the river in the 17th century that had a value of three pistoles (coins). Camping is available at Camping Municipal de Trois-Pistoles.

Saint-Fabien is located on the west edge of Parque du Bic, it has a few stores and Camping Municipal de Saint-Fabien.

Parque du Bic preserves a narrow strip of land from Saint-Fabien to Bic. Part of the Appalachian region, the park boasts distinctive limestone reefs and capes that cut into the water. The park is home to small herds of grey seals and harbour seals as well as a diverse brood of marine birds. There are three campgrounds in the area if you want to spend a day exploring. The road into the park is gravel and down a steep road. Ride with caution.

Your destination for the evening is Camping de L'Anse, which is located on the right side of the highway as you enter Rimouski.

Rimouski, population 42 240, is the commercial centre for the region. Every year Rimouski is home to the Festi Jazz International de Rimouski, which attracts Jazz aficionados from across the globe. Lepage Park, in downtown Rimouski, is named after Sir Rene Lepage, who founded the city in 1696. The campground offers laundry and internet access. If you need supplies for the evening, the nearest grocery store is five kilometres past the campground into town. Drop your gear off at the campground and enjoy a rare unweighted ride into town.

Kilometre Log

0.0 Leave Camping du Quai heading east on Rue De l'Ancrage.
0.8 Rue De l'Ancrage dead-ends into HWY 132 / Boulevard Cartier. Turn left.
1.3 Camping du Pont. Turn slightly right to gain Route De L'Anse-au-Persil / HWY 132.
8.8 Cacouna.
15.4 HWY 20 merges into HWY 132 here.
25.7 L'Isle-Verte.
44.2 Trois-Pistoles.
58.1 Saint-Simon.
73.6 Saint-Fabien.
76.3 West boundary of Parc du Bic.
80.4 Exit into Parc du Bic.
85.4 Exit into Parc du Bic.
88.8 East boundary of Parc du Bic.
89.6 Le Bic.
91.1 HWY 132 and HWY 20 diverge here. Stay left to remain on HWY 132.
99.3 Turn right off of HWY 132 / Boulevard Saint-Germain into Camping De l'Anse.

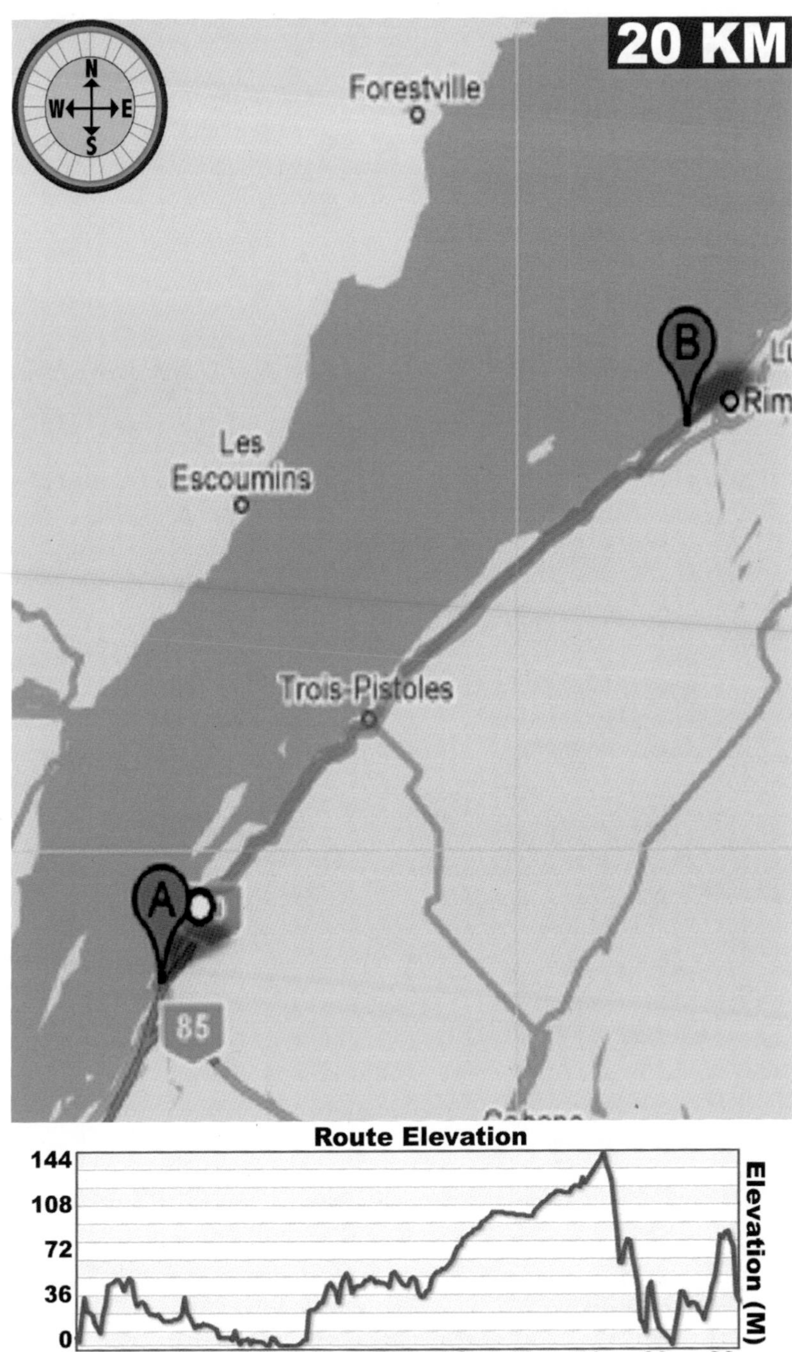

20 KM
N
W
E
S
Forestville
B
Rim
Les Escoumins
Trois-Pistoles
A
85
Route Elevation
144
108
72
36
0
10
20
30
40
49
59
69
79
89
99
Distance (KM)
Elevation (M)

Camping de L'Anse to Camping Val-Brillant's Camping Bois et Berges: (95.6 K)

Leave Rimouski on HWY 132. If you want to visit its downtown, it is parallel to HWY 132 near the city's large port.

Make sure to fill up on poutine as you are only two days away from the Québec / New Brunswick border. Today you will say goodbye to the St. Lawrence River and start heading south towards New Brunswick.

At Sainte-Flavée, HWY 132 splits to form a circle around the Gaspé Peninsula. Take a right turn here and expect a challenging day of cycling as you climb inland from the St. Lawrence River Valley. Enjoy a quiet highway towards your destination of Val-Brillant on Lake Matapedia. Pick up supplies for the evening in Sayabec and coast downhill into the Matapedia Valley.

Your destination for the evening is Camping Bois et Berges on the shore of Lake Matapedia in the Matapedia Valley.

Kilometre Log

0.0 Leave Camping L'Anse heading west on HWY 132 / Boulevard Saint-Germain.

5.6 Cross over the Rimouski River on HWY 132 / Boulevard Saint-Germain.

5.7 Cross the Rimouski River and HWY 132 / Boulevard Saint-Germain becomes HWY 132 / Boulevard René-Lepage E.

36.8 Enter Sainte-Flavie. Turn right onto HWY 132 / Route Jacques-Cartier.

40.7 Enter Mont-Joli, population 6 568, on Boulevard Gaboury / HWY 132.

47.6 Intersection of HWY 132 & HWY 234.

71.4 Intersection of HWY 132 & HWY 297 and Saint-Moise. Stay right on HWY 132.

83.8 Sayabec.

94.1 Enter Val-Brillant on HWY 132.

95.2 Turn left on Rue Saint-Louis.

95.5 Rue Saint-Louis intersects with Rue Saint-Pierre O. Turn right.

95.52 Turn left on Rue Saint-Louis.

95.55 Enter Camping Bois et Berges.

Québec Parliament Building

Rural Québec

Québec City

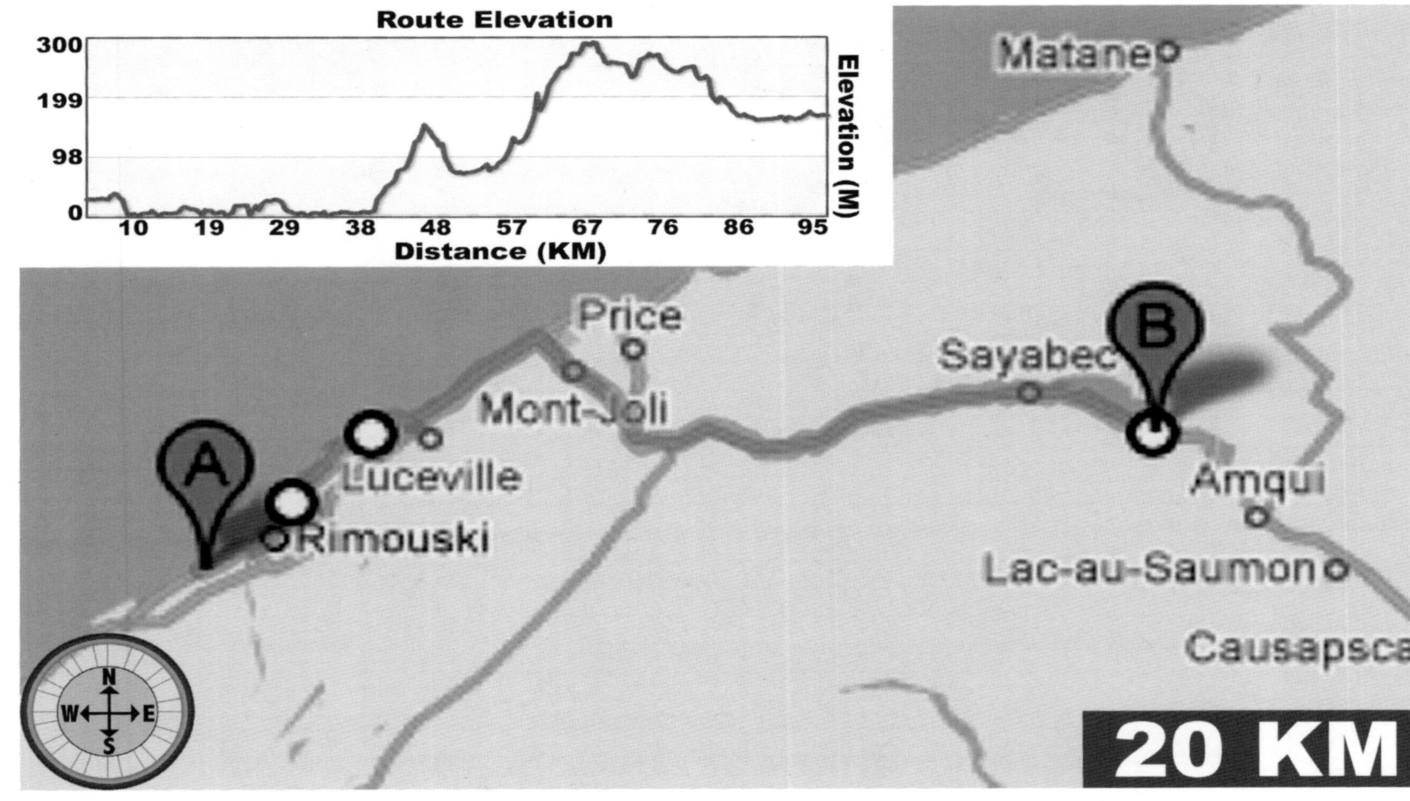
Route Elevation
300
199
98
0
Elevation (M)
10
19
29
38
48
57
67
76
86
95
Distance (KM)
Matane
Price
Mont-Joli
Luceville
Rimouski
Sayabec
Amqui
Lac-au-Saumon
Causapsca
A
B
N
W
E
S
20 KM

Camping Bois et Berges to Atholville's Sugarloaf Provincial Park: (111.0 K)

Leave Bois et Berges Campground on the shore of Lac-Matapedia, which feeds the Matapedia River and borders HWY 132 until it meets Restigouche River at the Québec / New Brunswick border. A dam in the river at Causapscal has created Lac-au-Saumon. Below the dam the Causapscal River joins the Matapedia River at a popular fishing spot called Junction Pool. Matapedia means, "meeting of the waters" in Mi'Kmaq. The Matapedia River is calm, clean and shallow. Enjoy your time biking down the Matapedia River Valley; it is picturesque and pleasurable.

Amqui, population 6 261, was the first town in Québec to ban single use plastic bags. It is a good place to get supplies for your day. Amqui in Mi'Kmaq means "a place where we have fun" or "where you play." Camping is available on the west side of town at Camping d'Amqui.

Causapscal, population 2 556, has a campground called Camping Causpascal. The town is located at the confluence of Matapedia River and Causapscal River.

Bike through Routhierville and check out the covered bridge that crosses over the Matapedia River. Covered bridges were traditionally built in geographic areas that had plentiful wood resources. As sun and weather are the biggest foes to wooden bridge integrity, closing in a bridge with a roof can greatly increase the structure's longevity. This is the only covered bridge that you will have a chance to see on the tour without a detour.

Matapedia lays at the confluence of the Matapedia and Restigouche Rivers. There is one small, well-equipped store in this town that stays open late. From the grocery store you can see the skateboard park. Behind it is a good spot to have a picnic and say goodbye to the Matapedia River.

Leave Matapedia heading east. Just outside of town you will cross the Restigouche River and enter into New Brunswick. As you cross into New Brunswick turn your clocks ahead one hour.

The Restigouche River is a world-class salmon river. For over 100 years, some of the richest and most powerful people in the world have come to this river valley to fish for Atlantic Salmon. The New Brunswick Department of Natural Resources sections up the river and leases stretches of the river to the highest bidder. It is rumoured that it can cost hundreds of thousands of dollars per year to obtain some of the best fishing spots. The general public is permitted to have a vessel on the river, but they are not permitted to drop anchor or disturb the water.

Just before Campbellton you'll find the town of Atholville, home of Sugarloaf Provincial Park and Campground. This park is home to a popular ski hill in the winter, which turns into Atlantic Canada's only lift accessible mountain bike park in the summer. Sugarloaf Mountain rises to 305 metres above sea level. Mountain bike rentals and groceries are available in Atholville.

Kilometre Log

0.0 Leave Camping Bois et Berges on Rue Saint-Louis and take an immediate left on Rue Saint-Pierre O.
1.2 Rue Saint-Pierre E merges with HWY 132.
13.4 Amqui.
23.2 Lac-au-Saumon.
34.2 Causapscal.
45.2 Sainte-Florence.
58.6 Routhierville.
90.1 Matapedia.
90.5 HWY 132 curves 90° to the left after Matapedia. Remain on HWY 132.
91.8 Turn right to cross the Matapedia River.
92.4 Welcome to New Brunswick. Turn left on HWY 11.
107.0 Enter Atholville on Notre Dame Street / HWY 134.
109.1 Turn right off of Notre Dame Street onto HWY 270.
110.3 Turn left onto Chemin Val d'Amour.
111.0 Sugarloaf Provincial Park Campground.

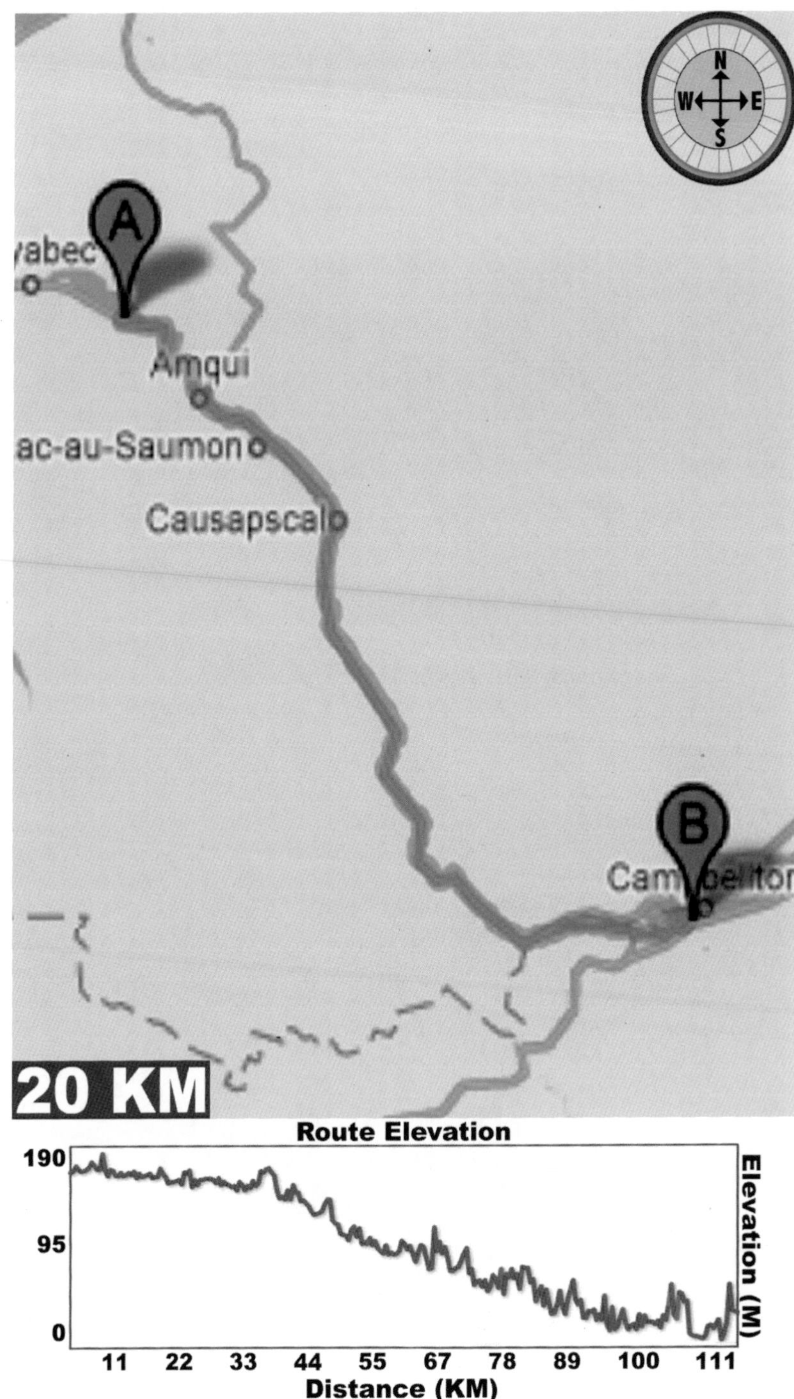
N
W
E
S
A
Amqui
Causapscal
B
20 KM
Route Elevation
190
95
0
11
22
33
44
55
67
78
89
100
111
Distance (KM)
Elevation (M)

Province:	New Brunswick
Population:	729 927
Area:	71 450 km^2
Industries:	Forestry, mining, farming, fishing.
Highlights:	Parlee Beach, the Restigouche River.

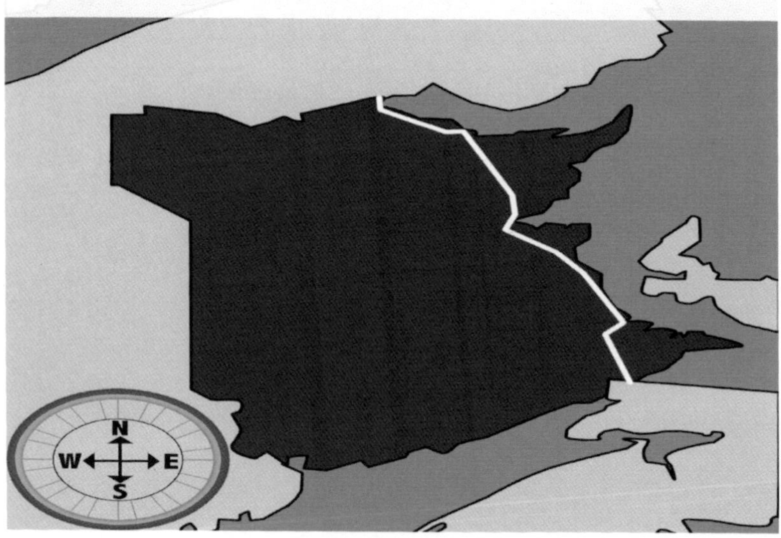

Sugarloaf Provincial Park to Camping Malybel: (108.6 K)

Campbellton, population 7 384, is located on the south shore of the Restigouche River. A high percentage of the people from Campbellton and much of New Brunswick speak both French and English. Check out Restigouche Sam, an 8.5 metre stainless steel salmon. Also, look for Hostelling International–Campbellton situated inside a lighthouse. Velo Xtreme is a good bike shop in Campbellton.

During the Seven Years War, the Resitgouche River was the site of the last naval battle between France and England for the possession of North America. The Battle of Restigouche ended on July 8, 1760 when France was defeated. Because French troops relied almost solely on supplies from the Mother Country, this loss was a devastating blow. It crippled their supply chain from Europe.

This area of New Brunswick is sparsely populated. Make sure that you have adequate supplies to last you as Eel River is the last spot to stock up on provisions before Belledune.

Historians maintain that settlers arrived in the area and upon observing the sand ridges in the area remarked, “Belle Dune,” which translates to “pretty dune” or Belledune. Belledune has a deep-water port serving the area. Groceries are available in town.

Expect to see many displays of Acadian culture in this area. Acadian refers to French descendants residing in Atlantic Canada.

Your destination for the evening is Parc Malybel in Beresford. This popular park offers a heated pool with waterslide as well as free internet. Beresford, population 4 624, has a pleasant beach that tourists flock to all summer long, as well as a grocery store.

Kilometre Log

0.0 Leave Sugarloaf Provincial Park biking east on Chemin Val d’Amour.

1.3 Turn left onto Sugarloaf Street.

1.8 Turn right on HWY 134 / Roseberry Street.

2.3 Turn left onto Subway Street / HWY 134. Welcome to Campbellton.

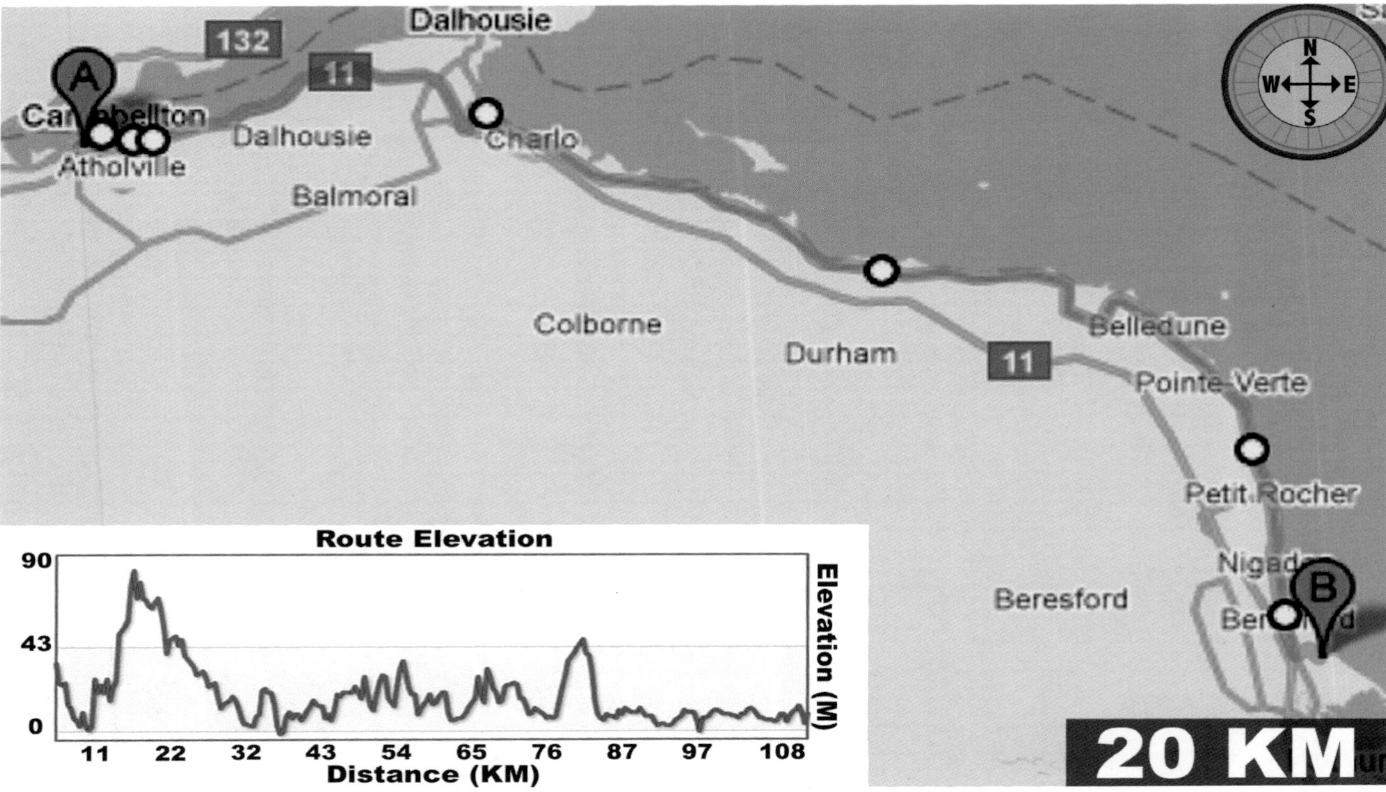
Dalhousie
132
11
A
Atholville
Dalhousie
Balmoral
Charlo
W
N
S
E
Colborne
Durham
11
Belledune
Pointe-Verte
Petit-Rocher
Beresford
B
20 KM
Route Elevation
90
43
0
11
22
32
43
54
65
76
87
97
108
Distance (KM)
Elevation (M)

2.4 Turn right onto Water Street / HWY 134.
3.3 Turn right off of Water Street / HWY 134 onto Ramsey Street / HWY 134.
4.6 Turn right on Salmon Boulevard to access HWY 11.
5.6 Cross HWY 11 on Salmon Boulevard. Turn left onto HWY 11 East.
9.1 Richardsville.
15.0 Intersection of HWY 11 & HWY 280.
27.2 Intersection of HWY 11 & HWY 275.
28.0 Cross over Eel River.
31.0 Eel River Cove. Turn right here and circle 270° clockwise to gain Cove Road / HWY 280.
33.2 Intersection of HWY 134 & Cove Road / HWY 280. Turn right here onto Chaleur Street / HWY 134.
35.7 Heron's Nest Campground.
36.7 Charlo.
40.7 Cross over Charlo River.
49.9 Benjamin River.
54.9 Black Point. Camping by the Bay.
57.9 Nash Creek.
81.8 Belledune.
95.4 Petit Rocher. Camping Murraywood.
104.8 Enter Beresford on HWY 134 / Principale Street.
107.1 Turn left onto Landry Street off of HWY 134 / Principale Street.
108.1 Landry street takes a right turn. Turn right.
108.6 Camping Malybel.

Camping Malybel to All Day All Night Camping: (98.9 K)

Bathurst is located on an estuary at the mouth of the Nepisguit River in Chaleur Bay which translates into "the Bay of Warmth." Check out the Bathurst War Museum if you have spare time. Bathurst is known for its phantom ship that appears in the Chaleur Bay. Legend has it that a ship burned in the waters of the bay and during certain weather and light conditions you can see the ship re-appear. A drawing of the burning ship is on Bathurst's welcome sign. If you need bike work done head to Nepisiguit River Company.

Leave Bathurst and head south on HWY 8 towards Miramichi. This well paved road cuts through desolate woodlands before depositing you at the north shore of the Miramichi River.

Cross the Miramichi River on the Centennial Bridge, and head into Miramichi, population 18 129. The highlight of Miramichi is its picturesque waterfront. This area's economy is focused on forestry, mining, fishing and tourism. If you need bike work done head to Incline Sports. No camping is available in Miramichi.

Purchase supplies in Miramichi before heading to All Day All Night Campground in Black River.

Kilometre Log

0.0 Leave Beresford's Camping Mayabel heading northwest to return to Landry Street.
0.6 Turn left on Landry Street.
1.7 Turn left off of Landry Street onto HWY 134 / Rue Principale.
5.5 Cross the Nepisguit River and enter Bathurst on HWY 134 / St. Peter Avenue.
8.3 Cross over Chaleur Bay.
9.2 HWY 134 / St. Peter Avenue becomes HWY 134 / Douglas Avenue.
9.7 Turn left onto Main Street / HWY 134.
10.2 Turn right on Murray Avenue / HWY 134.
10.8 Murray Avenue / HWY 134 turns left and becomes Bridge Street / HWY 134. Turn left.
11.7 Cross over the Nepisiguit River. After crossing the river immediately turn right onto HWY 134 / Miramichi Avenue.
13.7 Intersection of HWY 134 / HWY 11. Remain on HWY 134.
31.0 Allardville. Intersection of HWY 134 & HWY 160.
45.3 HWY 134 merges with HWY 8 and becomes HWY 8.
57.0 HWY 450 dead-ends into HWY 8.
83.7 Cross the Miramichi River on HWY 8.
84.8 Enter Miramichi on the south shore of the Miramichi River. Keep right at the cloverleaf and circle 270° clockwise to access Church Street and downtown Miramichi.
85.8 Turn right off of Church Street onto University Avenue / HWY 117.

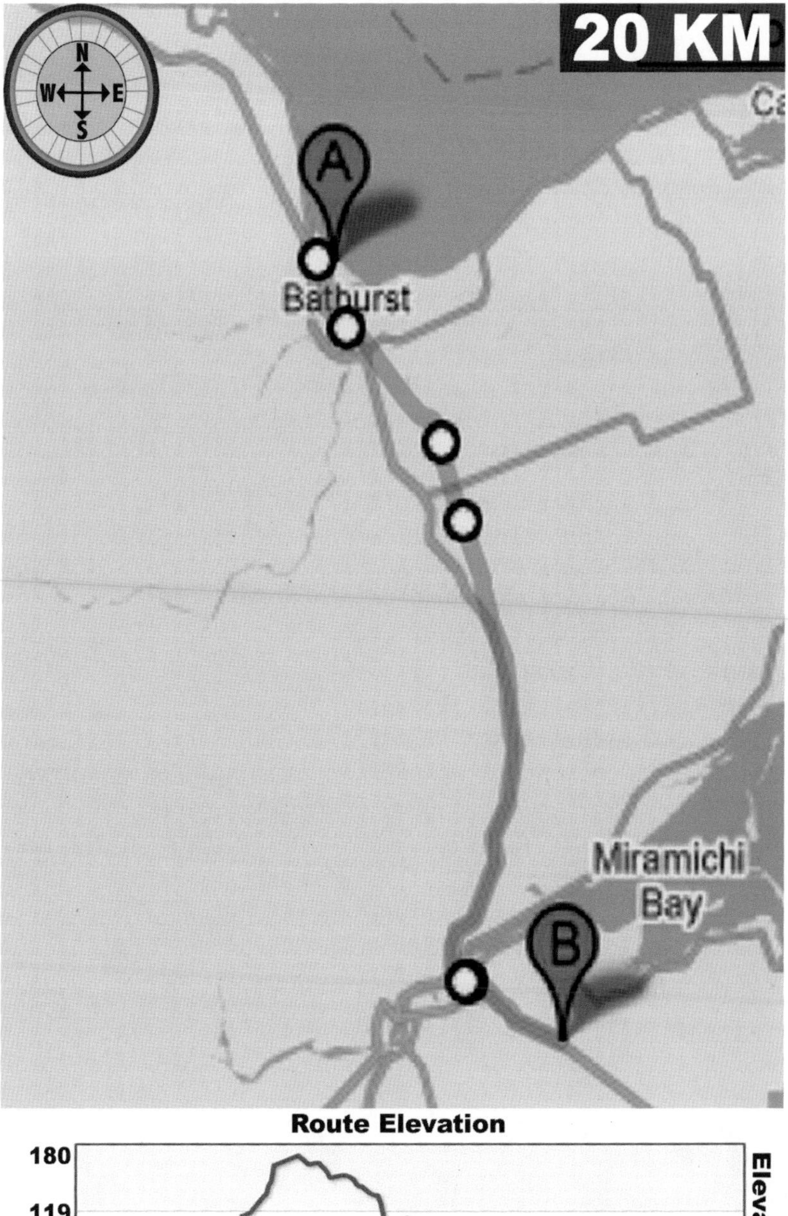

20 KM

Bathurst

Miramichi Bay

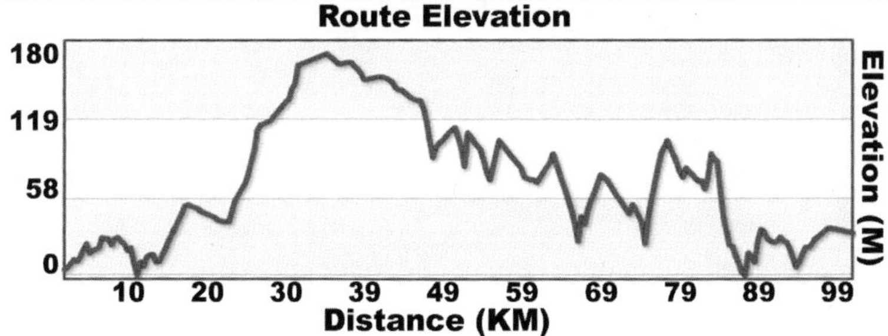

86.9 Exit onto HWY 11 E by passing HWY 11 and turning left.
88.1 HWY 11 curves to the right and becomes HWY 11 / King Street.
88.9 Cycle past Miramichi Airport on HWY 11 / King Street.
98.8 Enter Black River. Turn left on N Black River Bridge Road.
98.9 All Day All Night Campground.

All Day All Night Campground to Parlee Beach Provincial Park: (116.2 K)

Kouchibouguac National Park was established in 1969. The park covers 238 kilometres^2 and preserves the Maritime Plain Natural Region. Visitors come to the park to explore a fascinating mosaic of bogs, sparkling freshwater systems, sheltered lagoons, tall forests and 25^2 kilometres of shifting sand dunes. The park is home to a wide array of animals including cougar, Atlantic white-sided dolphin, moose and humpback whale. Camping at South Kouchibouguac Campground is available.

Don't be surprised to hear the residents speaking Mi'kmaq, English or French while on the streets or in a shop in Richibucto, population 1 290. The cities name means "river of fire" in Mi'kmaq. If you have time ask a local for directions to Cape Lumiere, a beautiful white sand beach with uniquely warm water.

Bouctouche, population 2 383 is located at the mouth of the Bouctouche River on the coast of the Northumberland Strait. This Acadian town is popular with tourists because of its natural beauty which has been ardently preserved by the residents. If you get a chance, visit the Irving Eco Centre, which includes a boardwalk over sand dunes. If you are looking for a campground try Bouctouche Baie Chalets et Camping.

Your destination for the evening is Parlee Beach Provincial Park on the edge of Shediac, population 5 497. Shediac is famous for the lobster that are harvested in the Northumberland Strait and the town has erected the worlds largest lobster sculpture at the west end of town. Grocery stores are available here.

Parlee Beach Provincial Park is a world-class beach destination. Favourable ocean currents give the area the warmest ocean water north of Virginia. The campground has 190 sites as well as a small canteen. Try to schedule some time to relax here at one of North America's finest beaches.

Close to Shediac is Moncton, population 64 128. It is known as the Hub City because of its central location in the Maritime Provinces. The city's most popular tourist attraction is Magnetic Hill, on the northwest side of the city. The hill is an optical illusion; the topography makes you feel like you are going uphill but you are actually going down!

Multiple bike shops are available in Moncton. The closest one to Shediac is Mike's Bike and Ski Shop. There are no bike stores in Shediac.

Kilometre Log

0.0 Leave All Day All Night Campground heading east on HWY 11.

12.6 Intersection of HWY 440 & HWY 11 and St. Margarets. No services.

28.9 Kouchibouguac. A small restaurant is available here.

30.2 Exit left off of HWY 11 onto HWY 134.

33.3 Intersection of HWY 134 & HWY 117. A left turn here will take you to Kouchibouguac National Park and South Kouchibouguac Campground. Remain on HWY 134.

42.5 Cross over St. Charles River.

48.7 Enter Richibucto on HWY 134 / Main Street. Cross Mooney Creek.

51.4 Pass over HWY 11 and exit right taking a 270° clockwise turn to access HWY 11 East.

52.8 Cross Richibucto River.

54.1 Enter Jardineville on HWY 11.

55.9 Turn left to access HWY 134 E, crossing HWY 11.

66.7 Sainte-Anne-de-Kent.

71.2 HWY 134 crosses HWY 11 to bring you into Saint-Pierre-de-Kent.

73.8 Cross HWY 11 on HWY 134.

77.5 Enter Bouctouche on HWY 134 / Rue Évangéline.

77.6 HWY 134 / Rue Évangéline dead-ends into Boulevard Irving. Turn right.

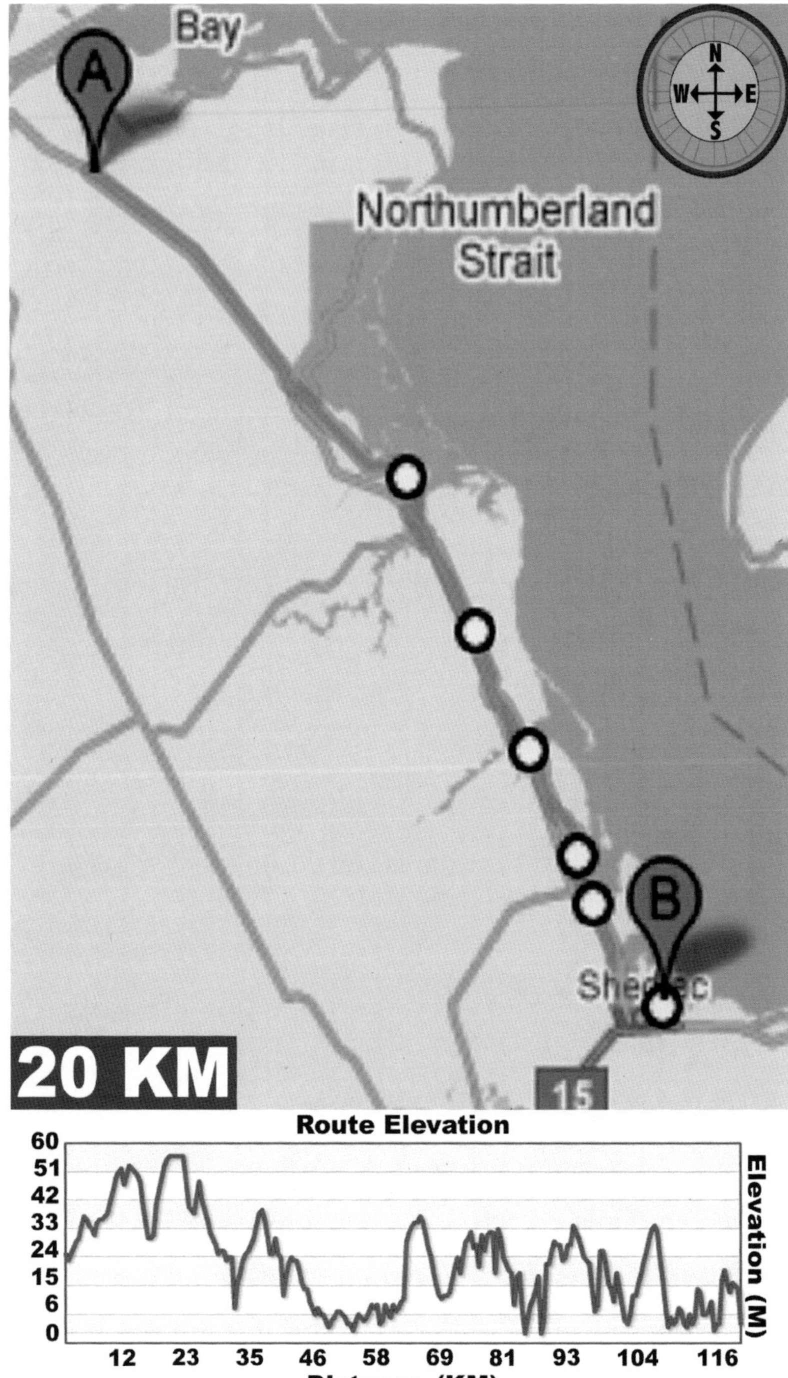

Bay
A
N
W
E
S
Northumberland
Strait
B
20 KM
15
Route Elevation
60
51
42
33
24
15
6
0
Elevation (M)
12
23
35
46
58
69
81
93
104
116
Distance (KM)

77.8 Turn left and cross the Bouctouche River.
80.6 Cross over a body of water and remain on HWY 134 / Rue Acadie.
95.2 Intersection of HWY 134 & HWY 535.
99.9 HWY 134 runs parallel with HWY 11.
103.5 Cross over the Shediac River.
107.4 Gilbert's Corner.
109.8 Turn left off of HWY 134 / Hanington Road onto HWY 133 / Main Street.
110.8 Cross over a bridge. Camping is available on the west side of the bridge. Both are expensive and cater to RV's.
114.5 Cycle through downtown Shediac then turn left on Parlee Beach Road.
116.2 Parlee Beach Provincial Park & Campground.

Parlee Beach Provincial Park to Amherst's Loch Lomond Campground: (74.2 K)

Enjoy a short ride into Amherst today. The grades of the highway are low but they go on for a long time, making the uphills easy and the downhills a pleasure.

Enter first into Sackville, population 5 411, on the shore of the Tantramar River next to the border to Nova Scotia. This lively town is home to Mount Allison University, which along with tourism drives industry in the town. Check out the Campbell Carriage Factory Museum, built in 1838. The museum depicts 19th century manufacturing practices. Also, the Boultenhouse Heritage Centre allows visitors to relive the days when Sackville was a busy seaport and shipbuilding centre. If you are looking for a campground, head to Marshview Trailer & Camping Park.

Leave Sackville and cross over the Missaguash River which forms the border of New Brunswick and Nova Scotia. Look for a large tourist information centre on your right as you cross the provincial border.

Amherst, population 9 505, was founded in 1764. It grew as a busy manufacturing town, gaining the name, "Busy Amherst." Many of the buildings that were used to manufacture products such as boots, trunks and pianos still exist today near the railroad station. Your destination for the evening is Loch Lomond Campground on the south side of Amherst.

Kilometre Log

0.0 Leave Parlee Beach heading south on Parlee Beach Road.

1.4 Parlee Beach Road crosses Main Street and becomes Ohio Road / HWY 140.

3.3 Turn right off of Ohio Road / HWY 140 onto HWY 15 W.

8.1 Circle 270° to gain HWY 132 S.

23.0 HWY 132 intersects with HWY 2 near the Greater Moncton Airport. Turn left to gain HWY 2.

36.6 HWY 2 intersects with HWY 933.

53.4 Sackville.

57.0 Cross over the Tantramar River.

65.1 Cross over the Missiguash River and enter into Nova Scotia. Here HWY 2 changes to HWY 104.

68.0 Don't take your first exit onto HWY 2 / Laplanche Street to enter Amherst. Remain on HWY 104.

70.3 Exit to Amherst and intersection of HWY 104 & HWY 6.

73.7 Exit to Amherst. Turn right onto Glooscap Trail / HWY 2.

73.9 Turn right onto Blair Lake Road.

74.0 Turn left onto Loch Lomond Lane.

74.2 Loch Lomond Campground.

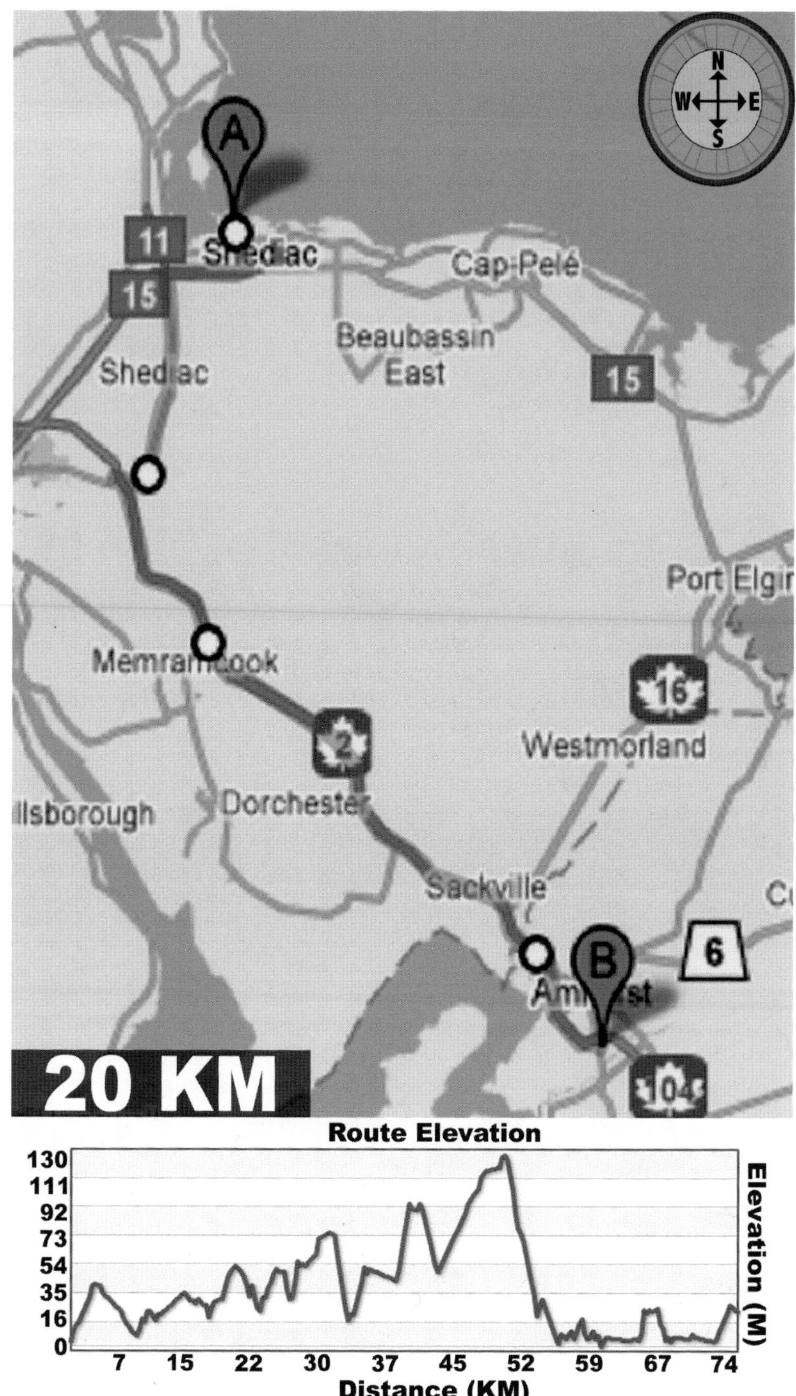

A
11
15
Cap-Pelé
Beaubassin
East
15
16
Westmorland
2
Sackville
B
6
104
20 KM
Route Elevation
130
111
92
73
54
35
16
0
7
15
22
30
37
45
52
59
67
74
Distance (KM)
Elevation (M)

Province: Nova Scotia
Population: 939 531
Area: 53 338 km^2
Industries: Fishing, mining, agriculture, arts.
Highlights: Halifax, The Citadel, St. Peters Lock, Lake Bras d'Or.

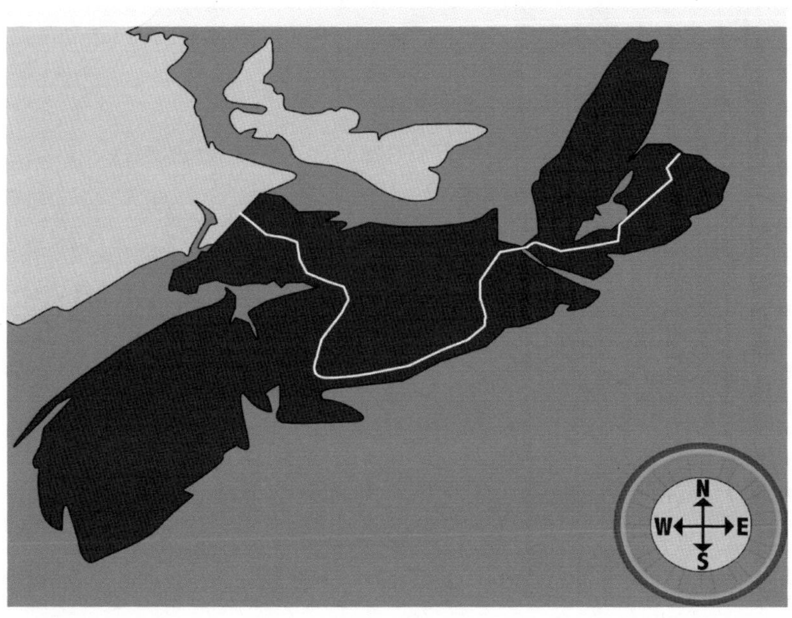

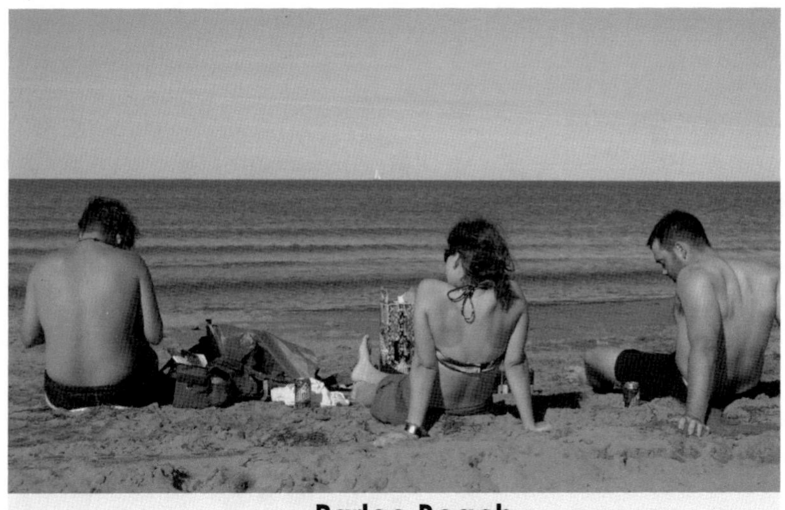

Parlee Beach

Loch Lomond Campground to Truro's Scotia Pine Campground: (112.8 K)

Prepare for a lonely day of cycling by packing adequate provisions of food and water.

HWY 104 turns into a toll-road today that cyclists are not allowed on. It is necessary to detour onto HWY 4, a sub-standard highway offering little in the way of commercial services. The road is quiet, however, so you can cycle without being crowded by vehicles. The turn off to HWY 4 is easy to miss so watch carefully.

After leaving Amherst you will cycle past the town of Oxford, the Wild Blueberry Capital of Canada. If you have a minute, head into Oxford and visit the Wild Blueberry & Maple Centre to learn about the tasty blueberry and maple industry that is vital to this town. Public internet is available at the Maple Centre. Oxford is located at the junction of Philip River, Black River and Little River. Oxford's name is derived from the shallow river that settlers would cross or "ford" on oxen.

Past Oxford, exit off of HWY 104 onto HWY 4. This lonely road climbs towards Folley Lake, a popular cottage destination. From Folley Lake, you will coast downhill and return onto HWY 104. There is a gas station and restaurant at this intersection.

Don't miss your exit as there is only one road into Truro, population 11 765. Truro's growth can be attributed to its location at the intersection of the Canadian National Railway between Montréal and Halifax and the Cape Breton and Central Nova Scotia Railway running between Truro and Sydney. The town is located on the shore of Cobequid Bay, an inlet of the Bay of Fundy.

Truro is famous for tidal bore on the nearby Salmon River, which occurs when incoming tides are funneled into a shallow, narrowing river via a broad bay. The effect of this phenomenon is large rumbling waves carrying immense amounts of water into riverbeds that stood dry mere seconds before.

Your destination for the evening is Scotia Pine Campground on the south end of Truro. The climb out of the Salmon River Valley is a hard ride at the end of the day. Get your supplies in central Truro before tackling the hill. The campground has wireless internet, a swimming pool and laundry facilities.

Kilometre Log

0.0	Exit Loch Lomond Campground heading east on Loch Lomond Lane.
0.2	Turn left onto Glooscap Trail.
0.4	Exit right onto HWY 104.
2.4	Cross over the Nappan River.
20.7	Intersection of HWY 104 & HWY 142 at Salt Springs Station.
30.9	Exit to Oxford.
31.8	Cross over Philip River.
39.7	Exit right for HWY 4 heading east.
40.3	Cross HWY 104 onto HWY 4.
51.4	Intersection of HWY 368 & HWY 4 at Mahoney's Corner.
57.2	Cross over Wentworth River.
57.9	HWY 307 merges with HWY 4 to become HWY 4. Remain on HWY 4.
59.8	Wentworth. There is a small store on the left side of the road.
62.6	Intersection of HWY 4 & HWY 246.

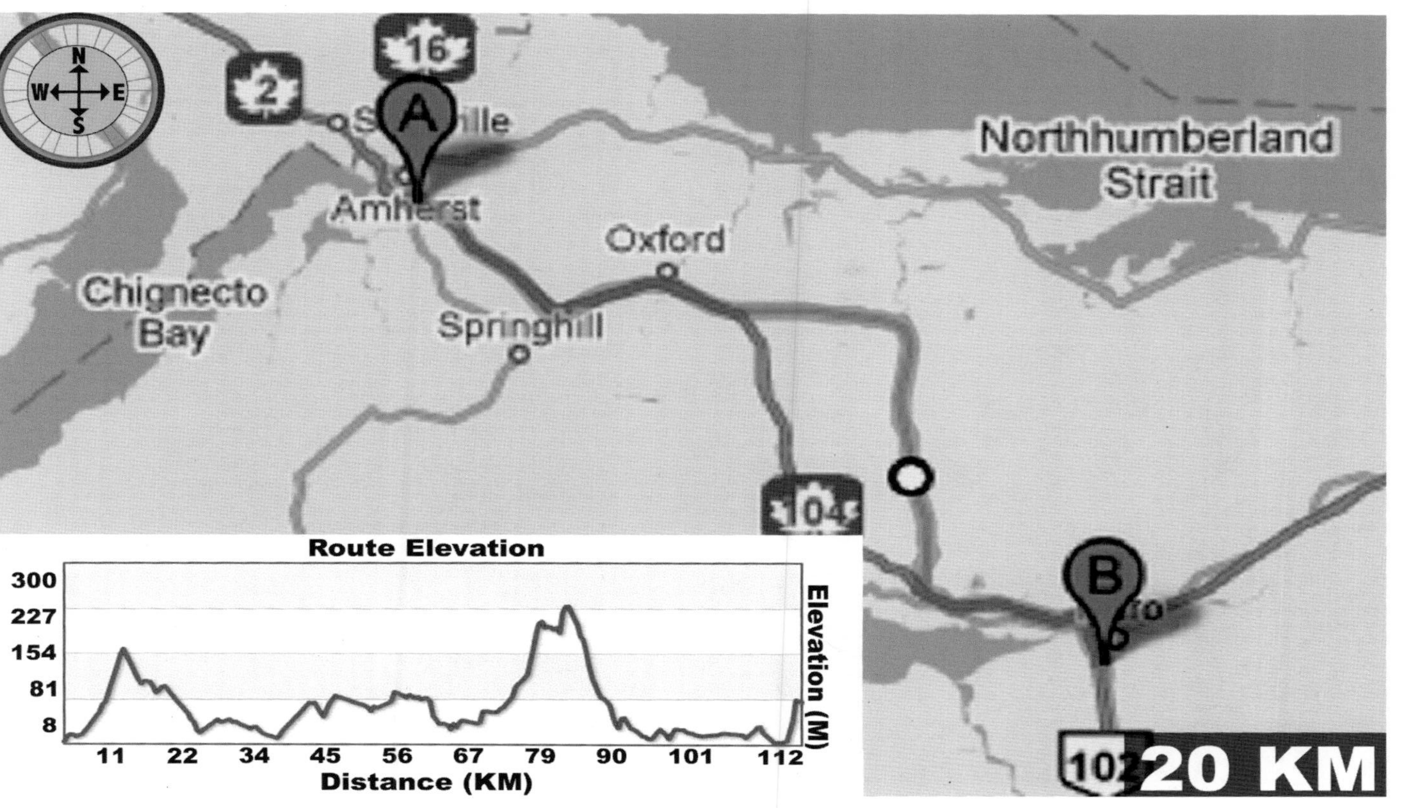

N
W
E
S
2
16
A
Amherst
Northhumberland
Strait
Oxford
Chignecto
Bay
Springhill
104
B
102
20 KM
Route Elevation
300
227
154
81
8
11
22
34
45
56
67
79
90
101
112
Distance (KM)
Elevation (M)

63.3 Turn right on Valley Road to access Hostelling International Wentworth.
72.4 Folly Lake.
81.3 Folly Mountain.
88.3 Pass over HWY 104. Exit to your right and ride 270° clockwise to gain HWY 104 E.
88.8 Service station here.
91.9 Glooscap Trail / HWY 2 / HWY 4 merges with HWY 104 via a cloverleaf to become HWY 104.
98.8 Cross over the Chiganois River.
105.8 HWY 102 intersects with HWY 104. Turn right here into Truro.
107.5 Cross over Salmon River.
108.2 Pass through a cloverleaf.
110.2 Pass through a cloverleaf.
112.3 Exit to your right onto Treaty Connector Road.
112.4 Turn right onto Treaty Trail heading north.
112.8 Enter Scotia Pine Campground.

Scotia Pine Campground to Dartmouth's Shubie Campground: (84.3 K)

From Scotia Pine, detour south towards Halifax because a visit to the storied capital city of Nova Scotia is worth some extra pedaling. If you are in a hurry, bike down HWY 104 out of Truro towards Antigonish where you can meet up with the *Canada By Bicycle* route just east of the city.

Arrive first in Dartmouth, population 65 741, which sits on the eastern shore of Halifax Harbour. Dartmouth is known as "the City of Lakes," as it has 23 within the city limits. The popular Canadian television show *Trailer Park Boys* is fictionally set in Dartmouth. Access Halifax from Dartmouth by either crossing the Angus L. MacDonald Bridge or on the city run Dartmouth-Halifax Ferry.

Named after former premier Angus L. Macdonald and designed by the same company that created the Lions Gate Bridge in Vancouver, the bridge was completed in 1955. The bridge averages 44 000 crossings per workday. A wide bike lane promotes expedient crossing for cyclists.

I recommend taking the ferry across the Harbour, so the route will guide you there. From Alderney Landing in Dartmouth you can ride inside the boat or on the roof in open air. This route is the oldest continuously running salt water ferry service in North America. The cost to ride the ferry is $2.25.

Mi'Kmaq people first congregated here to spend summers in the Bedford Basin west of Halifax. Their name for this area means "the biggest harbour," in reference to Halifax Harbour. During the Seven Years War, Halifax played a prominent role as a military base that countered the French fortress Loiusbourg in Cape Breton. During World War I, Halifax Harbour's sheltered waters protected convoys from attack prior to heading into the Atlantic Ocean.

The Halifax Explosion occurred on December 6, 1917, when SS Mont-Blanc, a French cargo ship loaded with wartime explosives, collided with SS Imo from Norway. Within 20 minutes, the cargo of Mont-Blanc exploded with a force greater than any man-made explosion in history. The ships were instantly destroyed and a massive fireball shot into the air. The devastating blast caused a tsunami wave that rose up to 18 metres above sea-level. Buildings shook and items fell off shelves in Truro. A fragment of Mont-Blanc's anchor shaft that weighed 517 kilograms was thrown 3.7 kilometres to the west.

The number of deaths could have been much higher if not for the heroic efforts of local train dispatcher Vince Coleman. Understanding the threat that a boat ablaze full of explosives posed, Coleman and his co-worker fled their work post. After leaving, Coleman remembered that a train was due in soon from Saint John, New Brunswick. He returned to his post to send a Morse code message to the train that undoubtedly saved the lives of the approximately 300 passengers on board. He perished after sending the message. The train was later used to transport the injured north to Truro.

If you have a look at the Canadian dime, you will notice a sailboat opposite the face of the Queen. This boat is a schooner named the Bluenose. The Bluenose was launched in Lunenburg, Nova Scotia, on March 26th, 1921, with Captain Angus Walters at the helm. The Bluenose spent the winter of 1921 fishing off of the Grand Banks. By completing a full season of fishing, the vessel had fulfilled the main requirement to compete in the International Fisherman's Series sailboat race. That October, Captain Walters sailed the ship to Halifax where it began its 17-year career as an undefeated racing boat. In 1935, the Bluenose went to England for the Silver Jubilee of King George V where thousands of people were welcomed aboard. This established the boat's international reputation. In 1937, the Canadian dime was changed to include an image of the Bluenose. In 1938, Captain Walters and crew sailed to one final victory. Walters purchased the boat, but by 1942 he could no longer afford the cost of maintenance and was forced to sell the boat to the West Indies Trading Company. This legendary boat was later run ashore and reduced to rubble.

Bluenose 2 was built as a marketing tool by a brewery in Halifax. The boat is now owned by the government of Nova Scotia and operated by the Lunenburg Marine Museum Society. During the summer, the Bluenose 2 visits ports all over Nova Scotia.

Don't leave Halifax without visiting the Halifax Citadel National Historic Site. Completed in 1856, the Citadel occupies the hill overlooking Halifax Harbour. The intended role of the Citadel was to guard against a land-based attack from the United States. The massive star-shaped fort's role was later changed to barrack accommodations and acted as a command centre. The Citadel was often the last view of Canada for thousands of outbound soldiers heading to Europe for World War II. Presently, the Citadel is operated by Parks Canada, recognized as a Historic Site and is complete with a museum and historical actors.

Your destination for the evening is Shubie Campground in Dartmouth. The campground is set in a tranquil location close to Dartmouth and Halifax Harbour. If you are looking for a hostel head to downtown Halifax's Halifax Backpackers Hostel or HI - Halifax Heritage House Hostel.

Kilometre Log

0.0	Leave Scotia Pine Campground heading south on Treaty Trail.
0.5	Turn left at Treaty Connector Road.
0.6	Turn right onto HWY 102.
0.9	Cycle past the Glooscap Heritage Centre and 40-foot statue of Glooscap.
9.9	Intersection of HWY 102 & HWY 289.
15.4	Cycle past Shortt's Lake.
22.9	Cross over Shubenacadie River.
23.6	Exit left to Stewiacke. Inquire here about tidal bore rafting.
28.1	Cross over Shubenacadie River.
52.3	Cross over Shubenacadie River.
58.9	Pass Halifax International Airport.
69.4	HWY 102 splits into HWY 102 & HWY 118. Turn left onto HWY 118.
78.7	Exit right and circle 270° clockwise to gain HWY 107 E.
81.5	Turn right off of HWY 107 onto Charles Keating Drive.
81.7	Turn left onto Waverley Road / HWY 318.
84.0	Turn right off of Waverley Road onto Jaybe Drive.
84.2	Turn left on John Brenton Drive.
84.3	Enter Shubie RV Park and Campground.

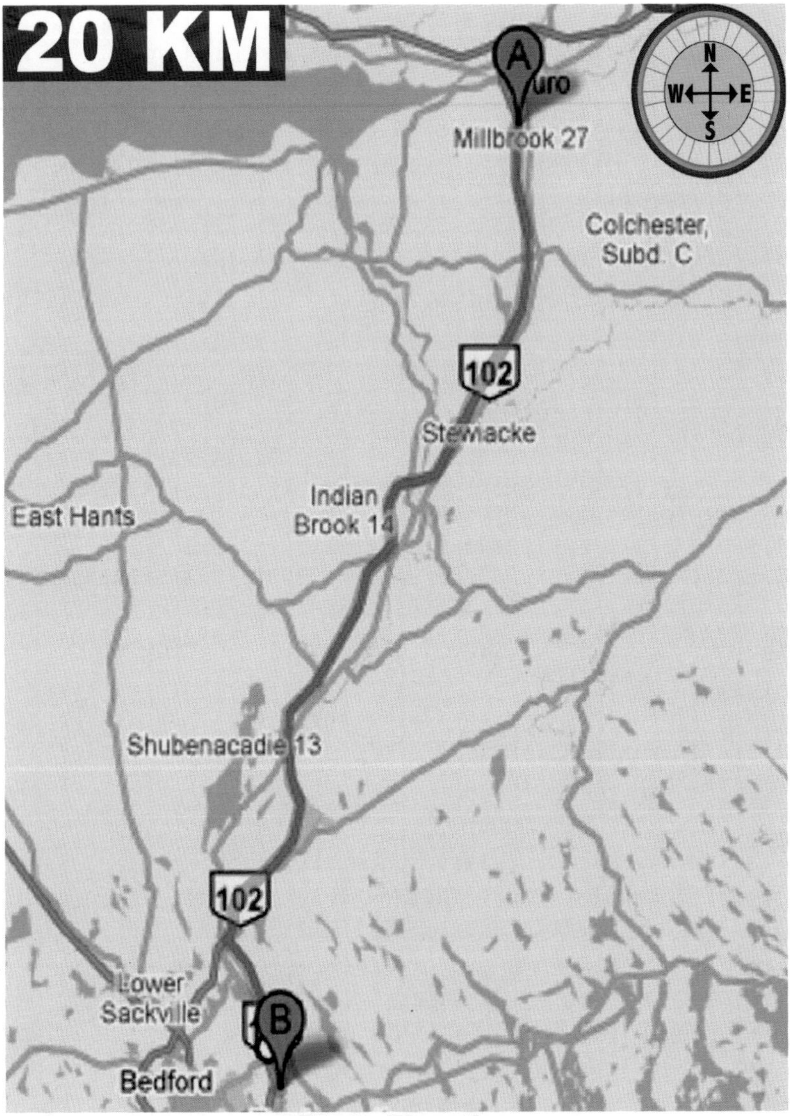

20 KM
A
uro
Millbrook 27
N
W
E
S
Colchester,
Subd. C
102
Stewiacke
Indian
Brook 14
East Hants
Shubenacadie 13
102
Lower
Sackville
B
Bedford

Route Elevation
150
126
102
78
54
30
6
Elevation (M)
8
17
25
33
42
50
59
67
75
84
Distance (KM)

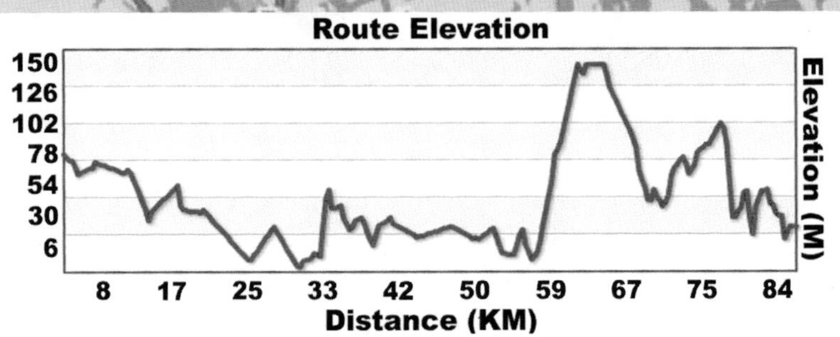

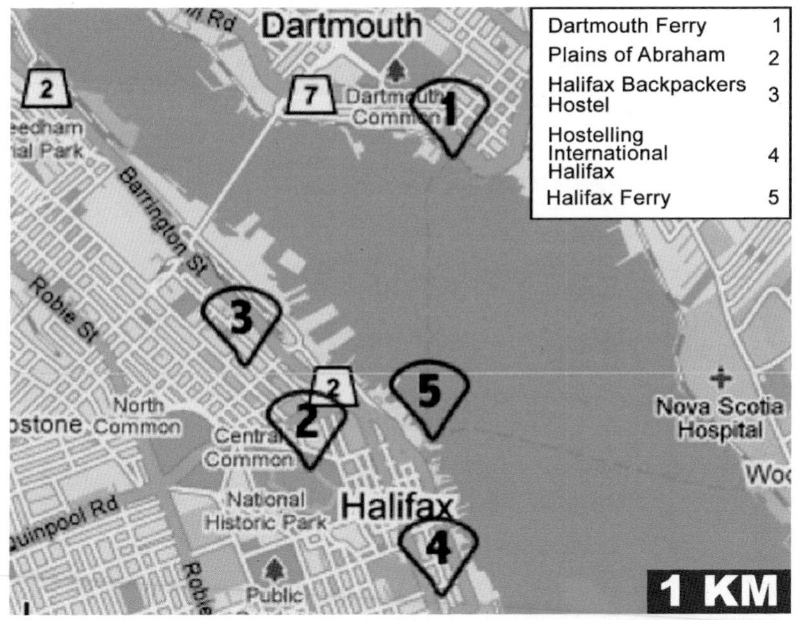

Shubie Campground to Sheet Harbour's East River Lodge, Campground & Trailer Park: (113.1 K)

The road down the south shore of Nova Scotia is a pleasant ride. Traffic is light and the people are friendly. In years past, fishing was the major industry of the communities along this coast. With fish stocks depleted, the area is now inhabited mainly by retirees.

For the first half of the day, HWY 107 runs parallel to HWY 7. HWY 107 is the more direct route to Sheet Harbour.

A good place for lunch on your way to Sheet Harbour is Musquodoboit Harbour, the commercial hub for the area between Sheet Harbour and Halifax. Groceries and restaurants are available here. There is a small museum and tourism office located in the centre of town on HWY 7. Make sure your water bottles are full when you leave, as there is little between here and Sheet Harbour.

As you approach Sheet Harbour you will see signs for Taylor Head Provincial Park and Spry Bay Provincial Park. Spry Bay is a small park with a picnic area. Taylor Head boasts 16 kilometres of unspoiled coastline and many hiking trails. Camping is not available at either park.

Your destination for the evening is Sheet Harbour's East River Lodge, Campground & Trailer Park on the shores of East River. Sheet Harbour is named after Sheet Rock, a flat, white rock found near the harbour. Groceries are available in town.

Kilometre Log

0.0 Leave Shubie RV Park and Campground heading north on John Brenton Drive.
0.2 Turn right on Jaybe Drive.
0.3 Turn right on Waverley Road / HWY 318.
2.0 Bike past Red Bridge Pond. Waverley Road / HWY 18 turns into Braemar Drive / HWY 318 here.
2.5 Turn left off of Braemar Drive / HWY 318 onto Maple Drive.
2.8 Turn left onto Plymouth Road.
3.1 Turn right on Mountain Avenue.
3.9 Turn left off of Mountain Avenue onto HWY 7 / Main Street.
7.0 HWY 107 merges with HWY 7 / Main Street to become HWY 107 / HWY 7 / Main Street.
11.6 HWY 107 / HWY 7 / Main Street splits into HWY 7 & HWY 107. Stay right on HWY 107.
16.4 Cross over Lake Echo on HWY 107.
23.5 Cross over Porters Lake on HWY 107.
33.6 Cycle over Petpeswick Lake on HWY 107.
36.2 HWY 107 merges with HWY 7. Turn right onto HWY 7.
38.8 Musquodoboit Harbour.
48.4 Salmon River Bridge.
65.0 Ship Harbour.
77.2 Turn right on Murphy's Road for Murphy's Camping by the Sea.
83.6 Cross the Tangier River.
84.8 Tangier.
95.7 Spry Bay.
109.4 Enter Sheet Harbour on Marine Drive.
112.2 Turn left on Pool Road. If you cross the green bridge you have gone too far.
113.1 Turn right to enter East River Lodge Campground & Trailer Park.

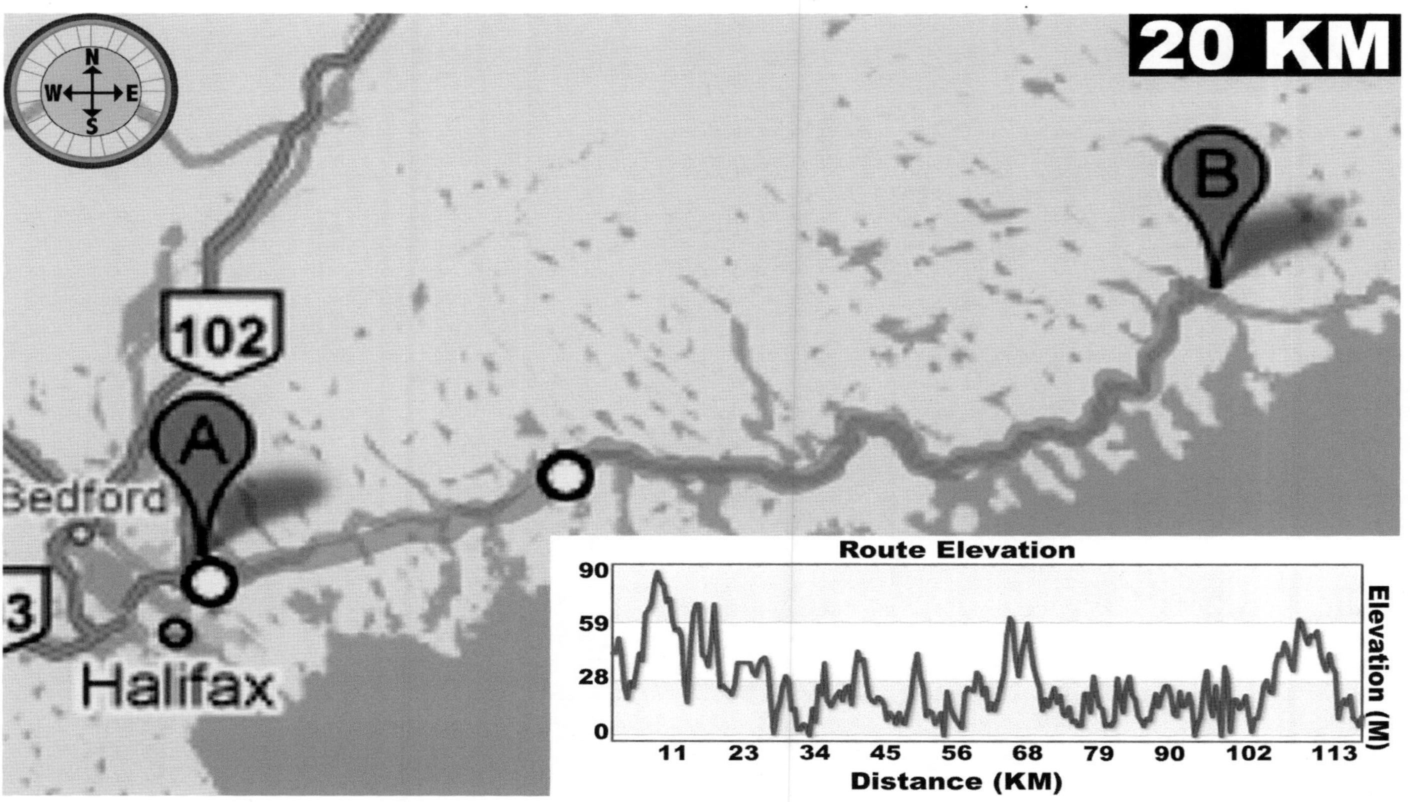
N
W
E
S
20 KM
102
A
B
Bedford
3
Halifax
Route Elevation
90
59
28
0
11
23
34
45
56
68
79
90
102
113
Distance (KM)
Elevation (M)

East River Lodge, Campground & Trailer Park to St. Mary's Riverside Campground: (81.5 K)

Enjoy another day of tranquil cycling through rural Nova Scotia. The Atlantic Ocean will appear more frequently today than yesterday. Once again, the area is sparsely populated. There is a grocery store at your destination but only a few commercial establishments in between Sheet Harbour and Sherbrooke. Pack accordingly.

There is a small restaurant in Moose River that is a good bet for lunch.

Just west of Marie Joseph is Marie Joseph Provincial Park. The park is a roadside picnic area with a view of offshore islands. Scattered picnic tables overlook the rocky shoreline.

Your destination for the evening is St. Mary's Riverside Campground in Sherbrooke. Sherbrooke is famous for being the home of Sherbrooke Village, the largest museum in the province.

Sherbrooke Village depicts a typical Nova Scotian village from 1860 to pre-World War I. The site has 80 buildings, 25 of which are open to the public. You can visit the wood turner shop, blacksmith, pottery shop and printery, all within the village.

St. Mary's Riverside Campground has laundry and internet.

Kilometre Log

0.0 Leave East River Lodge Campground & Trailer Park cycling south on Pool Road.

0.9 Turn left on HWY 7 / Marine Drive.

1.0 Cross over East River.

1.5 HWY 374 intersects with HWY 7 / Marine Road. Remain on HWY 7 / Marine Road.

13.4 Port Dufferin.

30.6 Moser River.

47.4 Marie Joseph Provincial Park.

48.8 Marie Joseph.

54.2 Liscomb Mills on Liscomb River.

64.2 HWY 7 / Marine Drive turns north at Liscomb.

80.2 Sherbrooke. Cross over St. Mary's River on HWY 7 / Marine Drive.

80.4 Turn right onto Main Street.

80.6 Turn left onto Court Street.

80.8 Turn right onto Sonora Road.

81.5 St. Mary's Riverside Campground.

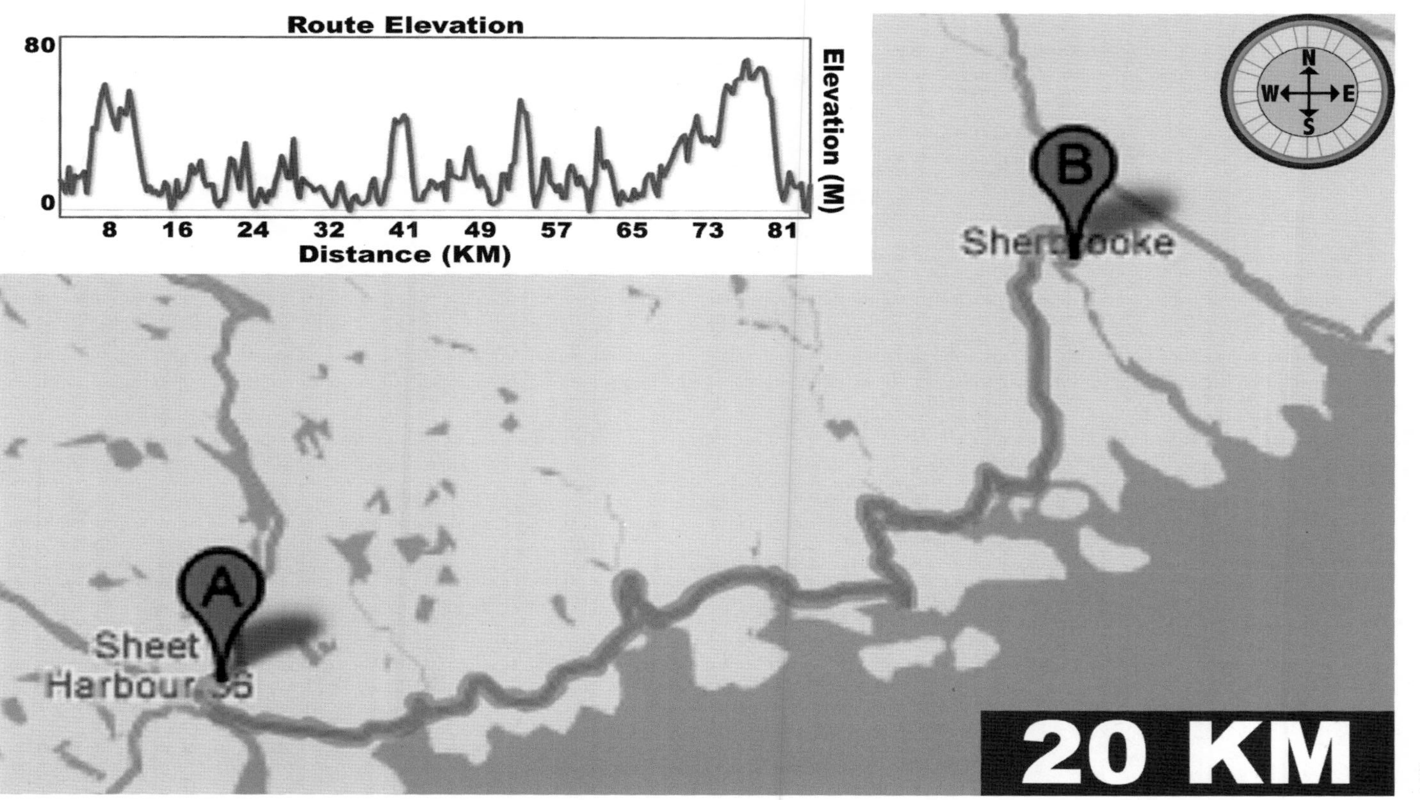
Route Elevation
80
0
8
16
24
32
41
49
57
65
73
81
Distance (KM)
Elevation (M)
N
W
E
S
B
A
Sheet
Harbour
20 KM

St. Mary's Riverside Campground to Hyclass Campground: (95.8 K)

Leave Sherbrooke and head north along the St. Mary's River. You are biking against the river and gaining elevation so expect a challenging ride.

The route detours Antigonish to save some kilometres. Antigonish, population 4 236, is home to St. Francis Xavier University, a bike store, Whidden Park Campground and a large grocery store if you wish to stop.

HWY 316 parallels South River as you bike towards HWY 104. Before arriving in South River you will pass through St. Andrews, a small town with a handsome church that beckons you into town. Distance signs in this area are erratic and not correct. HWY 316 is quiet and well paved.

There are a few small stores in South River as well as Ma Webb's Steakhouse, an oasis for hungry cyclists.

There is a small general store in Monastery where you can acquire provisions for the evening. Your destination is Hyclass Campground. This campground sits on the shore of St. Georges Bay and offers great views of the ocean. Wireless internet and laundry are available.

Kilometre Log

0.0 Leave St. Mary's Riverside Campground heading north on Sonora Road.

1.0 Turn right on Marine Drive / HWY 7.

5.2 Stillwater and Nimrod's Camping. Marine Drive turns right here. HWY 7 continues straight. Continue north on HWY 7.

26.7 Cycle past Lochiel Lake on your left side.

31.8 Turn right off of HWY 7 onto HWY 276.

37.2 Goshen. HWY 276 turns into HWY 316 here. Remain headed east on HWY 316.

44.5 Cycle past South River Lake.

61.6 St. Andrews.

66.5 HWY 316 dead-ends into HWY 104 at South River. Turn right here onto HWY 104.

88.8 Exit to Monastery. Turn right here to access Sunrise Trail / HWY 4 through Monastery and onto Hyclass Campground.

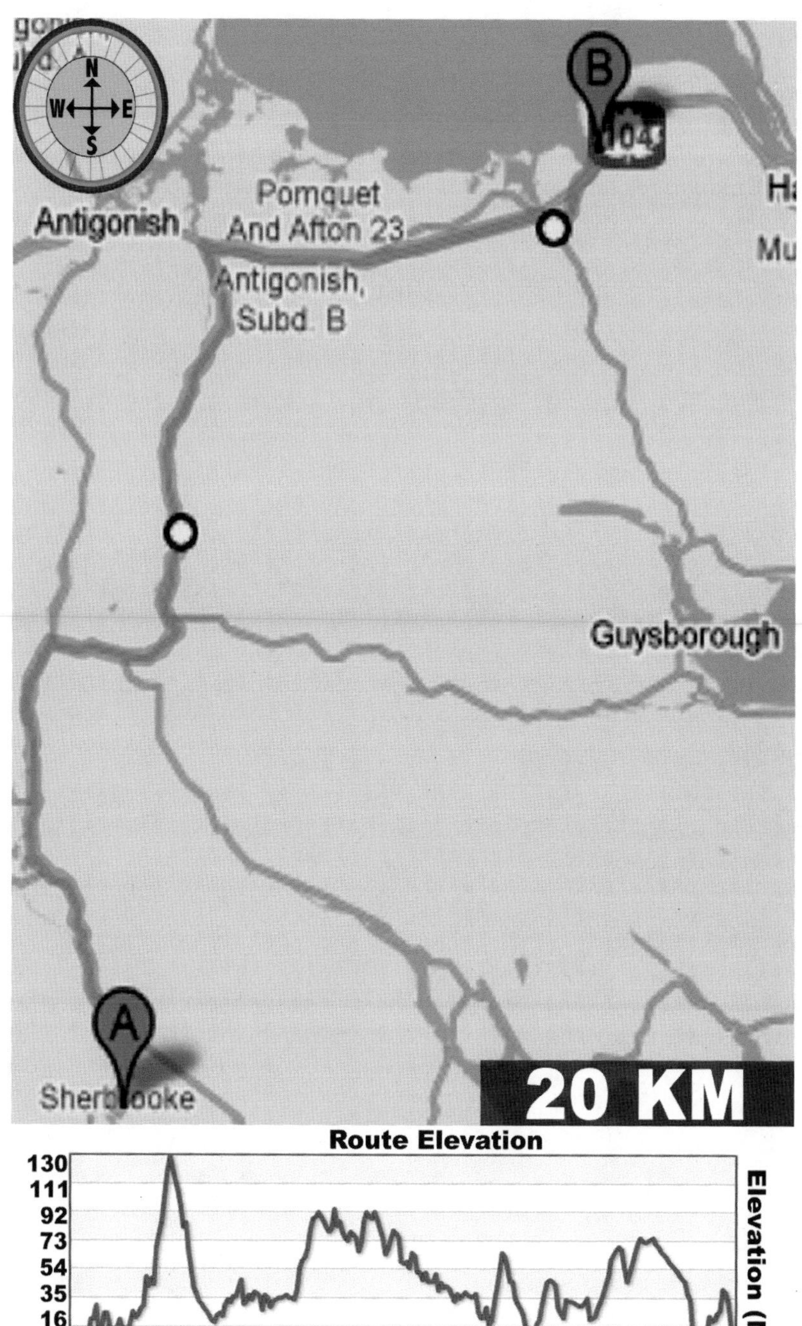
N
W
E
S
B
104
Antigonish
Pomquet
And Afton 23
Antigonish,
Subd. B
Guysborough
A
Sherbrooke
20 KM
Route Elevation
130
111
92
73
54
35
16
0
Elevation (M)
10
16
29
38
48
57
67
76
86
95
Distance (KM)

90.6 Cross over the Tracadie River.
93.5 Cross HWY 104.
95.8 Turn left into Hyclass Ocean Campground.

Hyclass Campground to St. Peters Battery Provincial Park: (70.8 K)

Today you will cycle to St. Peters on the shores of Cape Breton Island's Bras d'Or Lake.

Cape Breton Island is separated from Nova Scotia by the Strait of Canso but artificially connected by the Canso Causeway. A causeway is a land bridge that spans across water. Although often cheaper to build than a bridge they can cause significant environmental damage because they impede or stop the flow of water. The Canso causeway was opened to public in 1955. It spans 1 385 metres over water with a maximum depth of 65 metres.

Cape Breton's original residents were likely Maritime Archaic Indians, ancestors of the Mi'kmaq Indians that inhabited the island. In 1497 John Cabot became the first explorer of European descent to visit the area. Shipbuilding began in the 1790s and peaked in 1851, when the largest wooden ship ever built on the island, Lord Clarendon, was completed. During this time, many Highland Scots settled in the area. Their culture is still present, especially in rural communities.

Cape Breton Island has been home to many significant scientific discoveries. These include the invention of the telephone by Alexander Graham Bell, as well as the first trans-Atlantic radio message from Table Head in Glace Bay to a receiving station near Cornwall, England. Bras d'Or Lake was the sight of the first successful flight in Canada when the Silver Dart took off from Bras d'Or's frozen water on February 2nd, 1909.

Bras d'Or Lake is a salt water lake located in the middle of Cape Breton Island. The lake measures approximately 100 kilometres in length and 50 kilometres in width and has a relatively unpopulated shoreline. Watch the horizon for one of the many bald eagles that call this area home. Bras d'Or translates to "arm of gold," in French. Bras d'Or Lake is beautiful; you will remember it for the rest of your life.

After crossing the Canso Causeway you will enter Port Hawkesbury. Port Hawkesbury is a significant shipping hub, handling the second largest tonnage in Canada annually. Port Hawkesbury received a significant economic boost from the building of the Canso Causeway. Not only did it mean that goods no longer needed to be ferried across the strait, but it also gave the city a year round ice-free port. Groceries are available in town.

Your destination for the evening is Battery Provincial Park in St. Peters, population 2 634. St. Peters is an attractive town where everyone knows each other and waves to visitors. Groceries are available here.

St. Peters is famous for the St. Peters Canal on the north side of town. The canal was completed in 1869, connecting Bras d'Or Lake with St. Peters Bay in the Atlantic Ocean. It was used heavily for commercial shipping in the late 1800s and early 1900s, playing a significant role in the expansion of Cape Breton Island. The canal was designated a National Historic Site in 1925, and is now operated by Parks Canada. This canal is unique because in most canals, the flow of water is unidirectional meaning the high side of the canal is always the same. With St. Peters Canal, sometimes Bras d'Or Lake is higher than the Ocean and other times the Atlantic is higher than Lake Bras d'Or. This necessitates a double gate system.

Battery Provincial Park, overlooking St. Peters Bay, features a lighthouse that serves as a landmark for the entrance to St. Peters Canal. St. Peters is the birth place of world famous marine photographer Wallace R. MacAskill. Visit his home to view some of his works. MacAskill's famous Bluenose photo is still reproduced on the Canadian dime.

Kilometre Log

0.0	Leave Hyclass Ocean Campground heading north on HWY 4 / Sunrise Trail.
6.8	Turn right off of Sunrise Trail / HWY 4 onto Pellerien Road to access HWY 104.
6.9	Turn left onto HWY 104 E.
15.0	Enter Auld Cove, restaurants are available here.

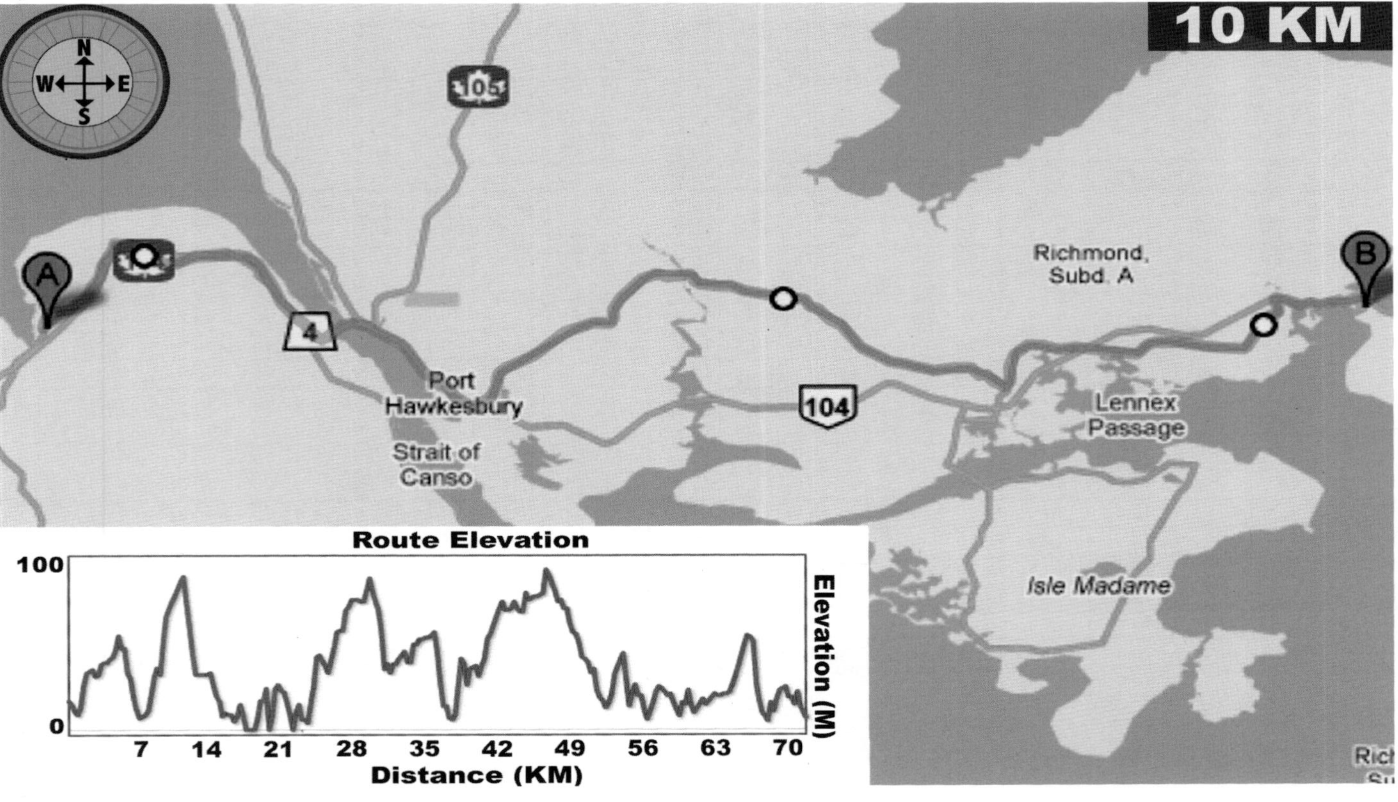
10 KM
N
W
E
S
A
B
105
4
104
Port Hawkesbury
Strait of Canso
Richmond, Subd. A
Lennex Passage
Isle Madame
Route Elevation
100
0
Elevation (M)
7
14
21
28
35
42
49
56
63
70
Distance (KM)

15.2 Exit Auld Cove staying left on HWY 104 / Sunrise Trail.
16.7 HWY 104 / Sunrise Trail turns left and crosses Canso Straight on Canso Causeway.
18.7 Intersection of HWY 19 & 105 & HWY 4. Stay right on HWY 4.
23.2 Enter Port Hawkesbury on Reeves Street.
24.6 Turn left off of Reeves Street / HWY 4 onto HWY 4 / Fleur-de-Lis Trail. Remain on this road until just before St. Peters.
56.4 Cross HWY 104.
66.4 HWY 4 merges with HWY 104. Turn right here.
69.3 Enter St. Peters on Grenville Street / HWY 4.
70.3 Cross over St. Peters Canal.
70.4 Turn right into Battery Provincial Park.
70.8 Battery Provincial Park.

Battery Provincial Park to Arm of Gold Campground: (104.1 K)

The road from St. Peters to Sydney is exceptionally challenging. Pack plenty of food and water as the road is sparsely populated.

Johnstown is world-famous because of its Sacred Heart Church and Our Lady of Guadalupe shrine. The Sacred Heart Church was completed in 1891, and has been serving the area ever since. It has a striking presence overlooking beautiful Bras d'Or Lake.

In 1946, Antigonish's Ronald MacLean was a chaplain in the Navy aboard the ship Uganda, when it docked in Acapulco, Mexico. There, he learned about the devotion of Catholic Mexicans to Our Lady of Guadalupe and the shrine erected in her honour near Mexico City. Years later, when MacLean became pastor at Johnstown, he commissioned the construction of a mosaic of Our Lady of Guadalupe. She was erected on the grounds of the Sacred Heart Church during the summer of 1963. Every year, parishioners pilgrimage to Mexico from Cape Breton to express their devotion.

Big Pond is the halfway mark between St. Peters and Sydney. Big Pond is the birthplace of Canadian singer Rita MacNeil and visitors flock to the area during the summer.

Sydney, population 24 115, was founded in 1785. Early in the 1900s, Sydney was home to one of the world's largest steel plants, powered by the many coalmines in the area. In the 1960s the coal and steel industries fell on hard times and were taken over by the federal and provincial governments. The coal mining and steel manufacturing industries were disbanded in 2001.

Cape Breton Island is growing in global popularity, attracting people from all over the world. As this happens, Sydney is growing along with it to service these tourists. Many cruise ships port in Sydney during the fall to view the autumn colors. Sydney's J.A. Douglas McCurdy Airport offers direct flights to Halifax and Toronto.

The Largest Ceilidh Fiddle in the World is situated at the Sydney Waterfront.

North Sydney is home to the ferry that sails to Port aux Basques, Newfoundland, twice daily, once in the morning and once at night. The sailing takes about eight hours. Food is available onboard. Make sure to call ahead and reserve a spot on the boat. There is also another ferry that travels between North Sydney and Agrentia during summer months. Argentia is approximately 130 kilometres from St. John's.

Your destination for the evening is either the ferry to Newfoundland or the Arm of Gold Campground in Sydney Mines, near North Sydney. The campground has free wireless internet, laundry and is located in proximity to the ferry to Newfoundland overlooking Bras d'Or Lake. Groceries are available in Sydney Mines.

Kilometre Log

0.0 Leave Battery Provincial Park heading north towards HWY 4 / Grenville Street.
0.4 Turn right on HWY 4 / Grenville Street.
8.5 Barra Head.
13.1 Soldiers Cove.
18.6 Hay Cove.
25.2 Johnstown.
33.7 Irish Cove.
41.4 Middle Cape.
47.8 Big Pond & Breac Brook.

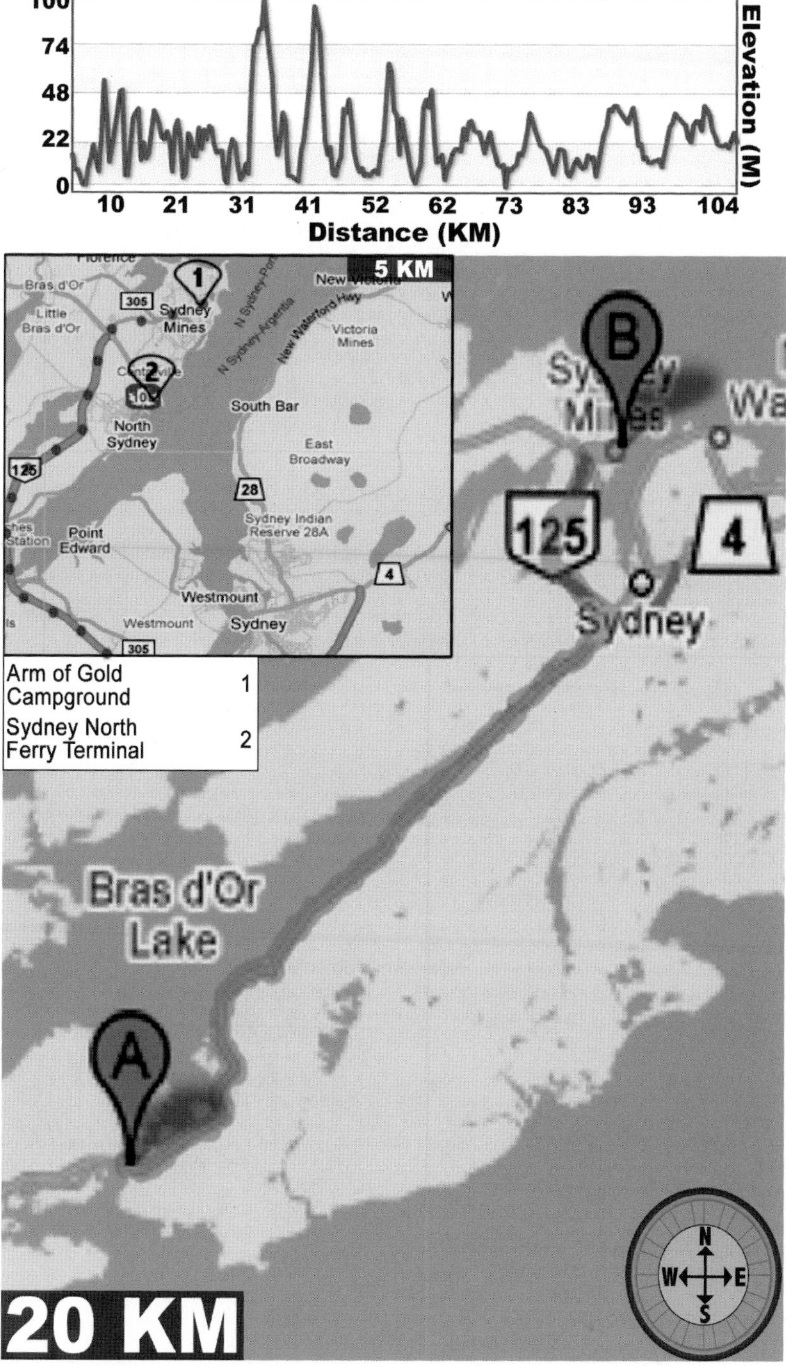

Route Elevation
100
74
48
22
0
10
21
31
41
52
62
73
83
93
104
Distance (KM)
Elevation (M)
5 KM
Bras d'Or
Little Bras d'Or
305
Sydney Mines
N Sydney-Argentia
New Waterford Hwy
Victoria Mines
North Sydney
South Bar
East Broadway
125
28
Sydney Indian Reserve 28A
Point Edward
Westmount
Sydney
4
Arm of Gold Campground 1
Sydney North Ferry Terminal 2
B
125
4
Sydney
Bras d'Or Lake
A
20 KM
N
W
E
S

53.8 Ben Eoin Beach RV Resort & Campground.
68.2 HWY 216 merges with HWY 4.
75.9 Sydney Forks.
80.2 Enter Sydney on Kings Road.

To access Sydney continue biking on Kings Road.

81.4 Cross HWY 125.
81.5 Turn left to access HWY 125.
82.2 Cross Sydney River on HWY 125.
90.0 Balls Creek.
97.2 North Sydney.
100.0 Intersection of HWY 125 & HWY 105. Turn right if you want to access the ferry. To continue to Golden Arm Campground continue straight on HWY 125 as it turns into HWY 305 / Main Street.
103.1 Turn left on Cottage Street.
103.2 Turn right on Jacob Street.
103.6 Turn left on Crescent Street.
103.9 Turn right on Church Street.
104.1 Arm of Gold Campground & Trailer Park.

Sacred Heart Church

Province:	Newfoundland and Labrador
Population:	508 925
Area:	72 908 km^2
Industries:	Fishing, mining, tourism.
Highlights:	Table Mountain, Corner Brook, Newfie culture, Toutins, George Street, St. John's.

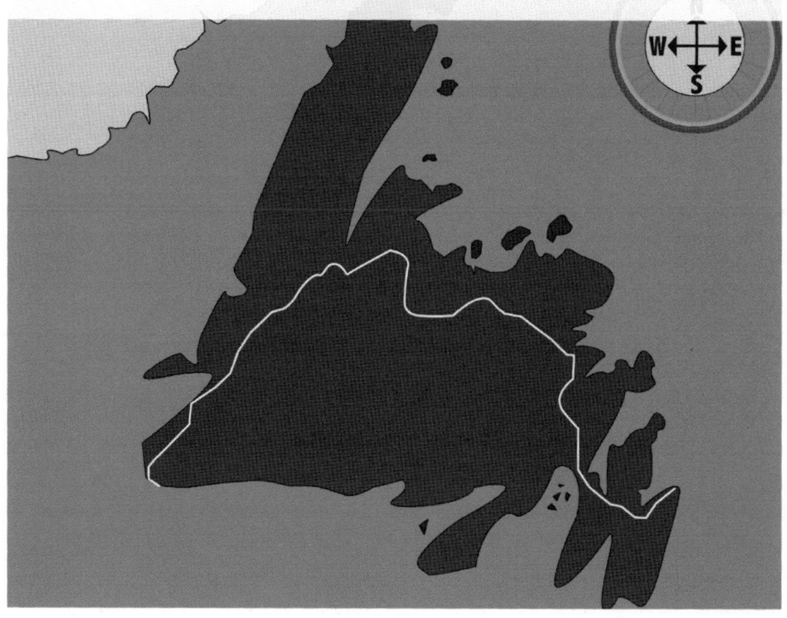

Port aux Basques to Midway Motel: (108.1 K)

Emerge from the ferry into rocky Newfoundland and turn your clocks forward half an hour. The ferry terminal is located just south of Port aux Basques, population 4 319. Port aux Basques received its name because of its sheltered harbour that was utilized by Basque whalers from France and Spain during the early 1500s. Purchase enough groceries to last until Corner Brook here. There are a few small stores and restaurants between Port aux Basques and Corner Brook, but they are inadequate for a hungry cyclist.

Attractions in Port aux Basques include the Gulf Museum, which displays 2 astrolabes that were historically used by astronomers, navigators and astrologers to predict the position of the sun, moon and planets. Ask a local for directions to Grand Bay West Beach, a great place to sunbathe or swim, weather permitting.

Leave Port aux Basques heading north and bike past J.T. Cheeseman Provincial Park, which is named after local politician John Cheeseman. Visitors are drawn to this park for sandy Cape Ray Beach, seashell collecting and bird watching. Camping is available here. Call or visit the Newfoundland Provincial Park website to reserve a site.

Just past Cheeseman Park you will see Table Mountain on your right, which stands at an elevation of 518 metres. It is a long mountain with a flat top that conduits winds from the summit to the weather-beaten forest below, with gusts exceeding 160 km/h. Winds near Table Mountain frequently cause road closures and have blown RV's right off of the road! After biking past Table Mountain, you will bike through the symmetrical Twin Mountains that are intersected by the highway.

Your destination for the evening is Midway Motel. As the name states, the motel marks the mid-point between Port aux Basques and Corner Brook. Rooms are affordable and there is a good restaurant next door. If you are feeling ambitious and desire a campground, keep cycling to Barachois Pond Provincial Park.

N
W
E
S

St George's Bay

Division No. 4, Subd. B

1

Division No. 4, Subd. A

1

B

A

1

Channel-Port-aux Basques

Isle aux Morts

Burnt Islands

Rose Blanche

20 KM

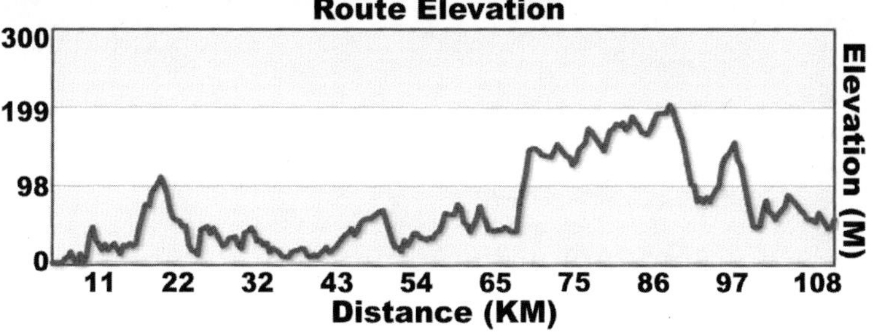

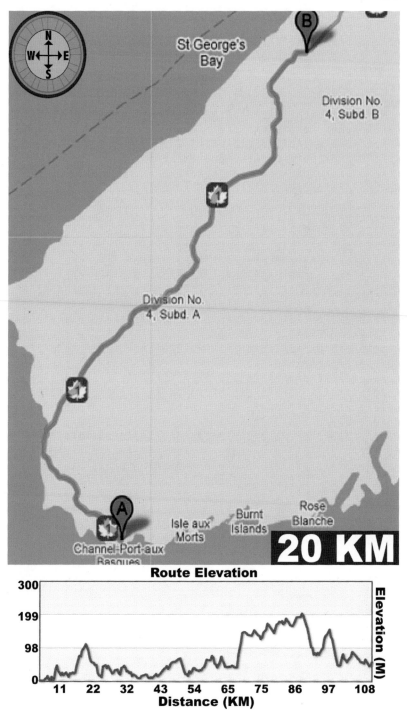

Kilometre Log

0.0 Exit the ferry and look for signs for HWY 1. Start biking on HWY 1.
2.0 HWY 470 intersects with HWY 1. Stay left on HWY 1.
11.5 Exit to J.T. Cheeseman Provincial Park.
17.2 HWY 408 intersects with HWY 1.
35.6 Cross Little Codroy River.
36.4 HWY 407 intersects with HWY 1.
38.9 HWY 406 intersects with HWY 1. Service station available here.
60.8 Coal Brook.
95.7 HWY 405 intersects with HWY 1.
99.7 HWY 404 intersects with HWY 1.
106.1 HWY 404 intersects with HWY 1.
108.1 Midway Motel.

Midway Motel to Kinsmen Prince Edward Campground: (118.8 K)

Leave the Midway Motel heading north on HWY 1. There is only one service station on the highway today so pack lots of food and water.

James Cook first explored and surveyed this area in 1767. Copies of his maps are available at the Captain James Cook Monument in Corner Brook. The city is situated on a steep hill near where the Humber River flows into the Atlantic Ocean.

The arts play a prominent role in Corner Brook culture. The city is a popular stop for touring musicians, comedians and theatrical productions.

HWY 1 runs well above sea level. The descent into Corner Brook is steep and fast. Fortunately, when you exit Corner Brook you will bike along the water and meet up with the highway with minimal effort.

The Corner Brook Museum and Archives exhibits the social, cultural and natural history of Corner Brook and the Humber Valley. Cycle Solutions is a full service bike store. Hotel Corner Brook has the cheapest rooms in town.

Purchase supplies in downtown Corner Brook before heading to the Kinsmen run Prince Edward Campground & RV Park, east of town. Laundry is available at the campsite.

Kilometre Log

0.0 Leave Midway Motel heading north on HWY 1.
25.5 Intersection of HWY 1 & HWY 403.
29.8 Service station.
35.9 Cross Barachois Brook.
36.7 Intersection of HWY 1 & HWY 490.
40.7 Barachois Pond Provincial Park.
48.4 Intersection of HWY 1 & HWY 480.
60.5 Intersection of HWY 1 & HWY 460.
105.1 Exit to HWY 450 / Lewin Parkway. Remain on HWY 1.
108.7 Exit right off of HWY 1 onto Massey Drive. Turn left to cross under HWY 1 to access Confederation Drive.
109.5 Turn left on West Valley Road.
111.5 West Valley Road turns into Park Street, which is a one-way that you can not travel down. Turn right onto Central Street.
111.6 Turn left onto West Street.
112.2 Turn right onto Main Street.
112.6 Cross Lewin Parkway and Main Street turns into Humber Road.
112.8 Stay left to remain on Humber Road.
115.3 Humber Road merges with Riverside Drive.
117.4 Turn left on North Shore Highway / HWY 440.
118.8 Kinsmen Prince Edward Campground.

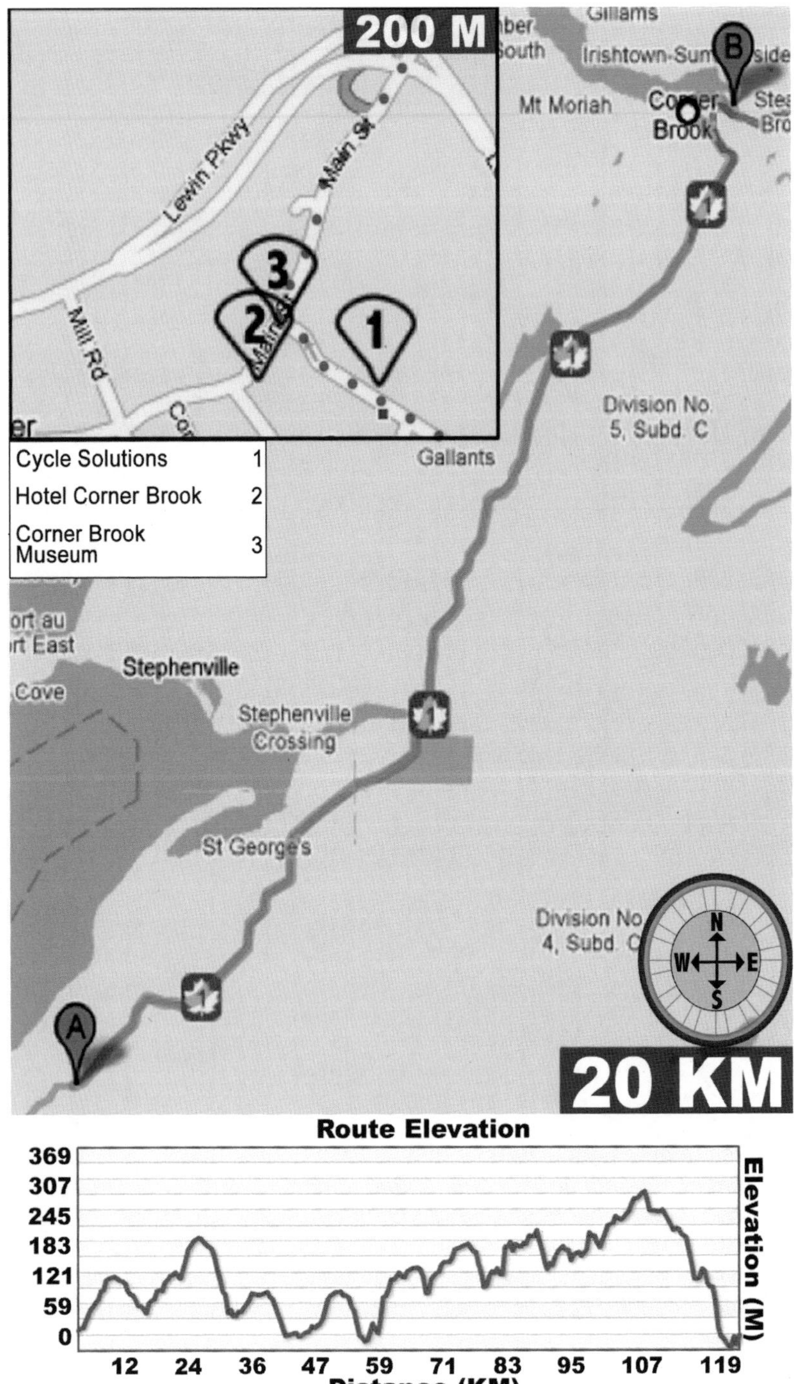

Route Elevation

Elevation (M)	Distance (KM)
369, 307, 245, 183, 121, 59, 0	12, 24, 36, 47, 59, 71, 83, 95, 107, 119

Moose

When cycling through Newfoundland, don't be surprised if you see a giant moose. The largest member of the deer family is not native to the island. In 1904, four moose were released near Gros Morne National Park. Presently, there is an estimated population of 120 000 moose on the island. The average weight of an adult moose is around 450 kilograms. Males have distinct antlers that weigh up to 20 kilograms each. The moose is a popular source of protein for Newfies, but they can be hazardous as cars collide with them on highways, especially at dusk and dawn.

If you see a moose, do not approach them. They are usually timid, but can be dangerous especially in the fall during breeding season.

Icebergs

Watching icebergs is a popular tourist activity in Newfoundland. These mammoth pieces of ice are truly spectacular. Icebergs are parts of glaciers that break off and flow south in ocean currents. Icebergs can weigh up to 10 000 000 tonnes and can be made of ice that is up to 15 000 years old.

The glaciers from which these icebergs originate are generally located in Greenland but some are from Canada's eastern Arctic islands.

The best time to view icebergs in Newfoundland is from March until July.

Kinsmen Prince Edward Campground to Deer Lake Municipal Campground: (49.2 K)

Leave Prince Edward Campground heading east on HWY 1. Bike past Marble Mountain ski hill, which rises over 500 metres above the Humber River. Marble Mountain was home of the alpine skiing events when Corner Brook hosted the Canada Winter Games in 1999. Restaurants and gas stations are available on the highway near the ski hill in Steady Brook. Humber River will be to your left throughout the day.

As you bike east, the Humber River widens and becomes Deer Lake. At the north tip of Deer Lake is the town of Deer Lake, population 4 827. The major industry in Deer Lake is pulp and paper, which began operation in 1925. A hydro-generating station was built on the Humber River to service the pulp and paper mill. The generating station is still in operation today. Camping is available in Deer Lake at the Deer Lake Municipal Campground. There is a small grocery store in South Brook and a few convenience stores along the way, but Deer Lake is your last opportunity to shop at a large supermarket until Grand Falls-Windsor.

In order to ensure that cyclists have a place to shower each evening, it was necessary to schedule an evening in Deer Lake as the next campground is in South Brook, 134 kilometres further. Sparsely populated Burchy Lake is 61 kilometres east of Deer Lake. It is a pleasant place for a break, swim or to spend the evening.

Kilometre Log

0.0 Leave Kinsmen Prince Edward Campground heading south on HWY 440.
1.4 Turn left on Riverside Drive.
2.6 Riverside Drive crosses HWY 1. Turn left to gain HWY 1.
7.0 Steady Brook.
18.2 Deer Lake is to your left.
22.9 Exit to Pasadena.
27.5 Exit to Pasadena.
45.2 Enter Deer Lake.
47.1 Exit right off of highway.

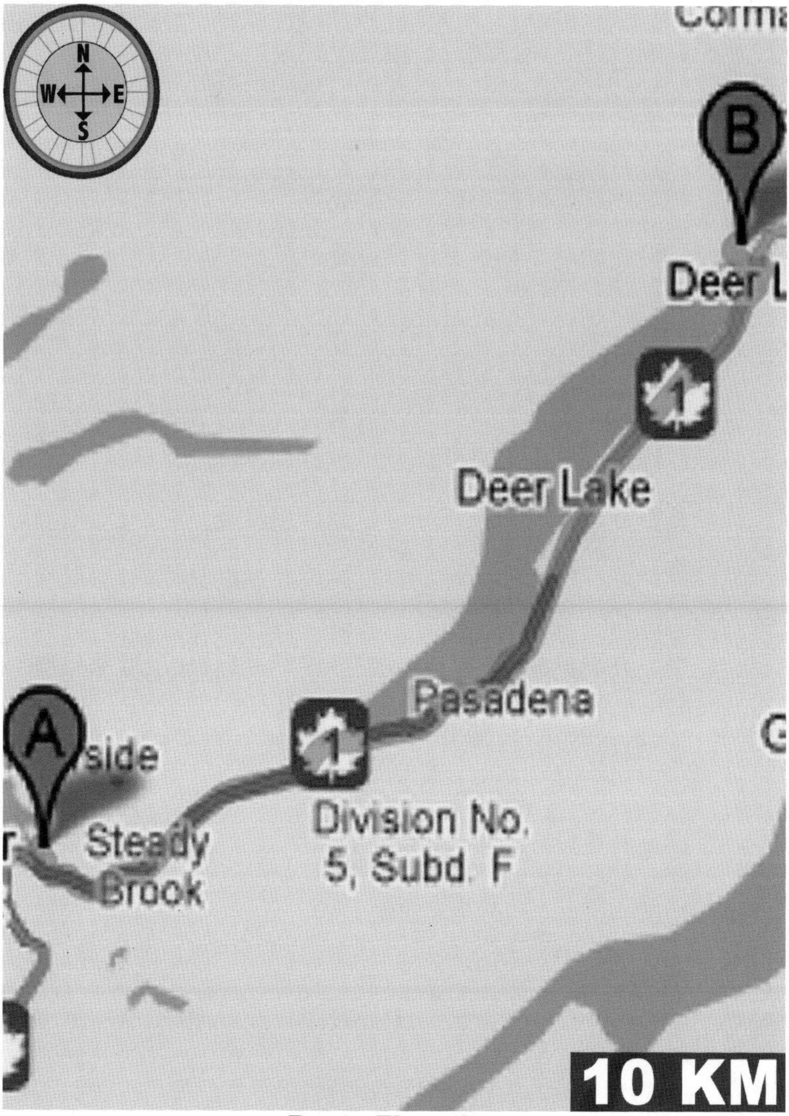

N
W
E
S
B
A
1
Deer Lake
Pasadena
Steady
Brook
Division No.
5, Subd. F
10 KM

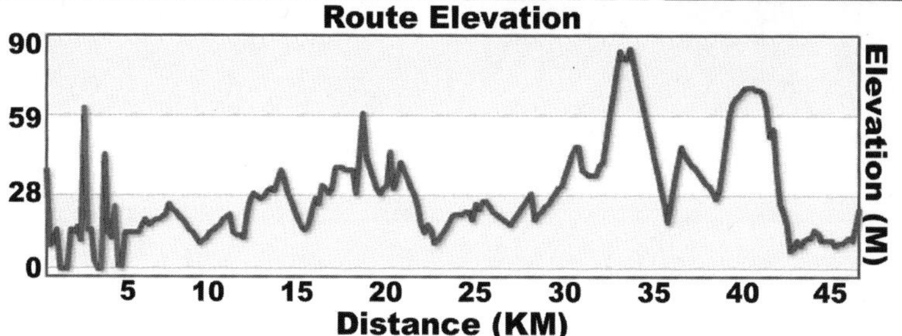
Route Elevation
90
59
28
0
5
10
15
20
25
30
35
40
45
Distance (KM)
Elevation (M)

47.2 Turn left to cross HWY 1, circling 180° counter-clockwise.
47.7 Turn right on Lake Side Drive.
48.0 Lake Side Drive turns into Nicholsville Road.
49.2 Deer Lake Municipal Campground.

Deer Lake Municipal Campground to Kona Beach Campground: (133.8 K)

Just past Deer Lake is the exit for Gros Morne National Park. Gros Morne is world-famous for its natural beauty. Visitors have the opportunity to hike through uninhabited mountains and spend the evening at campgrounds with ocean views.

There is a small service station on the east side of Burchy Lake.

Bike along barren highway to South Brook and nearby Kona Beach Campground. A small grocery store, restaurant and motel are present in South Brook. Kona Beach Campground has laundry facilities and a nice beach.

Kilometre Log

0.0 Leave Deer Lake Municipal Campground heading south on Nicholsville Road.
1.3 Nicholsville Road turns into Lakeside Drive.
1.5 Cross HWY 1. Circle 270° clockwise to access HWY 1.
3.9 Cloverleaf intersection of HWY 1 & HWY 430.
5.4 Exit to Deer Lake Regional Airport.
32.1 Intersection of HWY 1 & HWY 401.
47.5 Intersection of HWY 1 & HWY 420.
53.3 Birchy Lake. Good place for a picnic or a rest.
63.0 Birchy Narrows.
99.0 Intersection of HWY 410 & HWY 1 as well as Junction Inn & Restaurant.
119.2 Intersection of HWY 1 & HWY 390.
131.9 Intersection of HWY 1 & HWY 380 / Exit to South Brook.
133.8 Kona Beach Park Campground.

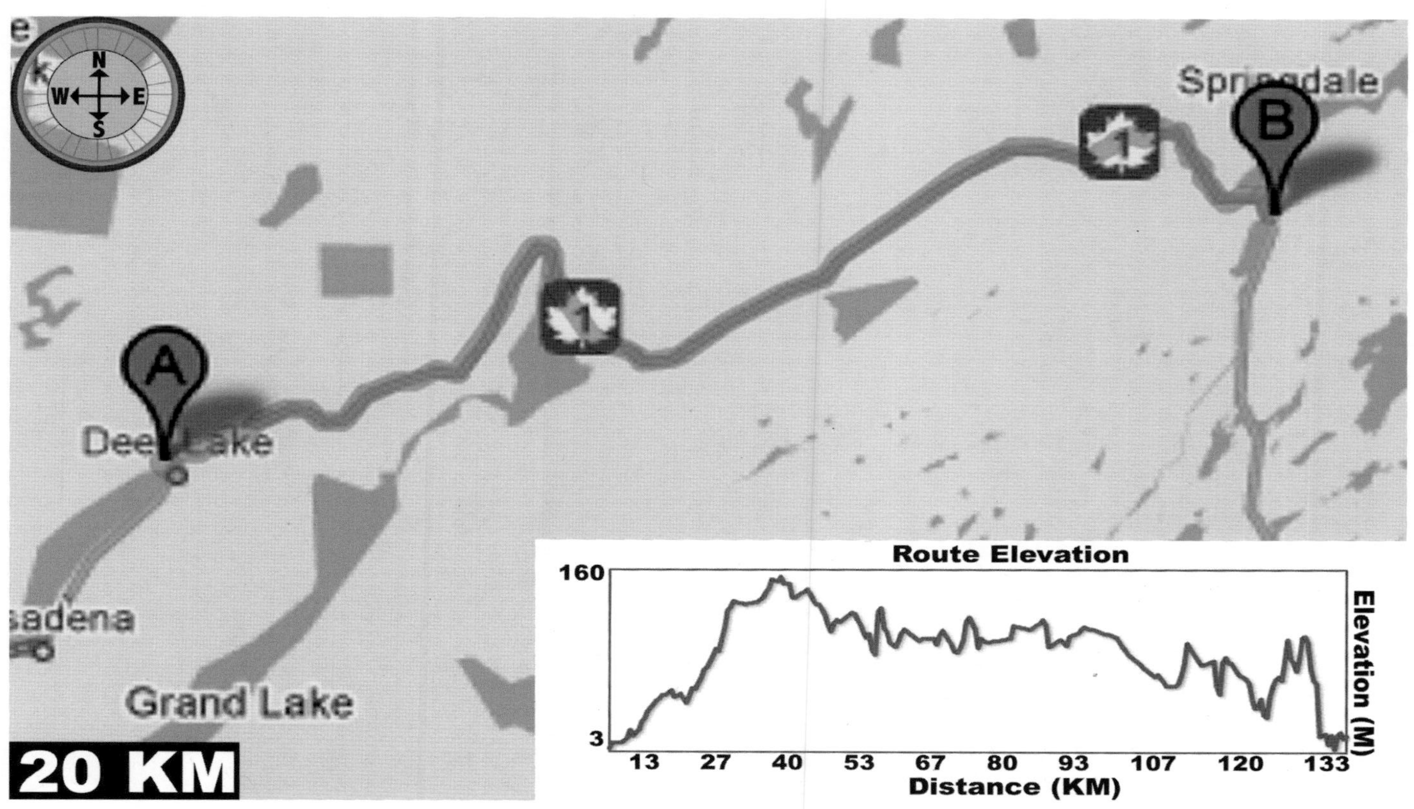
N
W
E
S
A
B
1
1
Grand Lake
20 KM
Route Elevation
160
3
13
27
40
53
67
80
93
107
120
133
Distance (KM)
Elevation (M)

Kona Beach Campground to Fallsview Municipal Park Campground: (97.4 K)

Catamaran Park is 8 kilometres before arriving in Badger on HWY 1. It is home to a campground, laundry and indoor pool.

There are restaurants and a few small stores in Badger, population 813, which is located at the forks of Badger Brook and Exploits River.

Grand Falls-Windsor was founded in 1991, when the towns of Grand Falls and Windsor were amalgamated. Grand Falls was established in 1905, when the area was deemed suitable for a pulp and paper mill because of its access to timber, possibility of hydroelectricity generation and the existence of a deep-water port in nearby Botwood.

In 1909, only employees of the mills and workers from private business were allowed to live in Grand Falls. Anyone who came to Grand Falls looking for work settled north of the railroad tracks in what was known as Grand Falls Station. In 1938, Grand Falls Station changed its name to Windsor in honour of the British Royal Family.

Pulp and paper are still the main industry in Grand Falls-Windsor, which is known as a "Garden City" and is a notoriously pleasant place to live. Visit the Grand Falls Fishway and Salmonid Interpretation Centre, which is next to the legendary Grand Falls waterfall. Camping is available at Beothuck Park.

After Grand Falls-Windsor, cycle into Bishop's Falls, population 3 399. The town sits on the banks of the famous salmon-filled Exploits River. Bishop's Falls has Newfoundland's oldest and longest railway trestle over the Exploits River.

Your destination for the evening is Fallsview Municipal Park. The lower level of the park offers visitors a spectacular view of Bishop's Falls.

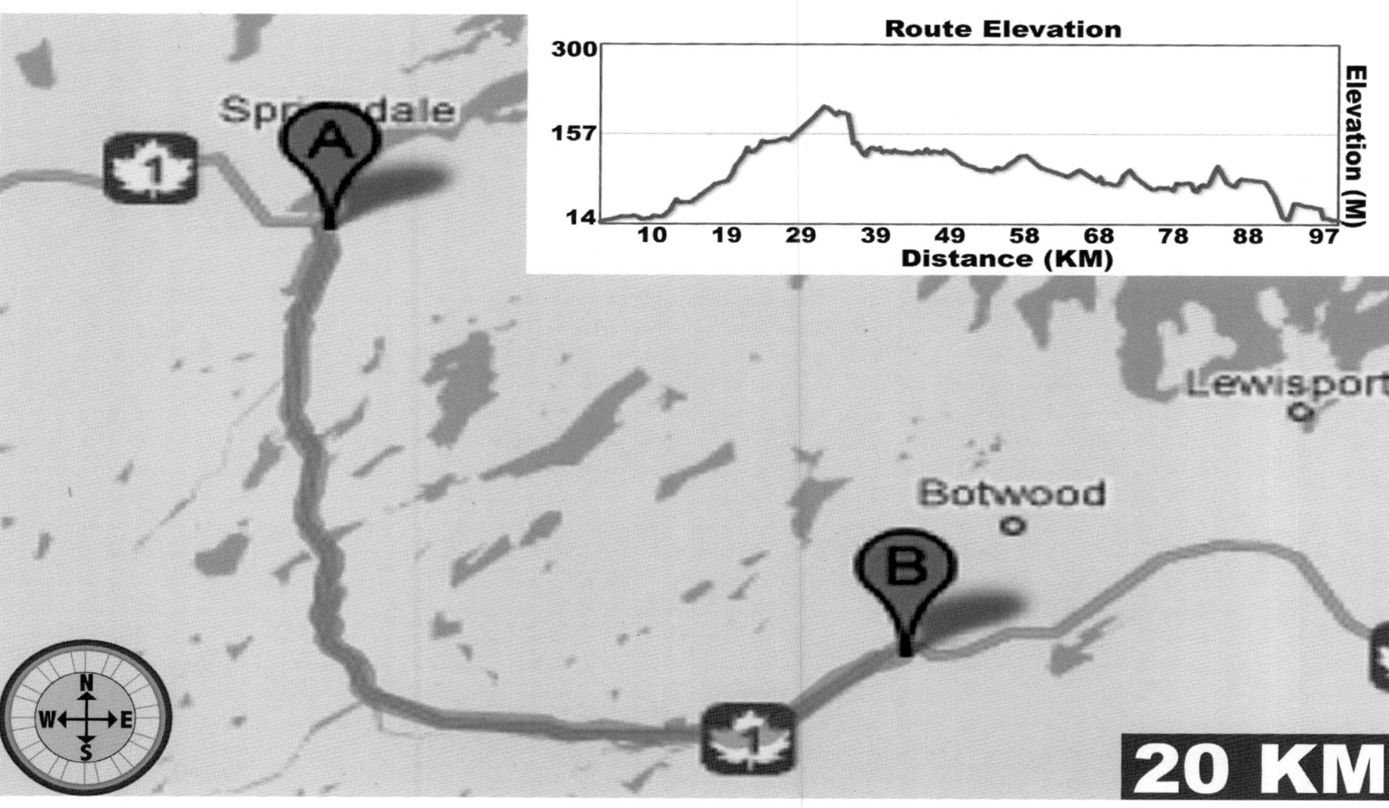
Route Elevation
Elevation (M)
300
157
14
10
19
29
39
49
58
68
78
88
97
Distance (KM)
Spr
dale
A
B
1
1
Botwood
Lewisport
N
S
W
E
20 KM

Kilometre Log

0.0 Leave Kona Park Campground heading south on HWY 1.
43.6 Catamaran Park Campground.
50.9 Badger.
51.4 Cross Badger Brook.
77.5 Enter Grand Falls-Windsor on HWY 1.
94.2 First access to Bishop's Falls on Centre Access Road. Turn right.
94.7 Turn left off of Centre Access Road onto Main Street / HWY 350.
97.2 Turn right onto Powerhouse Road.
97.4 Fallsview Campground.

Fallsview Municipal Park to Gander's Country Inn Campground: (79.8 K)

Notre Dame Provincial Park is nestled in a lush forest that borders on the serene waters of Junction Pond. Moose, beaver, snowshoe hare and many other animals call the park home. Camping is available here.

Your destination for the evening is Country Inn Campground, on the outskirts of Gander.

The Gander International Airport is a large catalyst for growth for Gander, population, 9 951. Because of its location in the far northeast of North America, the airport has become an important stop for planes heading across the Atlantic to Europe. Many of Gander's streets are named for famous aviators. Head to the North Atlantic Aviation Museum to sit in the cockpit of a DC-3, one of the most significant aircrafts ever produced.

During World War II, American and Canadian fighter jets stopped at Gander before heading off to war. Following the war's end, the airport was used as a refueling stop for commercial flights. During this era the town earned its name as the "Cross-roads of the world."

During the middle of the century it was common to hear languages from all over the world around town. Legend claims that Fidel Castro once tobogganed with youth on the slopes overlooking Gander Lake.

Gander played a prominent role in coping with the aftermath of the September 11th attacks in New York City. 6 600 passengers spent over three days in Gander while waiting for airspace to re-open. Residents of Gander and surrounding communities housed, fed and entertained the travelers in what became known as Operation Yellow Ribbon.

Gander sits on the north shore of Gander Lake, which has been measured at 274 metres and is estimated to be much deeper.

Country Inn Campground is located just outside of Gander. Gander is the last chance for supplies until Clarenville.

Kilometre Log

0.0 Leave Fallsview Campground heading north on Powerhouse Road.
0.2 Turn right on Main Street / HWY 350.
2.1 Exit right onto a cloverleaf to gain HWY 1. Head east on HWY 1.
2.6 Cross Exploits River.
3.1 Intersection of HWY 1 & HWY 351.
3.6 Intersection of HWY 1 & HWY 360.
33.3 Intersection of HWY 1 & HWY 340.
34.5 Notre Dame Provincial Park.
39.4 Cross Neyles Brook.
54.3 Cross Salmon River.
55.9 Glenwood.
56.1 Cross Gander River.
76.2 Intersection of HWY 330 / Magee Road & HWY 1. Turn left here.
79.8 Turn left off of HWY 330 / Magee Road into Country Inn Campground.

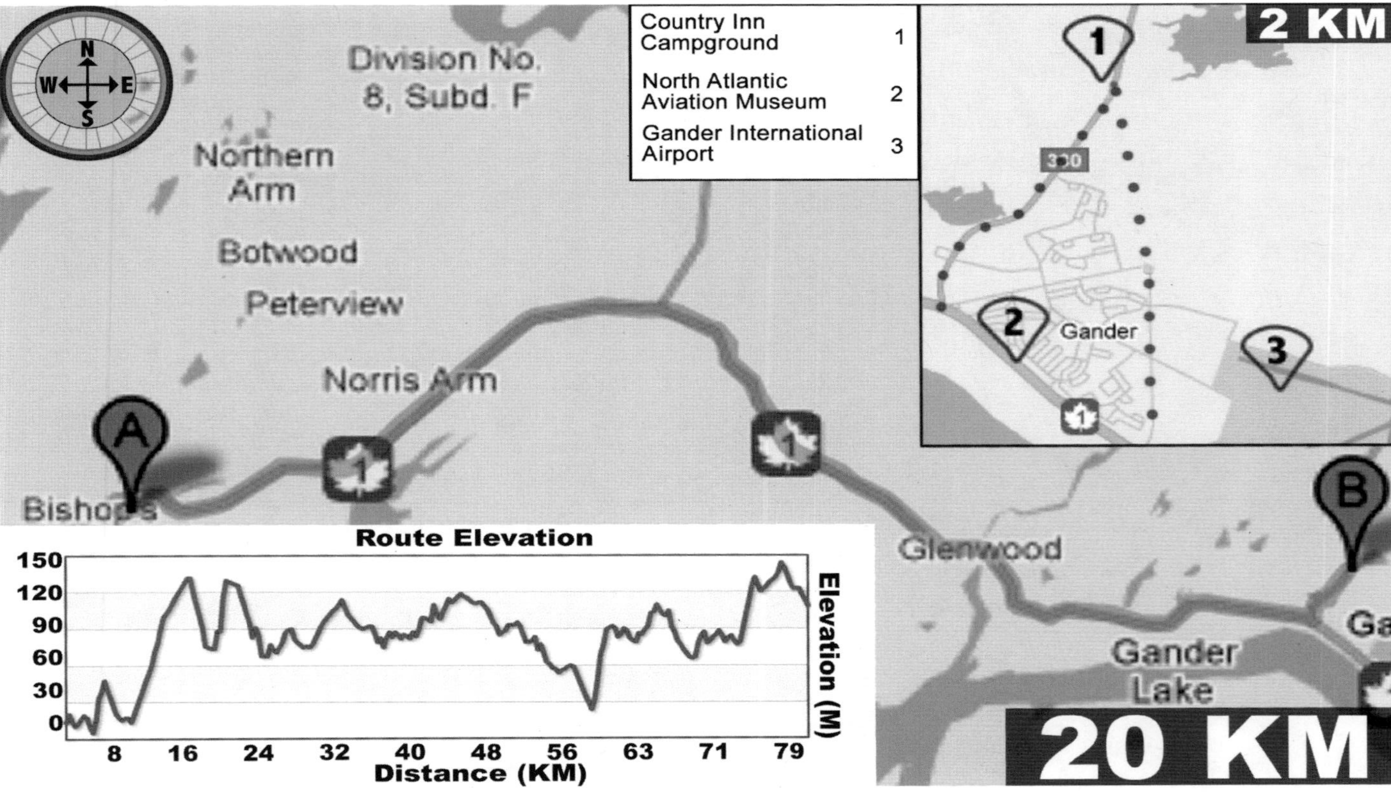
N
W
E
S
Division No. 8, Subd. F
Northern Arm
Botwood
Peterview
Norris Arm
Bishops
A
1
1
Glenwood
B
Gander Lake
20 KM
Country Inn Campground 1
North Atlantic Aviation Museum 2
Gander International Airport 3
2 KM
1
330
2
Gander
3
1
Route Elevation
150
120
90
60
30
0
8
16
24
32
40
48
56
63
71
79
Distance (KM)
Elevation (M)

Grand Banks Cod

When explorer John Cabot returned to Europe after visiting the waters around present-day Newfoundland, he reported that codfish were so abundant that you could catch them by hanging a wicker basket off the side of your ship.

For hundreds of years the inhabitants of Newfoundland based their economy almost solely on the cod. The supply of cod seemed endless to the fisherman that harvested the fish that lived in giant schools with populations in the hundreds of millions. The fish spawned in distinctive areas, making them an easy target for fisherman to scoop up with giant nets trolled behind their boats. Until the mid 1900s cod fishing was performed at a scope that was sustainable, allowing fish to reproduce.

In 1951, a large British ship sailed into the Atlantic and changed the lives of Newfoundlanders forever. This giant ship was 280 feet long and was loaded with technology that was developed in World War II. Below its deck was a fish processing facility and giant bank of freezers allowing the ship to fish around the clock for weeks at a time.

These super-sized fishing boats that caught many tons of fish an hour for months on end became the new norm. This new, unsustainable rate of catching fish completely demolished the cod stocks.

By 1992, adult cod population was 1% of what it had been during its glory years. The cod population has virtually disappeared and many experts theorize that the ecosystem may have been changed so greatly that they will never return.

Country Inn Campground to Terra Nova National Park's Newman Sound Campground: (81.0 K)

Today you will bike from Gander into Newman Sound Campground in the centre of Terra Nova National Park.

Terra Nova National Park is a place where the Atlantic Ocean meets the boreal forest. Terra Nova is Latin for Newfoundland. The rocky shorelines support colonies of common tern, herring gulls and bald eagles. Inland, there is boreal forest consisting of mostly black spruce and balsam fir, which hosts black bear, otter, lynx and beaver.

There are two campgrounds in Terra Nova National Park. Newman Sound is the largest while Malady Head is a quieter campground.

Although there is a grocery store off of HWY 1 before the entrance to Terra Nova National Park in Glovertown, it is far down a hill with a large climb back up to the highway. Bring supplies from Gander.

Kilometre Log

0.0	Leave Gander heading south on Magee Road.
0.1	Turn left to access HWY 330 / Gander Bay Road.
0.2	Turn right onto HWY 330 / Gander Bay Road.
1.8	Gander Bay Road intersects with Memorial Drive and becomes Cooper Road.
2.9	Cooper Road dead-ends into HWY 1. Turn left here.
3.9	Gander International Airport.
16.7	Cross Souris Brook.
31.7	Square Pond RV Park.
42.1	Intersection of HWY 1 & HWY 320.
43.7	Cross Gambo Creek.
59.1	Exit to Glovertown.
62.9	Cross Terra Nova River.
66.2	Exit to Traytown.
67.2	Small restaurant and lodge.
67.6	Enter Terra Nova Provincial Park.
68.2	HWY 310 intersects with HWY 1.
79.2	Terra Nova National Park Marine Interpretive Centre.
80.4	Turn left into Newman Sound Campground.
81.0	Newman Sound Campground.

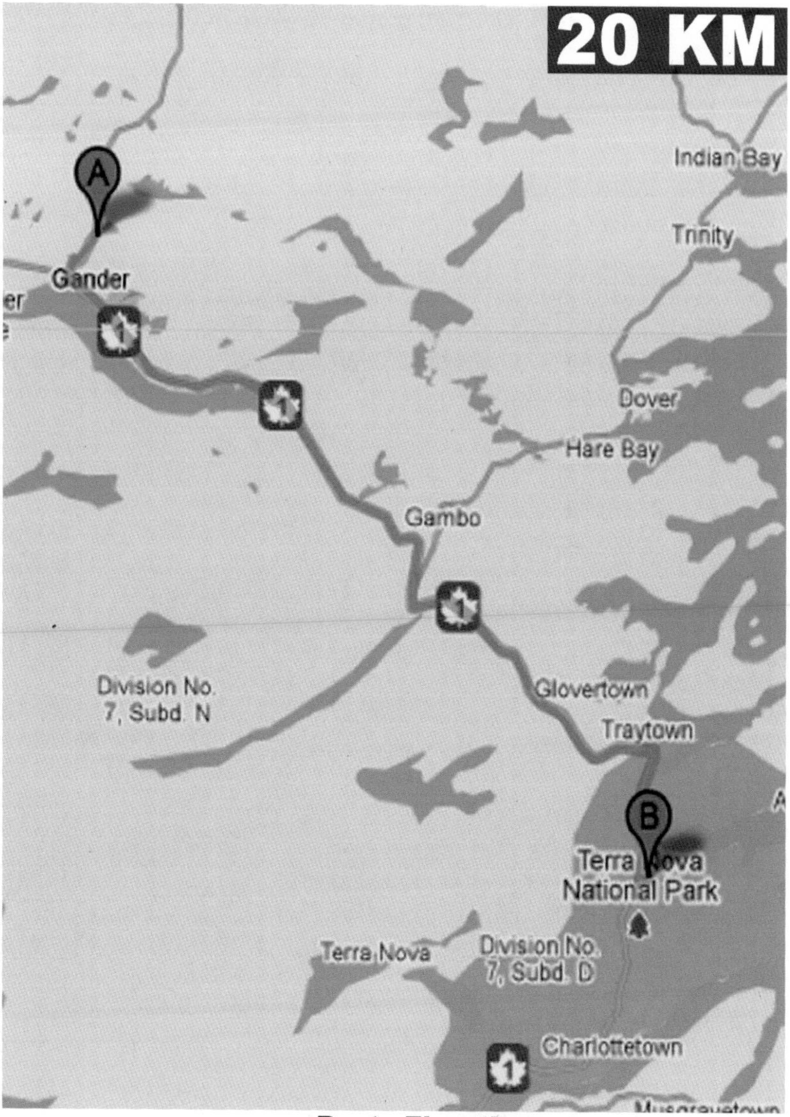

20 KM
Indian Bay
Trinity
Gander
Dover
Hare Bay
Gambo
Division No.
7, Subd. N
Glovertown
Traytown
Terra Nova
National Park
Terra Nova
Division No.
7, Subd. D
Charlottetown

Route Elevation
150
120
90
60
30
0
8
16
24
32
40
48
57
65
73
81
Distance (KM)
Elevation (M)

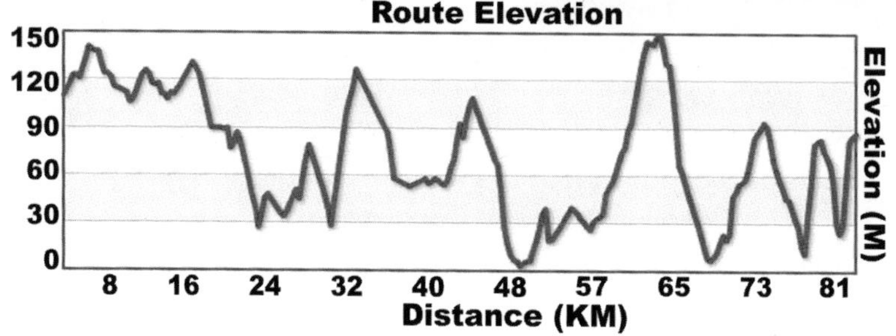

Newman Sound Campground to Arnold's Cove's Tanker Inn: (114.6 K)

Today you will continue biking through Terra Nova National Park before heading south to Arnold's Cove. Take a minute to check out the picnic area's scenic views of Terra Nova National Park.

Clarenville, population 5 274, is known as the hub of the east coast because it lies in the middle of the Avalon, Burin and Bonavista peninsulas. Clarenville has the distinction of being the North American starting point for the Trans-Atlantic Cable. It was laid in 1955, linking the town to Oban, Scotland, which allowed phone calls to be made across the Atlantic Ocean. All services in Clarenville are located just off of the highway.

Come By Chance is also located off of the highway. It is an oil-refining industrial town.

Your destination for the evening is the Tanker Inn Motel in Arnold's Cove, population 1 003. Groceries are available in Arnold's Cove. It marks the beginning of the Avalon Peninsula, the most densely populated area on the island of Newfoundland.

Kilometre Log

0.0 Leave Newman Sound Campground and head west towards HWY 1.
0.6 Turn left on HWY 1.
4.1 HWY 301 intersects with HWY 1.
28.0 Exit Terra Nova National Park.
36.2 Port Blandford at the intersection of HWY 1 & HWY 233.
63.7 Exit to Clarenville at the intersection of HWY 230 / Manitoba Drive & HWY 1.
67.2 Exit to Clarenville.
68.1 Small store.
74.4 Deep Bight.
85.2 HWY 204 intersects with HWY 1.
93.7 HWY 1 intersects with HWY 210. Restaurants are available here.
103.8 Exit to Come By Chance.
111.8 Exit right into Arnold's Cove onto Main Road.
112.1 Main Road turns left. Turn left here.
114.6 The Tanker Inn.

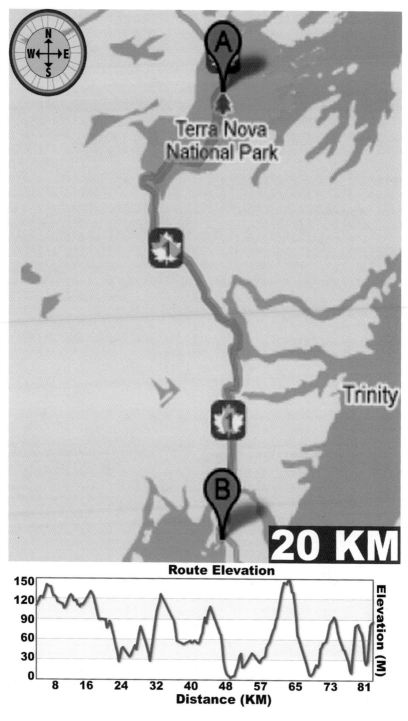

N
W E
S
A
Terra Nova
National Park
1
Trinity
1
B
20 KM

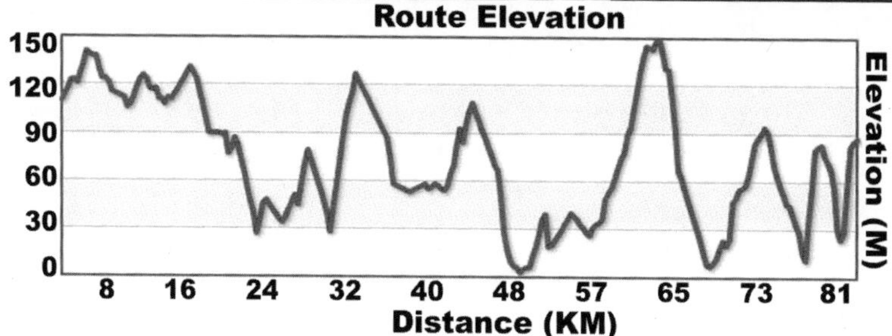

The Tanker Inn to Butterpot Provincial Park: (108.2 K)

Butterpot Provincial Park received its name from a prominent, rounded hill located within its boundaries. Long before the area was a park, nearby residents hunted animals and gathered firewood and berries here. High acidity levels in the soil combined with a forest fire that badly scorched the area in 1889, rendered much of the park unable to support growth. This has resulted in a diverse variety of habitat that is home to wildflowers and berries as well as boreal forest. Tourists flock to the area for trout fishing, picnics and to hike the park's extensive trail system. The campground has 175 sites and laundry on-site.

Purchase your groceries for the evening at the small store in Arnold's Cove.

There is a hotel called Moorland Motel and restaurant at the intersection of HWY 100 and HWY 1. This is your last chance to acquire food and beverage before arriving in St. John's. This intersection links the North Sydney–Argentia Ferry to St. John's. Expect big rig traffic to increase from here to St. John's. It is 47 kilometres from the Argentia Ferry to the intersection of HWY 1 and HWY 100.

Kilometre Log

0.0	Leave Arnold's Cove biking north on Main Road.
2.1	Turn right towards HWY 1.
2.2	Turn right on HWY 1.
28.0	Intersection of HWY 1 & HWY 201 (E) / 203 (W). Turn left for Bellevue Beach Camping.
43.1	Intersection of HWY 1 & HWY 201 (N) / 202 (S).
55.3	Intersection of HWY 1 & HWY 100.
76.1	Intersection of HWY 1 & HWY 75.
88.3	Intersection of HWY 1 & HWY 90.
97.6	Intersection of HWY 1 & HWY 62.
100.1	Intersection of HWY 1 & HWY 13.
106.2	Turn left into Butterpot Provincial Park on Daniels Road.
108.2	Butterpot Provincial Park Campground.

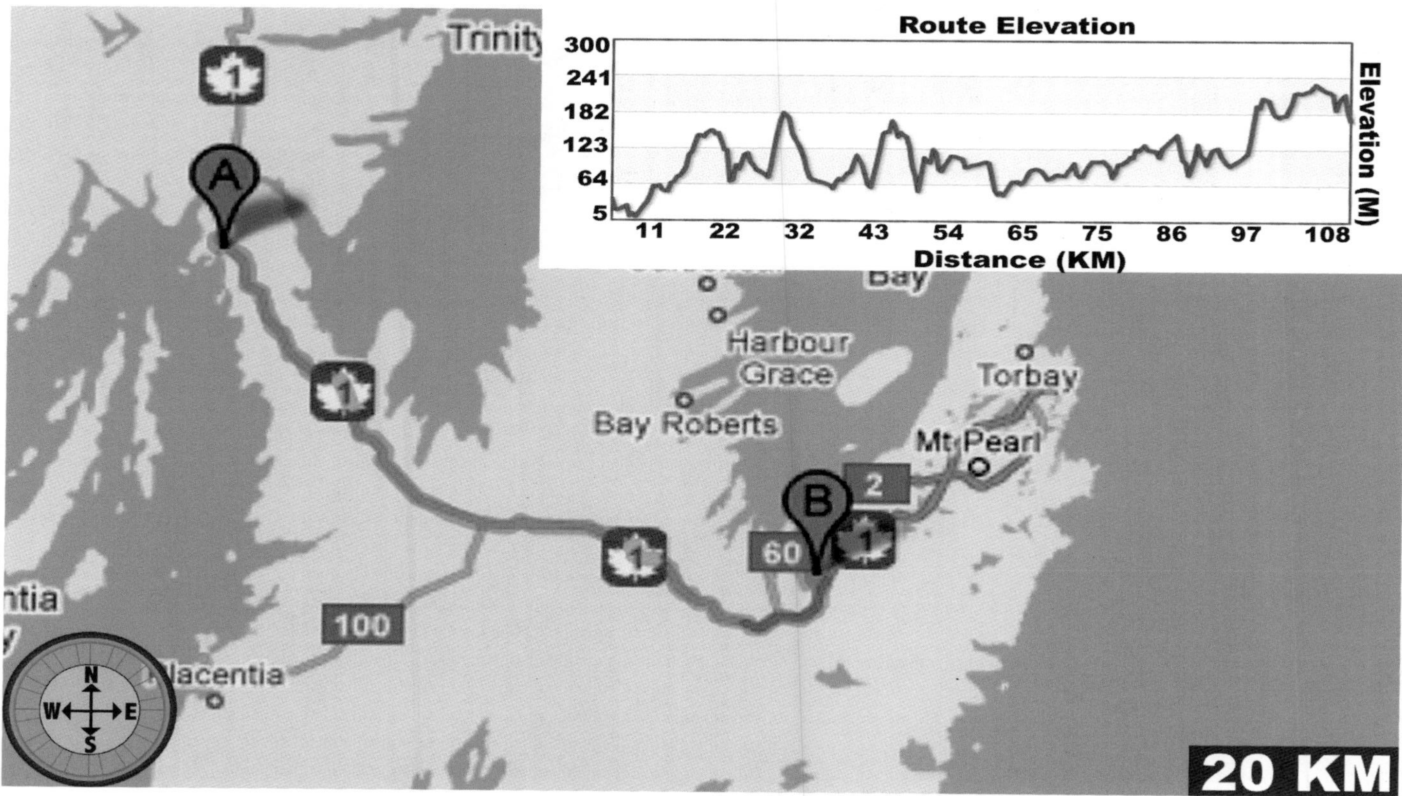

Route Elevation
Elevation (M)
300
241
182
123
64
5
11
22
32
43
54
65
75
86
97
108
Distance (KM)
Trinity
Bay
Harbour Grace
Bay Roberts
Torbay
Mt Pearl
Placentia
A
B
1
2
60
100
N
E
S
W
20 KM

Butterpot Provincial Park to C.A. Pippy Park Campground: (39.8 K)

St. John's, population 100 646, is the provincial capital of Newfoundland and Labrador. Sir Humphrey Gilbert declared Newfoundland an English colony in 1583. The generally accepted story for its name is that John Cabot became the first European to sail into the harbour, on June 24, 1497, the feast day of Saint John the Baptist. Others believe that the name came from Basque fishermen. The bay of St. John's is similar to the Bay of Pasaia in Basque Country. The bay of Pasaia is home to a town called San Juan, which translates to "St. John" in English.

St. John's Harbour is a geographical oddity. A small inlet leads into an expansive harbour, sheltering the boats in port from the often angry Atlantic Ocean.

Traditionally, St. John's economy has focused on fishing but this has changed within the last two decades. Presently, St. John's economy is being spurred on by oil and gas being extracted offshore.

The city itself is focused around the St. John's Harbour and Water Street, North America's oldest street. From the harbour and Water Street, St. John's rises in elevation. Houses in the city are painted a unique array of colours that are sure to leave an impression.

Don't leave St. John's without hiking up to Signal Hill, the site of the final battle of the Seven Years' War. In 1762, the French surrendered to the British here.

Coloured flags were the primary mode of communication between the boats and signalmen from the 1600s until the mid 1900s. Cabot Tower was built in 1897, to commemorate the 400th anniversary of John Cabot's discovery of Newfoundland. Today, Signal Hill is a National Historic Site. Enjoy some of the hiking trails through the area. To get there, head northeast down Duckworth Street until it turns into Signal Hill Road and continue following it towards Signal Hill.

If you enjoy a cold pint, you owe it to yourself to head to Quidi Vidi Brewery. It is located in an old fish processing plant. They offer daily sampling tours of the brewery. It is located just north of downtown.

To celebrate your arrival in St. John's, head to George Street. It is believed that George Street has more bars and pubs per square foot than any street in North America. The small street is only open to vehicle traffic from 8 AM until noon, allowing the bars to re-stock their supply. George Street is busiest on weekends.

Your destination for the evening is C.A. Pippy Park. This large park located north of downtown St. John's is home to a campground, the Newfoundland Freshwater Resource Centre and the Fluvarium. It gives visitors an introduction to the freshwater ecology of Newfoundland.

If you want a roof over your head check out Foggy Rock Hostel or City Hostel.

St. John's International Airport is easily accessible from downtown St. John's.

Kilometre Log

0.0 Leave Butter Pot Provincial Park heading south on Daniels Road.
2.6 Turn left onto HWY 1.
13.1 Intersection of HWY 1 & HWY 61.
16.4 Thomas Pond.
20.7 Paddys Pond.
24.5 Cross HWY 2 / Harbour Arterial Road.
27.5 Intersection of HWY 1 & HWY 60.
32.1 Intersection of HWY 1 & HWY 50.
34.1 Enter Pippy Park.
34.5 Intersection of HWY 1 & Team Gushue HWY.
37.5 Take Exit 46 on your right off of the highway onto Allandale Road.
39.1 Turn right onto Nagles Place.
39.8 Enter C.A. Pippy Park Camgpround.

Congratulations on reaching St. John's. I hope you had a safe trip and *Canada by Bicycle* was accurate and easy to use. If you have any corrections, advice or just want to say hello look me up @ www.canadabybicycle.com

Steve Langston

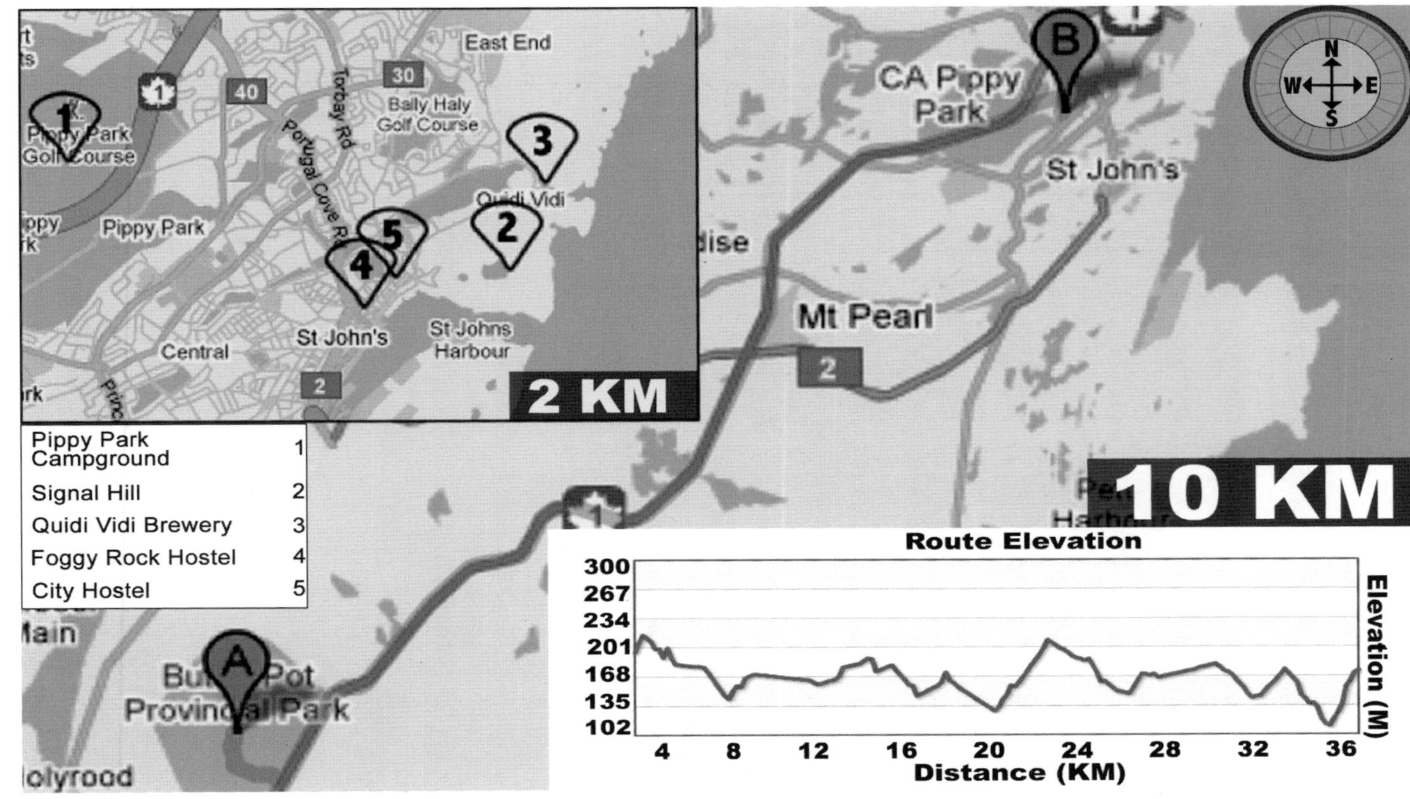

East End
30
40
Torbay Rd
Bally Haly
Golf Course
Portugal Cove Rd
Pippy Park
Golf Course
Pippy Park
Quidi Vidi
St John's
St Johns
Harbour
Central
2
2 KM
Pippy Park Campground 1
Signal Hill 2
Quidi Vidi Brewery 3
Foggy Rock Hostel 4
City Hostel 5
CA Pippy
Park
St John's
Mt Pearl
2
10 KM
A
B
N
W
E
S
Route Elevation
300
267
234
201
168
135
102
Elevation (M)
4
8
12
16
20
24
28
32
36
Distance (KM)

NUMBERS

WestJet 1-888-9378-538
Air canada 1-888-247-2262
Vancouver Samesun Hostel 604-682-8226
H/I Vancovuer Downtown 604-684-4565
Manning Lodge 250-840-8822
Discover Camping BC 1-800-689-9025
Kelowna SameSun Hostel 250-861-3001
Revlestoke's SameSun Hostel 250-837-4050
H/I Lake Louise 403-670-7580
Banff SameSun Hostel 403-762-5521
H/I-Calgary City Centre 1-866-762-4122
Manitoba Provincial Park Campgrounds 1-888-482-2267
Ontario Provincial Park Campgrounds 1-888-668-7275
Velorution Sault Ste. marie 705-253-9388
Ottawa Barefoot Hostel 613-237-0335
Ottawa Jail Hostel 613-235-2595
H/I-Montreal 1-866-843-3317
Montreal Backpackers Hostel 514-298-4615
Montreal Jazz Hostel 514-448-4848
Auberge International de Quebec 418-694-0755
Planete Backpackers 418-264-4615
Riviere du Loup International Hostel 418-862-7566
Hostelling International Campbellton 506-759-7044
H/I - Halifax Heritage House Hostel 902-422-0116
Halifax Backpackers Hostel 902-431-3170
Marine Atlantic Newfoundland Ferry 1-800-341-7981
Midway Motel 709-645-2650
Hotel Corner Brook 709-634-8211
Newman Sound Campground 1-877-737-3783
Arnold's Cove Tanker Inn 709-463-2313
Butterpot Provincial Park 1-877-214-2267
Moorland Motel 709-759-2550
Quidi Vidi Brewery 1-800-738-0165
St. John's City Hostel 709-754-4789